MANAGEMENT
STRATEGIES
IN
ATHLETIC
TRAINING

Richard Ray, EdD, ATC
Hope College
Holland, Michigan

Human Kinetics Publishers

Library of Congress Cataloging-in-Publication Data

Ray, Richard, 1957-
    Management strategies in athletic training / Richard Ray.
        p.   cm.
    Includes bibliographical references and index.
    ISBN 0-87322-582-1
    1. Athletic trainers.   I. Title.
    RC1210.R38   1994
    617.1'027--dc20   93-5167
                                                          CIP

ISBN: 0-87322-582-1

Acquisitions Editor: Rick Frey, PhD; **Developmental Editor:** Judy Patterson Wright, PhD; **Assistant Editor:** Ed Giles; **Copyeditor:** Ginger Rodriguez; **Proofreader:** Dawn Barker; **Photo Editor:** Valerie Hall; **Production Director:** Ernie Noa; **Typesetting and Text Layout:** Sandra Meier; **Paste-Up Artist:** Tara Welsch; **Text Designer:** Jody Boles; **Cover Designer:** Jack Davis; **Cover Photo:** University of Virginia, HOK Sports Facilities Group, Alan Karchmer; **Illustrator:** Kathy Boudreau-Fuoss; **Printer:** Braun-Brumfield

Interior photo credits—Tom Renner: pp. 5, 9, 29, 35, 63, 68, 104, 114, 127, 161, 196, 216; Stephen Warmowski/*The Daily Illini*: 1, 47; Arizona State University Sports Information: 21; Brigid Nagle/*The Daily Illini*: 85; Wilmer Zehr: 94; Dave Cross/Miami Dolphins: 111; Lisa Davis/*The Daily Illini*: 139; Mark Jones/Tintype Studio/University of Illinois Sports Information: 144; M. Cowan/*The Daily Illini*: 177; Glen Johnson/Johnson Photography: 180; Kristin Oostendorf/*The Daily Illini*: 203.

Printed in the United States of America

10   9   8   7   6   5   4   3   2   1

Human Kinetics Publishers
Box 5076, Champaign, IL 61825-5076
1-800-747-4457

Canada: Human Kinetics Publishers, Box 24040, Windsor, ON N8Y 4Y9
1-800-465-7301 (in Canada only)

Europe: Human Kinetics Publishers (Europe) Ltd., P.O. Box IW14, Leeds LS16 6TR, England
0532-781708

Australia: Human Kinetics Publishers, P.O. Box 80, Kingswood 5062, South Australia
618-374-0433

New Zealand: Human Kinetics Publishers, P.O. Box 105-231, Auckland 1
(09) 309-2259

This book is dedicated to all my teachers, but especially

To Mom and Dad, my first teachers, with devotion and thanks.

To Lindsy McLean and Otho Davis, with respect and pride.

To my students, with hope for the future.

To Carol, with love and joy.

CONTENTS

Preface   ix

Acknowledgments   xiii

chapter 1: Why Athletic Trainers Organize:
**   The Theoretical Basis of Management   1**

Student Objectives   1
Opening Case   2
Foundations of Management   2
Three Management Roles   7
Improving the Athletic Trainer's Managerial Effectiveness   13
Applications to Athletic Training: Theory Into Practice   15
Case Study 1   15
Case Study 2   16
Summary   17
Annotated Bibliography   17

chapter 2: What Athletic Trainers Do: Program Management   21

Student Objectives   21
Opening Case   22
Vision Statements   22
Mission Statements   23
Planning   25
Program Evaluation   38
Applications to Athletic Training: Theory Into Practice   40
Case Study 1   40
Case Study 2   43
Summary   43
Annotated Bibliography   44

chapter 3: Who Athletic Trainers Work With:
**   Human Resource Management   47**

Student Objectives   47
Opening Case   48
Organizational Culture   49
Organizational Structures   50
Staff Selection   54
Staff Supervision   65
Performance Evaluation   69
Applications to Athletic Training: Theory Into Practice   76
Case Study 1   76
Case Study 2   77
Summary   79
Annotated Bibliography   80

chapter 4: What Athletic Trainers Use:
**   Financial Resource Management   85**

Student Objectives   85

Opening Case   86
Budgeting   87
Purchasing   95
Inventory Management   103
Applications to Athletic Training: Theory Into Practice   105
Case Study 1   105
Case Study 2   106
Summary   107
Annotated Bibliography   108

**chapter 5: Where Athletic Trainers Work:
Facility Design and Planning**   **111**

Student Objectives   111
Opening Case   112
Conceptual Development   112
Elements of Sports Medicine Facility Design   124
Applications to Athletic Training: Theory Into Practice   133
Case Study 1   133
Case Study 2   134
Summary   135
Annotated Bibliography   135

**chapter 6: Helping Athletic Trainers Remember:
Information Management**   **139**

Student Objectives   139
Opening Case   140
Why Document?   141
Two Kinds of Information in Sports Medicine   143
Filing Sports Medicine Records   157
The Computer as an Information Management Tool   158
Applications to Athletic Training: Theory Into Practice   170
Case Study 1   170
Case Study 2   171
Summary   171
Annotated Bibliography   172

**chapter 7: Helping Athletic Trainers Pay the Bills:
Athletic Injury Insurance**   **177**

Student Objectives   177
Opening Case   178
Insurance Systems   180
Third-Party Reimbursement   184
Claims Processing   187
Purchasing Insurance Services   193
Applications to Athletic Training: Theory Into Practice   197
Case Study 1   197
Case Study 2   198
Summary   199
Annotated Bibliography   200

chapter 8: Protecting Athletic Trainers:
   Legal Considerations in Sports Medicine   **203**

   Student Objectives   203
   Opening Case   204
   Credentialing   205
   Legal Principles   208
   Legal Defenses   212
   Providing Testimony at Deposition or Trial   214
   Strategies for Avoiding Legal Liability   216
   Applications to Athletic Training: Theory Into Practice   218
   Case Study 1   218
   Case Study 2   219
   Summary   220
   Annotated Bibliography   221

Appendix A: WOTS UP Analysis for a Sports Medicine Program   225

Appendix B: State Credentialing Boards   237

Glossary   239

Author Index   251

Subject Index   253

About the Author   257

Athletic training has evolved through the years. Our predecessors early in the century were little more than clubhouse helpers for a select population of college and professional athletes. Following the establishment in 1950 of the National Athletic Trainers Association (NATA), however, credentialing and professional education standards have helped create a growing demand for our services. Athletic trainers are now allied health care professionals who provide injury prevention and management services for the public as a whole. As athletic trainers' employment settings and clientele have expanded, their need for administrative knowledge and skills has also expanded.

■ Why Is This Text Needed?

The days when an athletic trainer could get by without some administrative expertise are gone. The financial assets entrusted to the contemporary athletic trainer require prudent, thoughtful management. Athletic trainers can acquire some of the organizational knowledge and skill they need through on-the-job experience, but many entry-level athletic trainers will not get the information they need this way. The primary purpose of this book is to provide a standard for the kinds of knowledge and skills that every entry-level athletic trainer should master. Because the administrative problems that confront athletic trainers are growing in number and complexity, a reference book should be available to help athletic trainers cope with them while they provide high-quality services to their clients.

This text is also intended to enhance the administrative ability of athletic trainers already in practice. It contains a variety of topics and insights that many athletic trainers past the entry level don't consider in managerial or administrative terms. Practicing athletic trainers will learn to apply management theories to the administrative problems they have faced for years. This text will help them craft creative solutions to these problems.

This text brings together the body of knowledge about organization and administration and applies it to the profession of athletic training. Credentialing boards of national and state athletic training organizations could use this book as a source of valid questions for credentialing examinations. Currently available sources are either inadequate in focus because they are not intended for athletic trainers or inadequate in scope because they are typically single chapters in books intended for other purposes.

■ For Whom Is This Book Written?

The three primary audiences for this text are

- undergraduate students preparing for NATA certification,
- graduate students either preparing for NATA certification or working toward an advanced degree in athletic training, and
- practicing athletic trainers who may already be certified but who wish to either develop or update their knowledge and skill in athletic training administration.

■ How Is This Text Organized?

This book presents theories underlying the management principles that athletic trainers have historically been forced to learn through experience, utilizing anecdotes, practical suggestions, and case studies whenever possible to illustrate how management theory applies to the work of athletic trainers. An opening case precedes each chapter, and the content of the chapter relates to this opening case. Each chapter concludes with two case studies that require the reader to apply the theories presented in the chapter in situations they would be likely to encounter in actual practice.

■ Special Features

The following pedagogical aids help the reader master the content.

Chapter Objectives

Each chapter opens with a list of expected learning outcomes. These objectives are broad enough to form the behavioral objectives for an entire course in athletic training administration.

Key Words

Boldface italics highlight key words and important phrases to help the reader determine at a glance the concepts considered most important.

Glossary

Readers will find a glossary of important terms at the end of the book. In addition, students can use a running glossary that includes the same terms in the margins near the text where the term is used.

Sample Forms

Readers can modify sample forms for their own use.

Case Studies

Each chapter begins with an opening case study and concludes with two more. These cases will help the reader understand more fully the relationship between the theory and the application of various concepts discussed in the chapter. Instructors may wish to assign these cases as class assignments. Each case includes a hypothetical scenario. The cases at the end of the chapters are accompanied by a series of questions that require the reader to synthesize the information presented in the chapter and to develop alternative responses to each scenario. The analysis questions are open ended and encourage readers to be creative in developing possible solutions. There is no fixed number of "right" or "wrong" answers.

Chapter Summaries

The most important concepts of each chapter are summarized at the end of each chapter.

Annotated Bibliography

A complete bibliography of each reference used to develop the chapters, along with a brief annotation, will help readers decide if they wish to do additional reading on any given topic.

Index

The index of the entire text by author and subject facilitates easy reference.

ACKNOWLEDGMENTS

I am indebted to many people who gave their time and expertise to help make this book possible. I especially want to thank the professionals at Human Kinetics Publishers who not only offered many suggestions to improve the book, but also were kind and patient with this rookie author and his incessant phone calls. Many colleagues offered their advice and helped with chapter reviews, including Jeff Green, Dave Zessin, Dan Campbell, Jim Rudd, Dennis Corbin, Roger Kalisiak, George Kraft, Bob Carlson, Ken Gibson, Bill Anderson, and Barry Bandstra. Their expertise is acknowledged with gratitude. I am especially thankful for the thoughtful manuscript reviews offered by Jerry Bell and Bob Behnke. Their insights proved most useful in the editing stage of the project. Finally, I am deeply indebted to the administrative officers of Hope College, whose encouragement, interest, and support of my work has reinforced my contention that leadership makes a difference.

CHAPTER 1

"Being powerful is like being a lady. If you have to tell people you are, you ain't."

Jesse Carr

Why Athletic Trainers Organize: The Theoretical Basis of Management

STUDENT OBJECTIVES

▌ Define the concepts of power, authority, and leadership.

▌ Provide examples of how athletic trainers can use power, authority, and leadership to improve their managerial skills.

▌ Understand the different managerial roles assumed by athletic trainers.

▌ Understand the various strategies athletic trainers can employ to resolve conflicts with co-workers.

OPENING CASE

The staff meeting went just about as badly as Sharon was afraid it might. The athletic trainers she supervises (in the sports medicine clinic of which she is a part-owner) are angry. Sharon is also an athletic trainer, brought in by a physician and a physical therapist to help establish sports medicine services in a struggling outpatient physical therapy practice. When Sharon hired her staff of three certified athletic trainers, her partners required that they contribute a percentage of their health insurance premiums. They assured Sharon that this would be a temporary arrangement—2 years at most—until the other partners were confident that the expansion into sports medicine was going to pay off.

Sharon's athletic trainers were upset because, after 3 years, they were still being forced to contribute to their health insurance, even though the clinic's physical therapists didn't contribute a penny. Sharon agreed with their position. She felt they ought to be treated like the other professional staff. The problem she faced was that the physical therapist partner wanted to maintain the status quo while the physician was wavering between the two positions.

Sharon finally decided to call a partners' meeting, at which she threatened to pull out of the business unless the issue was resolved in favor of the athletic trainers. The vote was 2 to 1 in favor of Sharon's position. Unfortunately, Sharon's cordial working relationship with her two partners was partially eroded in the process. The physical therapist became coldly formal, and the physician was upset that Sharon had used a threat to get what she wanted.

▌ Foundations of Management

Elements of Sharon's dilemma are commonly experienced by athletic trainers, whatever the employment setting. Most athletic trainers have had to suffer through the tension that results from a "power play" in their organization. Though they typically lack formal education or training in management theory, athletic trainers need to be at least conversant with major theories of organizational behavior to make maximum use of the power, authority, and leadership that are normal components of their personal and professional profiles. Athletic trainers are often responsible for managing programs with large budgets and staffs. Until recently, intuition and on-the-job experience have been athletic trainers' only tools for attempting to solve administrative problems. Formal study of the principles underlying sound management practice should help athletic trainers perform their jobs better.

Power

power   The potential to influence others.

Scholars who devote their careers to the study of power cannot agree on a precise definition, but the definition most inclusive of the research done on the subject was put forth by Bass (1990). **Power** is the potential to influence.

Why is it important for students of athletic training administration to be able to define, recognize, and use power? Power is the glue that binds persons or groups in a relationship. It is the basis for both authority and leadership. Athletic trainers possess significant power in their relationships with coaches, administrators, clients, and other health care professionals. Sharon's case illustrates an athletic trainer recognizing her potential to influence others and acting on it. Sharon exercised power.

Athletic trainers can exercise power over those above them, below them, and at the same level in an organization. The two primary modalities for the exercise of organizational power are ***position power*** and ***personal power***.

Position Power

Athletic trainers, by virtue of their positions, possess resources they can use to influence the behavior of others in their organizations. Someone who supervises student athletic trainers, for example, can influence their behavior through the use of rewards and punishments—grades, financial aid, work-study money, desirable team assignments and internship placements, and the like. In an organization that follows a medical chain of command, the athletic trainer can use the power provided by that policy to change the behavior of a coach who may desire to usurp the athletic trainer's medical authority.

The ability to influence the behavior of a superior has been termed ***counterpower*** (Yukl, 1981). Counterpower is a tool that most athletic trainers need because they are typically viewed as support personnel who are less important than other organizational decision makers. Without counterpower, athletic trainers would be little more than technical consultants to more powerful coaches and athletic administrators, unable to influence the actions of these two important groups.

One of the ways athletic trainers can effectively use position power is by controlling the flow of information (Pettigrew, 1972). By controlling information athletic trainers can influence the perceptions and attitudes of their subordinates. For example, assistant athletic trainers often learn of changes in departmental policy through their head athletic trainers. And student athletic trainers depend to a large degree on instructors and supervisors to inform them of changes in the profession.

Athletic trainers can also make superiors reliant on them for certain types of information. For example, in the draft systems of professional sports, potential draftees are examined by both physicians and athletic trainers. How the results are passed on to decision makers can significantly influence whether an athlete is drafted. Ultimately, the athletic trainer exercises influence through providing or withholding information.

Personal Power

The athletic trainer's ability to influence others in the organization often depends more on personal characteristics and personality attributes than on formal authority. Indeed, athletic trainers who use charisma and personal appeal to influence others in their organizations are more likely to receive acceptance and support for their ideas. Coercive power and authoritarian

position power *Power vested in people by virtue of the role they play in an organization.*

personal power *The potential to influence others by virtue of personal characteristics and personality attributes.*

counterpower *The potential to influence the behavior of a superior.*

methods, on the other hand, are more likely to produce mere compliance, decreasing satisfaction and performance levels among the staff members these athletic trainers supervise (Yukl, 1981).

One of the most effective elements of athletic trainers' personal power is their reputation as experts. People are more likely to follow the recommendation of someone they perceive as an expert (French & Raven, 1959). Athletic trainers make judgments based on their expertise in sports medicine every day. Athletes who follow the treatment plan outlined by an athletic trainer probably have faith in the athletic trainer as an expert. When athletes fail to follow their treatment and rehabilitation plans, it is often because they have lost faith in the expertise of the athletic trainer supervising their programs. In these cases, the trainer must resort to position power as the basis for achieving compliance. Unfortunately, using the external motivators of position power is rarely as effective as using the internal motivators of personal power.

Authority

authority   *That aspect of power, granted to either groups or individuals, that legitimizes the right of the group or individual to make decisions on behalf of others.*

Authority is that aspect of power, granted to either groups or individuals, that legitimizes the right of the group or individual to make decisions on behalf of others. Implicit in this definition is the notion that authority is a subset of the broader construct of power. Although there are authors who disagree with this proposition (Friedrich, 1963; Kahn, 1968), most evidence clearly identifies authority as a type of power (Burns, 1978; Dejnozka, 1983; Good, 1973; Jacobs, 1970; Katz & Kahn, 1966; King, 1987; Lasswell & Kaplan, 1950; Organ & Bateman, 1986). If power is the glue that binds persons or groups together in a relationship, then authority is the applicator through which power is applied. Without authority, athletic trainers would lack position power.

legitimacy   *That aspect of power that gives the leader the right to make a request and provides the obligation of the subordinate to comply.*

Central to the meaning of authority is the concept of legitimacy. Authority is legitimate by its very nature (Good, 1973; Hollander, 1978; Karelis, 1987; Weber, 1962). **Legitimacy** is a check on the scope of an athletic trainer's authority. Consider Sharon's case at the beginning of this chapter. Even though she may have wanted to grant the request of her staff members, she didn't have the authority to do so without the consent of her partners. Any decision made without her partners' consent would have lacked legitimacy.

zone of indifference   *A hypothetical boundary of legitimacy, outside of which requests or orders will be met with mere compliance or refusal.*

Legitimacy is an especially important concept for athletic trainers who supervise others' work. Barnard (1938) postulated that each person has a ***zone of indifference***. People typically accept requests or orders within this zone without conscious questioning because they view them as appropriate given the status of the person making the request. Orders or requests outside the zone, however, lack legitimacy, and people may refuse to comply with them. Athletic trainers who supervise assistants or students should be cautious about asking them to do things outside the zone of indifference. It may be legitimate, for example, to ask a student athletic trainer to wash a whirlpool. Don't expect enthusiastic support if you ask the same student to wash your car!

Another property implicit in this definition of authority is that it involves decision making and is therefore action oriented. Like its parent, power, authority can only be observed when it is exercised. If Sharon had not acted on the vote of her partners in the health insurance case, she would have abrogated her authority in the matter. Athletic trainers are called on to make many administrative decisions during the course of a typical day. Should I order more tape? How should I arrange the team physician's injury clinic schedule? How many athletic trainers will be needed to cover the wrestling tournament? Athletic trainers exercise the authority they have been granted when they answer these questions with action. Indeed, many of their administrative problems stem from hesitation to use their authority.

There is one notable exception to the action orientation normally associated with authority. Some situations call for the athletic trainer to exercise authority by making a conscious decision *not* to act. Let's consider Sharon's dilemma as an example. Suppose that instead of being neutral her physician partner was against Sharon's point of view on the health insurance issue and in favor of the physical therapist partner's. In that case Sharon would know that calling a vote on the matter would likely result in a formal company position against full compensation of health insurance benefits for staff athletic trainers. The only prudent action she could take in this circumstance would be no action at all, other than to continue to try to convince her partners to support her. To request a vote would be counterproductive. The important point is that Sharon's inaction would be goal oriented. She would be letting the issue lay for the moment so she would be able to fight another day.

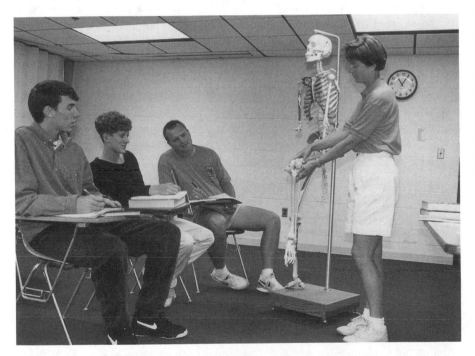

▌ Athletic trainers in educational settings are often called upon to exercise authority over student athletic trainers.

The athletic trainer's use of her authority can be a powerful tool to prompt task accomplishment. Authority provides a new athletic trainer an immediate power base to help her accomplish tasks. This is sometimes referred to as the **honeymoon effect**. Newly hired people in athletic training programs are often granted more authority to make decisions than they would be 6 months or a year after arrival. The honeymoon effect is an important factor in rejuvenating programs. Without it, new athletic trainers would have little impact since they wouldn't be able to implement new ideas as easily.

honeymoon effect *The period of time, usually immediately after arriving in a new position, in which persons are more likely to be granted extra authority to make decisions.*

There are several drawbacks to excessive use of authority to accomplish tasks in athletic training programs. Athletic trainers who rely too heavily on their authority are likely to find that their staffs respond with mere compliance and minimal effort (Organ & Bateman, 1986). The athletic trainer who constantly reminds his assistants ''who's the boss'' may be successful in extracting a minimal amount of work from the assistants, but he is also likely to experience a high rate of turnover. Athletic trainers who rely heavily on authority are also likely to find that their subordinates try to avoid them. The threat, perceived or real, of negative sanctions imposed by an authoritarian supervisor against subordinates is a common theme, even for those athletic trainers with no rational basis for their perceptions.

Leadership

Leadership is the process of influencing the behavior and attitudes of others to achieve intended outcomes. Like authority, it is a subset of the broader construct of power (Burns, 1978). There are nearly as many definitions of leadership as there are scholars who have studied the topic—over 130 distinct definitions exist (Burns, 1978). One of the few common denominators among this host of definitions is the assumption that leadership involves an intentional influence process by a leader over followers (Yukl, 1981). In addition, leadership is success oriented. If a ''leader'' attempts an action and doesn't get the support of followers, has leadership really taken place?

Why is a discussion of leadership important for athletic trainers? The exercise of leadership is the keystone of managerial success. Without the ability to influence attitudes and behaviors toward some predetermined goal, the athletic trainer will be an ineffective agent for change in her organization. Unfortunately, we often think of leaders as persons on the national or international stage. Churchill, Ghandi, and Roosevelt were certainly effective leaders. The more common form of leadership is a more local phenomenon, however. We are all surrounded by leaders in our homes, churches, communities, and the sports medicine settings in which we work. Without leadership, the organizations that employ us would stagnate and cease to be effective in providing needed services to their clients.

To help athletic trainers understand the importance of effective leadership and the effect it can have on their managerial success, it is useful to examine the two types of leadership found in most social structures, including the organizations that employ athletic trainers. Burns (1978) contends that there are two distinct forms of leadership: transactional and transformational. *Transactional leadership* involves the simple exchange of one thing for another in a relationship between two people. An athletic trainer pays her assistants in exchange for work. An athletic director agrees to send an athletic trainer to a conference in exchange for covering a state high school basketball tournament. Most administrative activities in organizations where athletic trainers work involve the transactional form of leadership. This book is devoted primarily to principles and techniques intended to improve the athletic trainer's ability to be a transactional leader. Transactional leadership is the stuff of management.

Nevertheless, a program or organization in which only transactional leadership takes place will probably not thrive. Organizational renewal and program

---

leadership   A subset of power that involves influencing the behavior and attitudes of others to achieve intended outcomes.

transactional leadership The simple exchange between leaders and followers of one thing for another.

improvement require transformational leadership. ***Transformational leadership*** transcends the day-to-day administrative requirements of operating an athletic training program by elevating standards through the creative use of change and conflict. The athletic trainer who can successfully prepare budgets, hire staff, purchase supplies, and schedule personnel is an effective transactional leader. The athletic trainer who recognizes the need to reduce the incidence of eating disorders among her athletes and who implements programs that successfully accomplish this task exhibits transformational leadership.

Transformational leadership almost always involves change in the organization. This change is likely to engender some degree of conflict. Consider the example of setting up an eating disorders program. Such programs cost money. Instructional materials must be developed or purchased. Group facilitators and therapists must be contracted. Funding will either have to come from existing programs or be raised specifically for the project. Decisions like these often bring athletic trainers into conflict with coaches and athletic administrators who are in competition for scarce financial resources. The athletic trainer who is a skilled transformational leader will be able to manage the conflict to meet the needs of coaches, athletic administrators, and athletes with eating disorders. As you can see, the transformational aspect of leadership is both challenging and essential if the athletic training program is to meet the changing needs of its clients.

transformational leadership That aspect of leadership that uses both change and conflict to elevate the standards of the social system.

▌Three Management Roles

Management is that element of the leadership process that involves planning, decision making, and coordinating the activities of a group of people working toward a common goal. Athletic trainers' regular management activities include scheduling, purchasing, hiring, evaluation, program development, accounting, and many others. In his classic text on the science of management, Fayol (1949) defined the following five elements of management: (1) planning, (2) organizing, (3) command, (4) coordination, and (5) control. Gulick and Urwick (1977) added staffing, directing, reporting, and budgeting to Fayol's original list. Dale (1965) felt that innovation and representation were also important management functions.

Mintzberg (1973) described three major roles that all managers, including athletic trainers, assume from time to time: (1) interpersonal roles, (2) informational roles, and (3) decisional roles.

management The element of leadership that involves planning, decision making, and coordination of the activities of a group.

Interpersonal Roles

Every athletic trainer who manages a department or program will probably be forced to assume three different ***interpersonal roles*** at one time or another. The first is the ***figurehead role***. As the person who has been granted formal authority for a particular program, the athletic trainer will be called on to perform certain routine functions such as providing signatures, public speaking, and answering requests for information. The figurehead role is often the most visible managerial task the athletic trainer will undertake. Although it is probably not as vital to the long-term health of the program as other managerial roles, it is important because of the public relations value that it can yield.

interpersonal role A type of managerial role, emanating from the possession of formal authority, that requires the manager to interact and form relationships with others in the organization.

figurehead role A type of interpersonal role that requires the authority holder to represent the group, usually in a visible public capacity.

The second managerial role the athletic trainer must assume is that of a leader. We have already discussed transactional and transformational leadership.

The third managerial role the athletic trainer must assume is that of *liaison*. The liaison role is a very important part of the athletic trainer's success or failure as a manager. Athletic trainers must work with a wide variety of people to run a successful athletic training program (see Figure 1.1). Although vertical liaison with co-workers above and below him in the organization is commonly understood to be a function of the athletic trainer, horizontal liaison with professional peers is vital to developing and maintaining goodwill

liaison role *A type of interpersonal role that requires the leader to interface with others in the group, including superiors, subordinates, and peers.*

▌ **Figure 1.1** Liaison relationships of the athletic trainer.

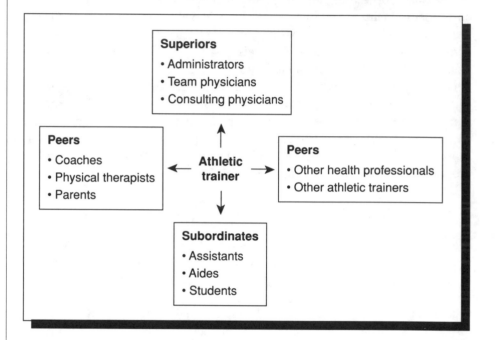

between the athletic training program and other departments of the organization and between the program and outside entities. Mintzberg (1973) hypothesized that social equals tend to interact with one another more often than with superiors or subordinates. Thus, athletic trainers need to develop relationships with athletic trainers at other institutions, health professionals in the community, coaches, consulting physicians, and parents. All these people will have an effect on the athletic trainer's managerial success. Chapter 3 discusses the athletic trainer's liaison function in greater detail.

Informational Roles

The first *informational role* the athletic trainer plays is as both a *monitor* and a *disseminator* of information. The athletic training program is constantly bombarded with information from a variety of sources on a variety of topics. Journals and trade publications present news of technological advances in preventing and treating athletic injuries. Newsletters and memoranda route organizational news and policy changes. Progress reports and clinical notes arrive in the mail from team and consulting physicians. The first response of the effective athletic trainer/manager is to filter the information. Is it

informational role *Those functions that require the manager to collect, use, and disseminate information.*

monitor role *A type of informational role that requires the leader to observe and keep abreast of changes that will affect the group and its activity.*

disseminator role *A type of informational role that requires the leader to communicate with members of the group.*

appropriate to share this memo with the staff? Who needs to know about the complications of Rick's knee surgery? Athletic trainers in a variety of employment settings decide these and similar questions daily.

After deciding what information should be passed along and to whom it should be passed, the athletic trainer must decide how to deliver it efficiently and effectively (see Figure 1.2). Some items can be posted on a bulletin

---

Communication Methods

- Bulletin boards
- Staff meetings
- Individual meetings
- Letters or memos
- Newsletters
- Telephone calls
- Electronic mail

■ **Figure 1.2** Tools for disseminating information.

board where the staff can scan the information at their leisure. Other items require more explanation and documentation and should therefore be put in writing and delivered individually. This is especially important if the information is confidential or if it is necessary to document that the information was actually passed along. For example, if a staff athletic trainer was not performing up to the standards set by the organization, it would be important to communicate these concerns in writing to keep them confidential and to document that the institution had warned the athletic trainer of dissatisfaction with his work.

The *spokesperson's role* is the third informational role that athletic trainers assume as part of their managerial repertoire. Mintzberg (1973) points out that effective managers must keep two important groups informed. The first group includes the organizational decision makers, also known as internal *influencers*. Internal influencers are people who either are members of or

spokesperson's role A type of informational role that requires the leader to communicate with organizational influencers and members of the organization's public.

influencers Organization decision makers.

■ Electronic mail is one information dissemination technique that sports medicine program leaders can use.

have close ties to an organization and who have the power to help shape policy and practice. Examples of internal influencers in various settings where sports medicine programs are found include the following:

High School Settings

- Coaches
- Team physicians
- Athletic directors
- Principals
- Central office administrators
- Board of education members

College and University Settings

- Coaches
- Athletic administrators
- Other university administrators
- Team physicians
- Trustees

Clinical Settings

- Clinic owners
- Hospital administrators
- Referring physicians
- Hospital trustees
- Supervisors

Professional Athletics Settings

- Coaches
- General managers
- Other club administrators
- Owners
- Team physicians

The second group the athletic trainer should communicate with in his role as spokesperson is the organization's public. Like the internal influencers, the members of the sports medicine program's public will vary by setting. Common to each setting are clients (patients, athletes, student-athletes), suppliers, community supporters (booster clubs, parents, fans, alumni groups), consulting health professionals, and the news media. The athletic trainer will be expected to communicate with each of these groups from time to time, taking on the role of the organization's expert in sports medicine. The expert spokesperson role is a source of considerable personal power for the athletic trainer.

Decisional Roles

The last group of roles athletic trainers must assume as part of their managerial responsibilities is probably the most important—it is made up of *decisional roles*. Decisional roles require the athletic trainer to use both personal and position power by exercising authority. The effective athletic trainer/manager will also use decisional roles to exercise transformational leadership by planning strategies to serve clients better.

The first decision-making role assumed by the athletic trainer is entrepreneurial. Although most of us envision an *entrepreneur* as someone who creates new businesses, the term refers here to an athletic trainer who designs and initiates changes for his programs and organizations. If the athletic trainer fails in this entrepreneurial role, the sports medicine program will probably stop improving. One of the ways athletic trainers can become entrepreneurs for the sports medicine program is by focusing both on small, solvable problems and on new opportunities and initiating improvements to take advantage of both. Every athletic trainer could probably come up with a list of 10 to 15 concrete steps that would improve their programs. Athletic trainers could also improve their programs by taking advantage of some of the opportunities they face. The key is the ability to make decisions about which changes to implement on the basis of what is feasible.

The second decision-making role involves the athletic trainer as *disturbance handler*. Disturbances requiring the attention and intervention of the athletic trainer almost always revolve around conflict. The role of conflict manager is often a difficult and uncomfortable one for athletic trainers for several reasons. First, conflict almost always involves change. Indeed, some scholars have defined the term *conflict* as change (Burns, 1978). Controlled change is a necessary ingredient for healthy program and organizational growth. Unfortunately, such change often occurs with some human costs attached.

Blake and Mouton (1984) have identified eight traditional methods managers should consider to resolve a conflict. Each is most effective under certain circumstances, and many cases may require a combination of two or more approaches.

Cooperation by Edict

This is the most frequently attempted and least frequently successful method. It requires that the athletic trainer have a high degree of control over subordinates, and its effects diminish rapidly. "My way or the highway" is a poor conflict management technique for most complex situations.

Negotiation

Negotiation between the two parties may resolve surface issues, but deep-seated conflict often remains unresolved since neither side gets everything desired. Negotiation often ends up throwing old precedents away and establishing new ones, so it should be used with caution.

---

decisional role That portion of a manager's work that requires her to use authority to make decisions.

entrepreneur role A type of decisional role in which the leader initiates and designs controlled change within an organization.

disturbance handler role A type of decisional role in which the leader manages conflict.

Leadership Replacement

Leadership replacement is a common technique when conflict resolution fails at one level and rises to the next level of the organization. Although new leaders can bring fresh perspectives to a problem, they lack a sense of the history and culture of the organization.

Personnel Rotation

Although this may be an effective conflict resolution method for a small staff, it is unlikely to change large-group norms. Changes due to personnel rotation are usually temporary in large groups.

Organizational Structural Changes

Such changes are often attempted to ameliorate conflict. Unfortunately, if the nature of the work remains the same, so does the conflict.

Liaison Persons

Liaison persons are often appointed or elected to represent the parties in a conflict. Although this can be beneficial, it can slow communication by adding another layer to the organizational structure.

Flexible Reporting Relationships

Using flexible reporting relationships can be an effective way to manage interpersonal conflict, especially if the conflict is between the program head and one of the subordinate staff. Having the staff member report to another staff member instead of the program head can often insulate the two players from each other.

Mediation and Arbitration

These conflict resolution techniques are the last resort since they involve bringing in a third party from outside the organization to impose binding solutions that both parties may accept, but that neither party is likely to desire or feel ownership in.

Thomas and Kilmann (1974) described five more general approaches to conflict resolution. To help resolve conflicts in the sports medicine unit, athletic trainers could choose one of these methods.

Competition

Competing resolves conflict between two or more members of the sports medicine unit through confrontation. Central to the concept of competition is the notion that one athletic trainer's position power will be imposed to the exclusion of the other's.

Accommodation

Accommodating involves conceding to the other party in the conflict.

Avoidance

Avoiding involves bypassing a conflict to prevent the unpleasant consequences normally associated with confrontation. Unfortunately, this method resolves nothing and conflict is almost certain to reappear at some point. Avoidance is one of the most frequent methods employed by managers in all kinds of settings.

Collaboration

Collaborating is the method most likely to result in lasting conflict resolution. It involves both parties to a conflict attempting to solve the problem together by investigating various possible alternatives. Collaboration requires creative solutions and typically results in meeting the needs of both parties.

Compromise

Compromise is similar to collaboration in that it attempts to meet the needs of both parties. The major difference is that compromising resolves the conflict by defining a position somewhere in between those of the two parties while collaboration develops new positions previously not considered by either party.

The third decision-making role played by the athletic trainer is as an *allocator of resources*. The athletic trainer generally has the formal authority to determine how time, money, supplies, equipment, and personnel should be deployed. If the athletic trainer/manager does not have this authority, frustration and managerial apathy are likely to result. Sharon's case at the beginning of this chapter is a good example. Although she wanted to allocate company funds toward full compensation of the athletic trainers' health insurance costs, she was unable to do so without being granted the formal authority of her partners. This frustrated not only Sharon, but also the staff athletic trainers.

The final managerial role the athletic trainer assumes is that of a *negotiator*. The athletic trainer negotiates on behalf of the organization he represents. Thus, the negotiator role is actually a combination of several different roles, including the figurehead, resource allocator, and spokesperson (Mintzberg, 1973). Although most arrangements the athletic trainer negotiates on behalf of the organization must eventually be ratified by someone closer to the top of the organizational structure, the athletic trainer must be granted a limited amount of authority to enter into meaningful discussions with another party. Typical arrangements negotiated by athletic trainers include prices for supplies and services, sponsorship for various activities, and grants for specific programs.

∎ Improving the Athletic Trainer's Managerial Effectiveness

Leaders usually, but not always, exercise authority by making legitimate requests. In response, staff might commit, comply, or resist. Athletic trainers

allocator of resources role A type of decisional role in which the leader exercises authority to determine how organizational assets will be deployed.

negotiator role A type of decisional role in which the leader uses authority to bargain with members of the internal or external audience.

can use many methods to decrease the likelihood of resistance and increase the possibility of commitment (Yukl, 1981).

Ways to Ensure Commitment

When making requests of subordinates, athletic trainers should take positive steps to ensure commitment.

Be Courteous and Respectful

Avoid emphasizing differences in status, intelligence, financial responsibility, and other factors related to rank.

Radiate Confidence

If the leader communicates doubt through verbal or nonverbal cues, the staff is unlikely to comply with enthusiasm.

Use Simple Language

When instructions must necessarily be complicated, check to be sure that subordinates understand them.

Make Reasonable Requests

Test requests for legitimacy by consulting with co-workers above you or at the same level in the organization. Referring to formally approved policies, rules, and negotiated agreements can help legitimize requests.

Provide Rationale

Providing reasons for your request will help reduce the perceived status gap between you and your staff.

Use the Chain of Command

Following established lines of communication decreases the possibility of message distortion. Make requests in writing whenever possible.

Use Authority Regularly

If you make legitimate requests regularly, your staff will be less likely to resist.

Exercise Authority to Confirm Task Accomplishment

If you do not demand compliance for legitimate requests, future noncompliance is more likely.

Be Open-Minded

Staff members who consider their leader to be a heartless automaton with no concern for their ideas or feelings are unlikely to respond to requests with enthusiasm.

■ Applications to Athletic Training: Theory Into Practice

The following two case studies will help you apply the concepts in this chapter to situations you may face in actual practice. The questions at the end of the case studies are open ended—there are many possible correct solutions. The case studies can be used as homework, exam questions, or for class discussion.

CASE STUDY 1

During the second half of an NCAA Division III tournament soccer game, the goalkeeper of the host team was involved in a collision and fell to the ground in pain. The school's athletic trainer evaluated the injury on the field and determined that the goalkeeper, who was unable to run or cut and could walk only with a pronounced limp, had suffered a Grade 2 ankle sprain. The trainer decided to remove the player from the game based on three factors: The athlete could not perform without significant dysfunction; the team had another game in a few days and the trainer wanted to begin immediate treatment in preparation; and the team was winning the game by two goals and appeared to be in control.

As the athletic trainer helped the goalkeeper from the field, the coach jogged out to meet them and asked the athlete how he felt. When he replied that his ankle was injured but not too badly, the coach said it was the athlete's decision whether to keep playing. The trainer interjected, telling the coach that she felt further play would jeopardize a rapid recovery. The coach looked again at the athlete and said the decision was his. The athlete replied that he would try to continue. The athletic trainer tried again to express her opposition, but the athlete was already walking back to the goal and the coach was leaving the field.

The athletic trainer was confused and upset, incensed that the coach would usurp her authority in the matter. The athletic department had a medical chain of command procedure that clearly authorized the team physician, or the athletic trainer in the physician's absence, as the final authority on playing status for injured athletes. She wasn't sure what else she could have done to change the outcome.

QUESTIONS FOR ANALYSIS

1. How do the concepts of power and authority apply to this case? Who had power, and how was it used? What was the basis for this power? Who had authority, and how was it used?

2. What might the athletic trainer have done differently (either before or during the incident) to avoid the situation?

3. What should the athletic trainer do now? Which conflict resolution methods are most appropriate for this case? Is there only one correct solution, or do several possibilities exist?

CASE STUDY 2

After interviewing for a job in a large Texas high school, Jim, a certified athletic trainer with 17 years of experience, decided he would accept a job offer there. His primary reason for accepting the job was that he was burned out in NCAA Division I athletics. He thought the high school position would give him the contact he enjoyed with athletes without the headaches of running a major university sports medicine program.

Jim arrived in Texas in June to allow plenty of time to organize his new program before the athletes came back in August. During the first week on the job, Jim began to realize that there were a few questions he should have asked during his interview. Even though the sports medicine program had an adequate budget, Jim was not allowed to order any equipment or supplies without the written permission of his athletic director. When Jim presented a list of supplies needed for the next year, the AD approved only half the items. In addition, he told Jim he would have to purchase them from the local sporting goods dealer. Jim complained that he needed all the items on the list and that if he purchased everything from the local vendor, the sports medicine budget would be spent before Christmas.

Another problem Jim faced during the first few weeks concerned a drug and alcohol education program he proposed for student-athletes. Jim wanted to involve all the coaches and team captains in a preliminary workshop and then to develop programs for individual teams. When he presented his plan, the AD smiled and said, ''That kind of thing has been tried before and it didn't work then. I don't see why it would work now. Besides, we don't have any serious problems like that in our school.''

When the athletes arrived in August Jim quickly gained a reputation as a caring and competent athletic trainer. Injured athletes came to know him as someone who would take good care of them and who could help them return to action as soon as possible. The fall sports coaches also appreciated Jim's talents and expertise. They liked the way he communicated with them and his hard work in keeping their teams healthy.

QUESTIONS FOR ANALYSIS

1. In what ways did the honeymoon effect work for Jim in his new job? In what ways didn't it work?

2. Which of Jim's early leadership actions were transactional? Which were transformational?

3. Which management roles did Jim assume during his first few months on the job? Which were most important in helping him establish relationships with the various groups at his new school?

4. Jim is obviously having trouble working with his new athletic director. Which conflict management strategies should he consider in attempting to work out his differences? Given the personality style of the AD, what are some likely outcomes of Jim's conflict management attempts?

5. If you were in Jim's position, would you have handled anything differently? What alternative actions would you have taken?

▌ Summary

Athletic trainers need formal instruction in management theory and technique if they are to become proficient administrators. The proper use of power, authority, and leadership can help the athletic trainer accomplish administrative tasks more effectively. Power is the potential to influence. Athletic trainers possess two forms of power: personal and position. Authority is that aspect of power, granted to either groups or individuals, that legitimizes the right of the individual or group to make decisions on behalf of others. Requests made on the basis of authority must be legitimate. Authority is action oriented unless the athletic trainer makes a goal-directed decision not to act in a given situation. Excessive reliance on formal authority can result in low subordinate satisfaction. Leadership is the process of influencing the behavior and attitudes of others to achieve intended outcomes. There are two forms of leadership: transactional and transformational. Transactional leadership involves the exchange of one thing for another between two people in a relationship. It makes up the majority of managerial tasks that athletic trainers perform. Transformational leadership raises the standards of the program or organization through the creative use of conflict and change. It is essential for the ongoing health and development of a sports medicine program.

Management is that element of the leadership process that involves planning, decision making, and coordinating the activities of a group of people working toward a common goal. Athletic trainers play many managerial roles, which can be generalized into three groups: interpersonal, informational, and decisional roles. Athletic trainers can improve their managerial effectiveness by using nine techniques: making polite requests, making requests in a confident tone, making clear requests, making legitimate requests, explaining the reasons for the request, using proper channels, exercising authority regularly, insisting on compliance, and being responsive to subordinate concerns.

▌ Annotated Bibliography

Barnard, C.I. (1938). *The functions of the executive*. Cambridge, MA: Harvard University Press.

> This well-known text focuses on the concept of legitimacy as it relates to authority. Barnard defines *authority* as a type of communication in a formal organization. Of particular note is his theory regarding the "zone of indifference," within which requests are not consciously questioned.

Bass, B.M. (1990). *Bass & Stogdill's handbook of leadership* (3rd ed.). New York: Macmillan.

> This classic text synthesizes the most recent findings in research into leadership. Major topics include leadership theories, personal attributes

of leaders, power and legitimacy, transactional exchange, leadership and management, situational moderators, and the leadership of diverse groups.

Blake, R.R., & Mouton, J.S. (1984). *Solving costly organizational conflicts.* San Francisco: Jossey-Bass.

This case-oriented approach to conflict management includes practical suggestions and examples of the Interface Conflict-Solving Model.

Burns, J.M. (1978). *Leadership.* New York: Harper & Row.

This Pulitzer Prize–winning book is recognized as a seminal work on leadership. Its major themes center on leadership, followership, authority, power, needs, and wants. It also presents in-depth case studies of noted historical leaders.

Dale, E. (1965). *Management: Theory and practice.* New York: McGraw-Hill.

This introductory management text provides lifelike accounts of managerial situations and explains basic management theory.

Dejnozka, E.L. (1983). *Educational administration glossary.* Westport, CT: Greenwood Press.

This reference work identifies and defines educational terms with an emphasis on school management and organization.

Fayol, H. (1949). *General and industrial management.* London: Pitman & Sons.

In one of the earliest texts to deal with management as a distinct discipline, Fayol describes various managerial functions and promulgates guidelines for successful management.

French, J.R.P., & Raven, B. (1959). The bases of social power. In D. Cartwright (Ed.), *Studies in social power* (pp. 150-167). Ann Arbor, MI: Institute for Social Research.

French and Raven present a mathematical model to describe the power relationship between two agents. The primary focus of the article is on the five bases of power: reward, coercive, legitimate, referent, and expert power.

Friedrich, C.J. (1963). *Man and his government: An empirical theory of politics.* New York: McGraw-Hill.

Friedrich's book analyzes politics and government. Chapters 9 to 13 discuss the interrelationship between power, authority, leadership, influence, and legitimacy.

Good, C.V. (Ed.) (1973). *Dictionary of education.* New York: McGraw-Hill.

Good provides a comprehensive dictionary of professional terms in education.

Gulick, L., & Urwick, L. (Eds.) (1977). *Papers on the science of administration.* Fairfield, NJ: Kelley.

This collection contains the original writings of some of the pioneers in managerial science, including Henri Fayol, Elton Mayo, and Mary Parker Follett.

Hollander, E.P. (1978). *Leadership dynamics: A practical guide to effective relationships*. New York: Macmillan.

Hollander defines *leadership* as an influence process. His primary thesis is that leaders influence through a system of social transactions in which leaders build up ''idiosyncratic credits.'' He discusses authority in terms of three sets of rules that are employed in social systems: mock rules, consensus rules, and contested rules.

Jacobs, T.O. (1970). *Leadership and exchange in formal organizations*. Alexandria, VA: Human Resources Research Organization.

This author's thesis is that traditional management theorists have over-emphasized the importance of property rights and management prerogatives as explanations of authority and have failed to recognize the importance of member consent.

Kahn, R.F. (1968). A note on the concept of authority. In G. Wijeyewardene (Ed.), *Leadership and authority* (pp. 6-14). Kuala Lumpur, Malaysia: University of Malaysia Press.

This paper was presented as part of a symposium on authority and leadership in Malaysia. The author defines various types of authority. Kahn argues that charismatic authority does not depend on success. He describes several examples of charismatic leaders who retained their followings despite failure to accomplish stated goals.

Karelis, C.H. (1987). The limits of leadership. *Liberal Education*, **73**(2), 20-33.

Karelis argues that people in authority should never substitute their own vision and values for those of the group. He differentiates between the concepts of leadership and authority and takes the nontraditional view that those in authority should not exercise leadership except in times of crisis. To do so, he argues, is to usurp the right of the group to control its own destiny.

Katz, D., & Kahn, R.L. (1966). *The social psychology of organizations*. New York: Wiley & Sons.

The authors' point of view in this book is that classical organizational theory does not adequately explain or predict organizational behavior. Their thesis is that open system theory is more predictive of what actually occurs in social systems. Chapters 8 and 11 consider authority as it relates to leadership in an organizational setting.

King, A.A. (1987). *Power and communication*. Prospect Heights, IL: Waveland.

King presents the constructs of power and communication in relation to speakers and audiences and suggests that language is a type of power. The author views authority as legitimacy granted to power holders by the masses.

Lasswell, H.D., & Kaplan, A. (1950). Power and society: A framework for political inquiry. *Yale Law School Studies*, **2**, 133.

This article is a collection of definitions produced as a part of the Research Project on Wartime Communication. It was developed in an effort to perfect the tools of mass communication research and to define and analyze the terms pertinent to such research.

Mintzberg, H. (1973). *The nature of managerial work.* New York: Harper & Row.

Mintzberg outlines major managerial theories, with particular emphasis on the contingency theory of managerial work. Chapter 4, which discusses the 10 roles that all managers must play in order to be successful, is especially valuable.

Organ, D.W., & Bateman, T. (1986). *Organizational behavior: An applied psychological approach.* Plano, TX: Business Publications.

The authors focus on four topics: basic behavioral concepts, patterns of conflict and reconciliation between individuals and organizations, social influence processes, and the organization as a behavioral entity. The section on the functions and limitations of authority contains useful suggestions for leaders about using multiple tools to influence subordinate behavior.

Pettigrew, A.M. (1972). Information control as a power source. *Sociology*, **6**, 187-204.

A report of an empirical study designed to help a gatekeeper filter information during decision making. The author concludes that the control of information is a critical source of power, especially when the information is technical in nature.

Thomas, K.W., & Kilmann, R.H. (1974). *The Thomas-Kilmann conflict mode instrument.* Tuxedo Park, NY: Xicom.

This instrument is designed to assess a manager's preferred conflict-handling behavior. Its scores help managers determine their assertiveness and cooperativeness in a conflict situation.

Weber, M. (1962). *Basic concepts in sociology* (H.P. Secher, Trans.). Secaucus, NJ: Citadell.

This book contains a synthesis of Weber's important writings about social conduct, legitimate authority, and the concepts of power and domination. Chapters 5 through 7 outline his thoughts on the concept of legitimacy as a prerequisite for authority.

Yukl, G.A. (1981). *Leadership in organizations.* Englewood Cliffs, NJ: Prentice Hall.

Yukl synthesizes the major theories of leadership. He includes sections on reciprocal influence processes, leadership behaviors and managerial activities, situational determinants of leader behavior, and participation and delegation.

CHAPTER 2

"The best is the enemy of the good."

Voltaire

What Athletic Trainers Do: Program Management

STUDENT OBJECTIVES

▌ Understand and be able to develop vision and mission statements for a sports medicine program.

▌ Understand the principles underlying sports medicine strategic planning.

▌ Develop and link sports medicine policies, processes, and procedures.

▌ Communicate and develop ownership in the sports medicine program among inside and outside stakeholders.

▌ Understand the principles of effective sports medicine program evaluation.

OPENING CASE

Janet arrived at work one morning to find a note from the director of rehabilitation services on her desk requesting her presence at a meeting later that morning. She wasn't sure why the director would want to meet with her. She had been doing a good job since arriving at the hospital 2 years ago. Still, she was apprehensive as she walked down the hallway to the meeting.

"Janet," the smiling director said, "you have been doing a fine job here at Memorial Hospital. As the only certified athletic trainer in the department, you are playing an important role in helping us establish our niche in the sports medicine market. Our physically active patients appreciate having an athletic trainer on staff who can work with them during their rehabilitation. I want you to take on a very important project. The hospital administration and I think we need to be more aggressive in marketing our sports medicine program. We want you to begin an outreach program to the three Ashton County high schools to help attract patients to our hospital. School doesn't start for a few months, so you have plenty of time to get organized. Thanks a lot and keep up the good work."

Janet had mixed emotions about the new assignment. On one hand, she was pleased that the director trusted her with this new responsibility. On the other hand, she had no experience with community outreach programs. She didn't know where to begin.

The predicament Janet finds herself in is a common one because all organizations change over time. Whether you are employed in a high school, college, professional, or clinical setting, you are bound to face organizational changes at some point in your career. These changes force us to examine our sports medicine programs from time to time to see if they are still consistent with both the needs of our clients and the mission of the institution that employs us. The concepts discussed in this chapter are intended to help athletic trainers plan, implement, and evaluate sports medicine programs.

▌ Vision Statements

The first step the athletic trainer must take when planning sports medicine programming is to develop a brief, succinct description of what the program should eventually become—a *vision statement*. The vision statement should be both ambitious and compelling (Block, 1987). It should spell out the athletic trainer's hopes and aspirations for the program. Janet might consider a vision statement for her community outreach program that looks like this:

vision statement A concise statement that describes the ideal state to which an organization aspires.

> *The Memorial Hospital Sports Medicine Outreach Program shall provide injury prevention, care, and rehabilitation services of recognized excellence to the high school students of Ashton County. Memorial Hospital is committed to becoming the leader in sports medicine services in the Ashton County area.*

As you can see, the vision statement contains four distinct elements (see Figure 2.1). First, the statement identifies the provider of the service: Memorial Hospital. Second, it identifies the actual service to be provided: injury

• Name the service provider.	• Identify the target clients.
• Name the service to be provided.	• Identify the level of quality.

Figure 2.1 The four elements of the sports medicine program vision statement.

prevention, care, and rehabilitation. Third, it identifies the target clients: the high school students of Ashton County. Finally, the statement includes a quality declaration that identifies aspirations for how the program will be received by internal and external audiences. While these elements may seem to be self-evident, they are important because of the way they function in the next step—the mission statement. The vision statement should become the ultimate standard by which the program is judged. Without a clearly articulated vision statement, developing the program mission and evaluating the effectiveness of the program become much more difficult.

▊ Mission Statements

After the athletic trainer has explored and identified his vision for the sports medicine program, he should expand upon this vision and create a mission statement. Pearce (1982) has defined the ***mission statement*** as ''a broadly defined but enduring statement of purpose that distinguishes a business from other firms of its type and identifies the scope of its operations in product and market terms.'' Gibson, Newton, and Cochran (1990) have suggested the following component parts of a mission statement. Adapted for a sports medicine program, they include

mission statement *A written expression of an organization's philosophy, purposes, and characteristics.*

- the particular services to be offered, the primary market for those services, and the technology to be used in delivery of the services;
- the goals of the program;
- the philosophy of the program and the code of behavior that applies to its operation;
- the ''self-concept'' of the program based on evaluation of strengths and weaknesses; and
- the desired program image based on feedback from internal and external stakeholders.

The mission statement for the sports medicine program should help the athletic trainer accomplish three things (Gibson, Newton, & Cochran, 1990). First, the mission statement should help the athletic trainer direct resources toward accomplishing specific tasks. This is especially important for athletic trainers because they are often called on to perform a broad variety of tasks for a divergent group of supervisors. Athletic trainers need a framework within which they can make decisions about the relative importance of one task versus another.

The second function of the successful mission statement is that it should inspire athletic trainers to do a good job. The mission statement should communicate that the work they do is important and needed. The athletic trainer ought to be able to believe in the precepts described in the mission statement. Want (1986) has suggested that successful mission statements help employees, including athletic trainers, understand the values and beliefs of the organization and thereby help establish employee commitment.

Finally, the mission statement should be action oriented and should stimulate a change in behavior. It should be written to require the formation of program goals and objectives. It should ideally challenge the athletic trainer to periodically evaluate the effectiveness of the sports medicine program.

Based on these principles, the mission statement for the Memorial Hospital Sports Medicine Outreach Program might read as follows:

> *The Memorial Hospital Sports Medicine Outreach Program delivers traditional athletic training and sports medicine services to the student-athletes of the three high schools located in Ashton County. The services to be delivered can be broken down into three primary types: injury prevention (taping, bracing, padding, orthotics construction), management of athletic injuries, and rehabilitation of athletic injuries. In addition, whenever possible, we will strive to integrate education about athletic injuries so that our clients can be empowered to lead healthier, injury-free lifestyles. We are committed to using whatever technology is available and affordable in the delivery of these services. We will remain committed to the continuous upgrading of the equipment used in the delivery of sports medicine services so our clients will be assured of the most modern care available in the area.*

> *The purpose of the program is fourfold. First, we hope to allow easy access to sports medicine services for high school student-athletes. Second, we hope to encourage a philosophy of sport that places a high value on health and wellness. Third, we hope to enable injured student-athletes to return to their sports as soon as is medically safe. Finally, we hope to be able to substantially reduce the risk of athletic injury for those high school students in our service area.*

> *The underlying philosophy for the outreach program is the same as for all the other programs of Memorial Hospital, that is, the needs of the patient shall always be the first consideration for all members of the hospital staff. Furthermore, we expect the athletic trainer(s) who will be providing these services to maintain the highest standards of quality consistent with the National Athletic Trainers Association* Code of Professional Practice *and the credentialing statutes of this state.*

> *We are committed to ongoing evaluation of our outreach program so our clients can be assured of the highest quality in sports medicine care. Furthermore, we are committed to addressing problems and concerns in a timely manner so the needs of our clients and employees can continue to be met.*

> *Finally, the Memorial Hospital Sports Medicine Outreach Program aspires to be a program of recognized excellence. It is*

our intention to support the program with human and financial resources necessary to accomplish the stated goals of the program. It is our desire to establish Memorial Hospital as the primary and most outstanding outlet for the delivery of sports medicine services in the area.

▌ Planning

The athletic trainer has long been thought of as a jack-of-all-trades. Although athletic trainers' roles have become more specialized since sports medicine clinics began in the late 1970s, most athletic trainers still handle a broad variety of job-related activities (see Figure 2.2). Because the athletic trainer's job has so many aspects, the athletic trainer must develop planning skills.

Planning is the athletic trainer's best hope for accomplishing sports medicine program goals. Without planning, the athletic trainer leaves the ultimate success or failure of the sports medicine program to chance (Castetter, 1986). Ackoff (1970) has defined the planning process as a special type of decision making with three characteristics: It takes place before any action occurs; it is needed to produce a future state that would be unlikely to occur without action; and the future state desired results from multiple, interdependent decisions.

planning *A type of decision-making process in which a course of action is determined in order to bring about a future state of affairs.*

▌ **Figure 2.2** Job-related activities of the athletic trainer.

strategic planning A type of planning that involves critical self-examination in order to bring about organizational improvement.

The Memorial Hospital case illustrates the need for careful sports medicine program planning. The hospital administration has placed the bulk of the planning responsibility in Janet's lap. The plan she develops, if adopted by the hospital administration, will eventually determine whether the program succeeds or fails. To plan effectively, Janet should break the task into its two component parts: strategic planning and operational planning.

Strategic Planning

Strategic planning is a process that identifies a course of action to be taken to bring about a future state of affairs. Although it is normally conducted at the top of an organizational structure, strategic planning at the program level can have many benefits.

First, strategic planning requires the athletic trainer to critically examine the sports medicine program and to ask two questions: Why does this program exist? What should the business of this program be? These questions are fundamentally important. Because all organizations and their programs change, they must be asked and answered on a regular basis, or athletic trainers may find that their sports medicine programs no longer serve the purposes for which they are most needed.

The second reason for ongoing strategic planning at the sports medicine program level is to determine if the program is consistent with the overall mission of the institution or organization. This is especially important in institutions or organizations subject to rapid change. Sports medicine clinics based in hospitals are especially vulnerable to the shifting missions of their institutions. The mission of a professional athletic team often changes dramatically when a new coach is hired. If the sports medicine program isn't periodically reviewed for mission congruence, problems will arise because the administration may view the purpose of the sports medicine program differently than the athletic trainer.

The third reason for strategic planning at the sports medicine program level is that it helps build support for the program. Strategic planning is, by definition, a process that involves persons at all levels of the organization. By asking students, staff athletic trainers, coaches, and administrators to take part in the strategic planning process, the athletic trainer will be forging important allies with an increased sense of ownership in the sports medicine program.

Finally, strategic planning should be a tool for improvement, helping to determine the relative strengths and weaknesses of the program and to transform it positively. In addition, the strategic planning process will help direct more action-oriented operational plans.

Many conceptual models could be used to develop a strategic plan for the sports medicine program. The model presented in Figure 2.3 adapts the process developed by Steiner (1979), but athletic trainers should further modify the methodology to meet the needs of the institution. In most cases, the combination of institutional mission, needs, and goals will help determine the most appropriate planning methods.

Major Outside Interests

The first groups whose interests must be considered when developing a strategic plan are those outside the institution or organization. Of these

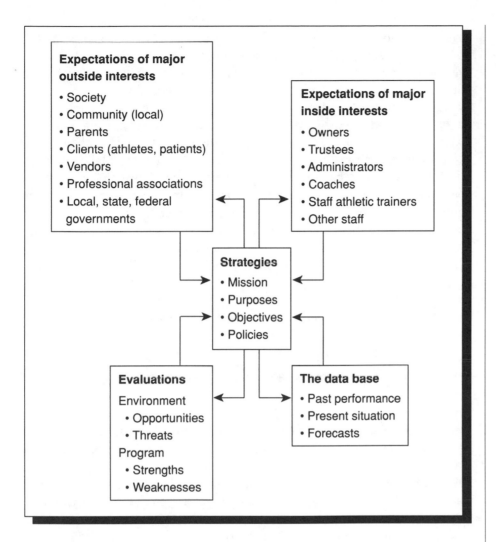

Expectations of major
outside interests
• Society
• Community (local)
• Parents
• Clients (athletes, patients)
• Vendors
• Professional associations
• Local, state, federal
  governments

Expectations of major
inside interests
• Owners
• Trustees
• Administrators
• Coaches
• Staff athletic trainers
• Other staff

Strategies
• Mission
• Purposes
• Objectives
• Policies

Evaluations
Environment
• Opportunities
• Threats
Program
• Strengths
• Weaknesses

The data base
• Past performance
• Present situation
• Forecasts

Figure 2.3 A model for strategic planning in sports medicine. *Note.* Adapted with the permission of The Free Press, a Division of Macmillan, Inc., from *Strategic Planning: What Every Manager Must Know* (p. 17) by George A. Steiner. Copyright © 1979 by The Free Press.

groups, the interests of clients should take precedence. In addition, the interests of parents; the local community; vendors; professional associations like the National Athletic Trainers Association (NATA) and the National Collegiate Athletic Association (NCAA); and local, state, and federal governments are important. Professionals who manage athletic training education programs must be familiar with the NATA Board of Certification (NATABOC) requirements[1] and the American Medical Association's Committee on Allied Health Education Accreditation (CAHEA) requirements for athletic training education program accreditation.[2] In some cases, the athletic trainer will need only simple information from one of these groups. For example, if a program is in a state that monitors the credentials of athletic

[1]Contact National Athletic Trainers Association Board of Certification, 3725 National Dr., Ste. 213, Raleigh, NC 27612.

[2]Those interested in entry-level athletic training education program accreditation should contact the Joint Review Committee on Educational Programs in Athletic Training, c/o Department of Physical Education, Indiana State University, Terre Haute, IN 47809. Those interested in advanced graduate level programs should contact the Professional Education Committee, National Athletic Trainers Association, 2952 Stemmons, Ste. 200, Dallas, TX 75247.

trainers, it doesn't require much planning to know that it must be staffed by athletic trainers with the necessary credentials required by law. Conversely, some of the information the athletic trainer will need to develop the strategic plan may be more difficult to gather. For example, as important vendors of medical services, local physicians may have a substantial interest in how the sports medicine program is planned. Only by meeting with these physicians and involving them in the planning process can the athletic trainer be assured of their enthusiastic endorsement of the program being planned.

The most important group whose interests must be considered is the program's client base. Without patients, athletic trainers and sports medicine programs would be unnecessary. The athletic trainer can incorporate clients' perceptions into the strategic planning process in several ways, including written questionnaires, telephone surveys, and suggestion boxes (see Figure 2.4). If the athletic trainer needs more detailed insight, it may be necessary

Figure 2.4 Methods for gathering feedback from clients on sports medicine services.

- Written questionnaires
- Telephone surveys
- Suggestion boxes
- Client involvement on planning committees
- Focus groups

to involve clients as members of planning committees. Another method for securing detailed feedback from clients on the quality of services and their desire for future services is to use the focus group technique. This technique involves gathering a group of approximately 10 clients who are representative of the total population of clients. A trained facilitator meets with the group and asks a series of open-ended questions about program quality and the clients' desires for the future. This process is generally repeated with several different groups as a reliability check. The information is then collated and used to help build the strategic plan.

Gathering valid and reliable information from clients is not a task for the untrained. The literature is full of poorly written and poorly analyzed client-based questionnaires. Sampling methods and statistical analysis of the data must meet modern scientific norms. Athletic trainers can turn to several sources of assistance for this phase of the strategic plan. Most colleges and universities have faculty members with expertise in social science research who are willing to consult. Many of the larger educational institutions have full-time planners available to assist with projects like these. Most large hospitals either have full-time planners or contracts with management consultants to help in the development of the strategic plan.

Major professional associations and the government are two important sources of information for assessing what outside interests are necessary to develop the strategic plan for the sports medicine program. Professional associations (such as NATA, the NCAA, the American Physical Therapy Association, and the National Federation of State High School Athletic Associations [NFSHSAA]) are important because they are often the source of professional credentials that act as "gatekeepers" for practitioners in sports medicine and they mandate quality standards for sports medicine programs. The NCAA and the NFSHSAA set the rules for each sport, including safety rules that impact athletic trainers and sports medicine programs. Both of these organizations have rules for administering physical examinations that have a marked effect on sports medicine programs.

Major Inside Interests

Athletic trainers are not typically found among the top management of an institution or organization. Top managers, including team owners, university administrators and trustees, and boards of education have certain expectations for the sports medicine program so it is important that the athletic trainer involve a representative sample of these persons as part of the planning team. Without the active support of these groups, the strategic plan for the sports medicine program is likely to fail. Consider the Memorial Hospital case as an example. Janet was left to plan the sports medicine outreach program by herself. She knows two things: First, at least a few and possibly more hospital administrators support the program; and second, she isn't sure which direction the program should take. The next logical step for Janet is to identify those administrators that support the concept and include them in the planning process. This will have two likely effects: It will strengthen ownership for the program among the people who will have to eventually approve or disapprove it, and it will provide Janet with some fresh ideas for the type of program the hospital wants.

❚ Focus sessions with sports medicine clients can yield valuable information for program improvement.

Another major inside group is comprised of the coaches. It is wise to include coaches in the planning effort because they have a legitimate need to be involved, or at least informed, in the health care of their athletes. The success of the team and their success as coaches often depends on the overall health of their athletes. Second, coaches have a powerful impact on the attitudes and behaviors of the athletes on their teams. If the coaches in the three Ashton County high schools don't have confidence in the expertise and care patterns that Janet will offer them through the outreach program, they are unlikely to be receptive to the advice she offers and Memorial Hospital is unlikely to receive many referrals. Janet is the hospital's primary marketing tool to these schools, and most of her contacts will be with students and coaches. The final reason coaches should be involved in the planning process is that they are an important power base in any athletic program. A successful coach can sometimes become one of the most powerful persons in the entire organization. It makes sense to try to use such power to build alliances with the sports medicine program.

The most important inside group to tap in developing the strategic plan is the institution's athletic trainers. They are the professionals inside the organization with the most sports medicine expertise. As such, they are the best sources of information about how the program should be developed. It is important, however, to involve the athletic trainers in the proper manner. Too often, meetings intended to develop strategic directions for sports medicine programs can break down into complaining about program problems with working conditions, salary, and professional standing in the institution. These issues are important, but if they become the focus of the athletic trainers' roles in the strategic planning process, the resultant plan will be little more than a shopping list of their demands, which is unlikely to foster administration support or improved care for injured athletes. Athletic trainers must constantly ask themselves during the planning process ''How can we improve the quality of service to the athlete?'' Questions that deviate significantly from this are unlikely to have strategic value.

The Data Base

This portion of the strategic planning model helps athletic trainers devise alternative action plans and estimate their potential value for meeting the goals of the sports medicine program. First, analyze the past performance of the program, considering trends in patient loads, injury rates, clinic profits or losses, and athletic trainer performance evaluations, among other information. Next, analyze the program's present situation. You'll need data about staffing level, budget, client population size, number of sports to be served, demands and expectations of outside and inside interests, and any applicable laws that affect the program.

forecast A process of predicting future conditions on the basis of statistics and indicators that describe the past and present situation.

Finally, develop a forecast of the future. Ammer and Ammer (1984) have defined the term *forecast* as a process of predicting future conditions on the basis of various statistics and indicators that describe the past and present situation. Forecasts are highly informed and educated guesses that should always be backed up with documented evidence. Athletic trainers should consider the predicted rise in the cost of medical goods and services and the future availability of professional staff, support employees, and consulting medical personnel when preparing the forecast. In addition, they should consider advances in technology because the available technology often drives the practice of sports medicine.

"WOTS UP"

The last data collection procedure to be accomplished in the strategic planning process is often referred to as a *WOTS UP analysis* (Steiner, 1979). WOTS UP is an acronym for "weaknesses, opportunities, threats, and strengths underlying planning." Because the WOTS UP analysis identifies strengths and weaknesses already present in the sports medicine program, it is most appropriate for programs that are already established (see Appendix A). It is very important that the WOTS UP analysis be conducted by a broad spectrum of participants. Interpretation of the data is subject to the biases of the interpreter so only by involving a representative group of both outside and inside interests will the WOTS UP analysis yield useful results.

The WOTS UP analysis often reveals important sources of both opportunities and threats for the sports medicine program. In the Memorial Hospital case, a WOTS UP analysis would probably help Janet identify allies she may not have previously considered. Many will have a vested interest in seeing the program succeed. She will also undoubtedly identify sources of opposition to the program that she will need to develop plans to deal with.

WOTS UP analysis   A data collection and appraisal technique designed to determine an organization's strengths, weaknesses, opportunities, and threats in order to facilitate planning.

Operational Planning

Once the athletic trainer has developed a strategic direction for the sports medicine program, the strategies must be translated into practice through the use of *operational plans*. Whereas strategic plans are meant to provide program direction over a long period of time, say 5 years, operational plans define the activities of the program for a much shorter period of time, usually no more than 1 or 2 years. The importance of functioning operational plans for the sports medicine program should not be underestimated. One of the most common pitfalls in every type of organization that undertakes strategic planning is the failure to effectively translate the strategic vision for the program into workable, useful operational plans (Garofalo, 1989). Three often misunderstood types of operational plans include policies, processes, and procedures.

operational plans   A type of plan that defines organizational activities in the short term, usually no longer than 2 years.

Policies

Castetter (1986) has defined *policy* as a plan for expressing the organization's intended behavior relative to a specific program subfunction. By definition, policies are broad statements of intended action promulgated by boards empowered with the authority to govern the operation of the organization.

Policies are not intended to answer detailed questions about how the sports medicine program operates. They are intended as road maps to guide the athletic trainer in developing and operating a sports medicine program in accordance with the desires of the policy board. Athletic trainers will rarely be empowered to dictate policies since they usually do not sit on the governing boards of institutions. They should, however, be consulted in the development or modification of institutional policies that affect the sports medicine program. A well-managed organization with a sports medicine program should have policies in place that express the intended behaviors of the program. The athletic trainer is obviously a crucial ingredient in advising those in

policy   A type of plan that expresses an organization's intended behavior relative to a specific program subfunction.

authority on the development and implementation of these policies. An example of a policy statement for the Memorial Hospital Sports Medicine Outreach Program might look like this one.

> *Memorial Hospital acknowledges its role in the following activities:*
>
> - *Reducing the incidence of injury among high school student-athletes*
> - *Making competent medical care readily and easily available to the student-athletes of Ashton County*
>
> *Additionally, Memorial Hospital recognizes that a program delivering sports medicine services to the three high schools of Ashton County will help it fulfill its mission to be the leader in sports medicine in the Ashton County area. Consequently, the Board of Trustees of Memorial Hospital has established the following policies:*
>
> *1.0 Provide sports medicine services at the site of athletic practice and competition for the three Ashton County high schools.*
>
> *1.1 Provide sports medicine coverage using only personnel who have been trained and credentialed as experts in sports medicine, including certified athletic trainers.*
>
> *1.2 Maintain an injury data base to determine the risk of injury to athletic participants.*
>
> *1.3 Provide hospital-based management of injuries requiring follow-up care.*
>
> *1.4 Provide education on the prevention of injuries and the development of healthy life-styles to the students of the three Ashton County high schools.*
>
> *1.5 Assist in the prevention of athletic injuries by providing physical examinations and screening services for the students of the three Ashton County high schools.*

Processes

process A collection of incremental and mutually dependent steps designed to direct the most important tasks of an organization.

Processes are the next step down from policies on the hierarchy of operational plans. **Processes** are the incremental and mutually dependent steps that direct the most important tasks of the sports medicine program (see Figure 2.5). Each process should be related to at least one, and possibly many, of the policies that govern the program. Each policy will undoubtedly have several supporting processes.

❚ **Figure 2.5** Processes of the sports medicine program.

• Injury prevention	• Injury rehabilitation
• Injury recognition	• Organization and administration
• Injury management	• Education and counseling

Procedures

Procedures provide specific interpretations of processes for athletic trainers and other members of the sports medicine team. They are not abstract. They should be written in clear and simple language so they will be interpreted the same way by different people. Procedures are the lowest level of the planning hierarchy. An example of how policies, processes, and procedures are linked for the Memorial Hospital program might look like this:

procedure A type of operational plan that provides specific directions for members of an organization to follow.

Policy 1.0
It is the policy of Memorial Hospital to provide sports medicine services at the site of athletic practice and competition for the three Ashton County high schools.

Process for the Injury Rehabilitation Subfunction
The sports medicine team, including the physician, athletic trainer, and physical therapist, shall work together to provide student-athletes with a rehabilitation program appropriate for their injuries. Consideration will be given to the location of the rehabilitation program (home, school, or hospital), equipment required to attain the desired rehabilitative effect, the insurance coverage provided by the student's family, and the insurance coverage provided by the school.

Procedure for Discharge from Rehabilitation
Physical therapists or athletic trainers shall discharge student-athletes from rehabilitation only after consulting with the attending physician. Discharge shall occur when the critical long-term goals established when the student-athlete was admitted have been met. All discharged student-athletes shall be given verbal and written instructions in the long-term care of their injuries. The names of all discharged student-athletes shall be placed on the mailing list for the Memorial Hospital Sports Medicine Newsletter. *All discharged student-athletes shall be called both at six months and one year postdischarge by an athletic trainer to check on the status of their injuries.*

Other Types of Operational Plans

Policies, processes, and procedures are types of operational plans common to almost every organization. They should be reviewed and modified as appropriate at least once every three years. Other types of operational plans have fixed life spans. Budgets are a type of operational plan that are usually one year in length. (See chapter 4 for an expanded discussion of budgets.) Two additional planning techniques that result in fixed-term operational plans are Program Evaluation and Review Technique (PERT) and Gannt charts.

program evaluation and review technique (PERT)
A method of graphically depicting the time line and interrelationships for the different stages of a program.

PERT: *PERT* (Penton/IPC Education Division, 1982), an acronym for *program evaluation and review technique*, is a useful tool to help athletic trainers develop plans for implementing programs. It is also useful for evaluating actual outcomes against expected outcomes. PERT is essentially a method of graphically depicting the time line for and interrelationships of different stages of a program. Users depict events as circles and activities as lines or arrows connecting two or more events. One of the advantages of using the PERT planning technique is that it allows athletic trainers to visually display events that occur simultaneously. PERT is most often used with large, complicated projects in business and industry, but it can also be applied to the smaller projects that athletic trainers are often called upon to develop and administer (see Figure 2.6).

Gannt chart A graphic planning and control technique that maps discrete tasks on a calendar.

Gannt Charts: A *Gannt chart* is a graphic planning and control method (Stoner, 1982). It has many potential applications in sports medicine because it takes discrete tasks and maps them on a calendar (see Figure 2.7). Athletic trainers can use a Gannt chart to demonstrate to their superiors the progress being made on particular projects (Randolph & Posner, 1988). When used in this way, it becomes a powerful tool for communicating sports medicine plans to crucial members of the internal and external audience. For example, in the opening case of this chapter Janet could use a Gannt chart not only to plan the implementation of the sports medicine outreach program, but also to provide her superiors with concise, easy-to-understand progress updates.

Both PERT and Gannt charts are challenging to construct for the untrained. Depending on the complexity of the project, the final result of graphically illustrating the milestones and critical path of a project can appear somewhat bizarre. The first few times you attempt these methods, use pencil and paper. As you gain expertise, try using a computer to help you create either PERT

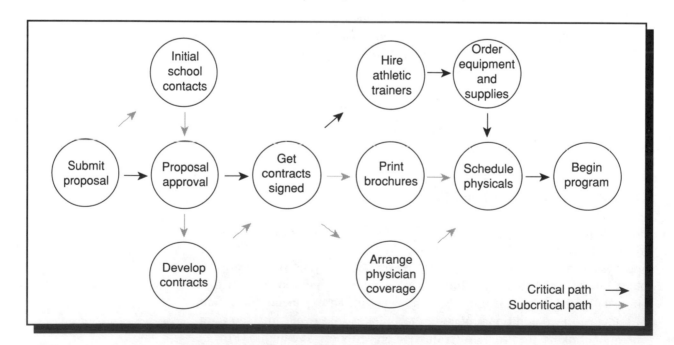

❙ Figure 2.6 PERT diagram for a hospital-based sports medicine outreach program.

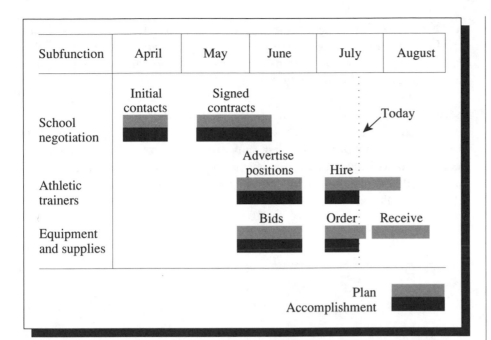

Subfunction	April	May	June	July	August

■ **Figure 2.7** Gannt chart for a new hospital sports medicine outreach program.

■ The PERT technique can help athletic trainers develop operational plans.

or Gannt charts. *The Software Encyclopedia* (1990) lists over 100 computer programs designed specifically for this purpose.

Communicating and Developing Support for the Plan

Unfortunately, all the work the athletic trainer expends developing the sports medicine program plan will be wasted unless other people inside and outside the organization accept it. One of the most difficult aspects of planning for the delivery of sports medicine services is developing a sense of ownership in the people who make up the major organizational power bases. Plans developed without such ownership are unlikely to remain politically viable for very long. The ability to translate plans into action and develop support for the program is the ultimate measure of political skill.

Block (1987) has developed a support-building strategy that could be useful to athletic trainers as they attempt to develop ownership for their sports medicine programs. The strategy is based on the **agreement-trust matrix** (see Figure 2.8). The first step in the process is to identify those people who will have an impact on the eventual success or failure of the sports medicine program. After these people have been identified, they are labeled as follows.

agreement-trust matrix   A model that identifies and types the most important people in developing support for a plan.

▌ Figure 2.8   Agreement-trust matrix. *Note.* From *The Empowered Manager* (p. 133) by Peter Block, 1987, San Francisco: Jossey-Bass. Copyright 1987 by Jossey-Bass and Peter Block. Reprinted by permission.

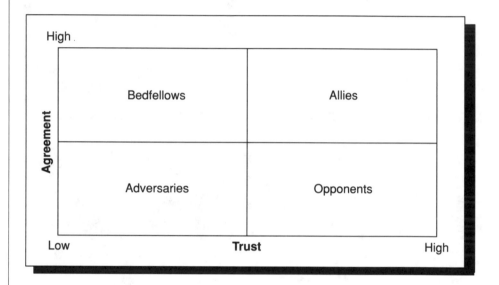

Allies

The **allies** of the athletic trainer exhibit a high level of agreement with the plans for the sports medicine program. In addition, they are people the athletic trainer trusts. They not only are supporters of the sports medicine program but also have an established record of honesty and truthfulness.

allies   Persons who exhibit a high level of support for a plan.

Opponents

Opponents of the athletic trainer should not be viewed as enemies. They are persons whom the athletic trainer trusts to give an honest opinion of the sports medicine program or its components, but who have opposing views to those of the athletic trainer. Opponents can often serve a useful purpose—their challenge can lead to more critical examination of the sports medicine program, resulting in stronger strategic and operational plans.

opponents   Persons who support a particular program but dispute the implementation of a plan related to that program.

Bedfellows

Bedfellows are those who agree with the plans of the athletic trainer for the sports medicine program but have a history of untrustworthy behavior. Bedfellows are generally quick to ally themselves with the sports medicine program, but they tend to be manipulative and to operate "behind the back."

bedfellows   Persons who exhibit support for a particular plan but who have a history of untrustworthy behavior and vacillation.

Adversaries

People with whom the athletic trainer has attempted negotiation that has been fruitless are known as ***adversaries***. Not only do they disagree with the athletic trainer's plan for the sports medicine program, they are untrustworthy and dishonest as well. It is important to be able to distinguish between adversaries and opponents. A common pitfall occurs when opponents who are honest, trustworthy persons of differing viewpoints are labeled as adversaries. Opponents can make the sports medicine program stronger. Adversaries are often strengthened through confrontation because it tends to lend legitimacy to the alternative vision they have for the sports medicine program. Negotiation will not alter their vision of how the program should function. If the athletic trainer has done a good job of including a wide spectrum of people in the planning effort, the number of adversaries ought to be relatively small.

Block (1987) suggests specific strategies for developing support among the four types of organizational players.

Allies

- Confirm the fact that the person agrees with the sports medicine plan.
- Profess appreciation for the quality of the relationship.
- Admit any faults and shortcomings of the sports medicine plan.
- Request the support and continued counsel of the ally.

Opponents

- Profess appreciation for the quality of the relationship. Emphasize the trust and honesty that have characterized the relationship.
- Explain the plan for the sports medicine program along with any supporting arguments for why it should be implemented.
- Define your interpretation of the opponent's views in a non-threatening manner.
- Attempt to engage the opponent in a problem-solving process to find common points.

Bedfellows

- Confirm the fact that the person agrees with the sports medicine plan.
- Convey your concern about the person's willingness to be open and honest. Express a willingness to share a portion of the blame and to find a way to improve the trust relationship so the program can move ahead.
- Clearly state your expectations for the person's behavior toward the sports medicine program. What is it that you want the person to do?
- Ask the person what expectations they have for you in order to improve the relationship.
- Attempt to establish a consensus for future working relationships with bedfellows.

Adversaries

- Explain the plan for the sports medicine program with any supporting arguments for why it should be implemented.

adversaries *Persons who are unsupportive of both a program and a particular plan related to the program.*

- Define your interpretation of the adversary's views in a nonthreatening manner.
- Explain any actions you have taken or will take to implement the sports medicine plan so everything is "out in the open."
- Avoid making demands that are unlikely to be met.

▌ Program Evaluation

Athletic trainers are called upon to assess various aspects of the sports medicine program on a regular basis. How is Bill's knee rehabilitation coming along? Is he on schedule? Was the drug education seminar we hosted last week effective? Will the behavior of the athletes change as a result? Questions like these help determine the quality of the sports medicine program. Unfortunately, even the most thorough and well-conceived strategic and operational plans don't always produce the desired results. To maximize the value of the sports medicine program, athletic trainers must engage in ***program evaluation*** regularly.

program evaluation A systematic and comprehensive assessment of the worth of a particular program.

Worthen and Sanders (1973) have defined *evaluation* as "the determination of the worth of a thing. It includes obtaining information for use in judging the worth of a program, product, procedure, or objective, or the potential utility of alternative approaches designed to attain specified objectives" (p. 19). The trainer should answer two underlying and related questions when evaluating the sports medicine program: What would the likely effects be if the sports medicine program ceased to exist, and How are the persons who have access to the program better off than those persons who do not have access to the program? Each of these questions is crucial—the answers will ultimately help the organization determine if it is committing an appropriate amount of human and financial resources to sports medicine. These questions, and indeed every area of the program evaluation, should be supported by documented evidence (see Figure 2.9). Evidence of sports medicine program quality can be, and should be, derived from several sources. Reviews of patient files, injury and treatment summary statistics, and client testimonials are examples of data that should be used. Educational programs should evaluate student graduation and certification rates. Surveys of client and alumni satisfaction can provide valuable evidence of perceived program quality because they allow respondents to reflect for a period of time prior to providing feedback. None of this evidence is sufficient in isolation. Considered together, however, it can help provide an overall assessment of the effectiveness of the sports medicine program. Although the athletic trainer

▌ **Figure 2.9** Types of evidence to support sports medicine program effectiveness.

- Patient files
- Injury summaries and statistics
- Treatment summaries and statistics
- Client testimonials
- Student athletic trainer graduation and certification statistics
- Critical incident reports
- Staff accomplishments
- Client surveys
- Alumni surveys
- Surveys of employers of alumni

will certainly be required to render judgments based on professional experience, others who will judge the program will need tangible proof that the sports medicine program is accomplishing its mission.

Two types of program evaluations athletic trainers may be called upon to perform are ***summative*** and ***formative*** (Fitz-Gibbon & Morris, 1987). The summative evaluation includes

- a summary statement of program effectiveness,
- a description of the program,
- a statement of documented achievement of program goals,
- unanticipated outcomes of the program, and
- comparisons with other similar sports medicine programs.

The formative evaluation includes

- identifying potential problems in the sports medicine program,
- identifying areas that need strengthening,
- identifying program strengths, and
- monitoring program objectives.

Ideally, athletic trainers should use rigid experimental research designs that include the use of control or nontreatment groups for every program evaluation. This is the best way to determine if the sports medicine program is having the intended effect. Unfortunately, many athletic trainers lack the research and statistical skills necessary to carry out such experimental designs. In addition, athletic trainers often find it impossible to carry out evaluation projects of this scope and complexity because they take too much time away from the other duties the athletic trainer must be accountable for. The athletic trainer should strive to include as much comparative information as possible in the program evaluation. This will help other stakeholders appreciate the quality of the sports medicine program compared to other programs of its type.

One way athletic trainers can provide evidence of comparative quality with sports medicine programs at other similar institutions is by using other athletic trainers as ***external evaluators***. Similarly, the Joint Review Committee on Educational Programs in Athletic Training uses athletic trainers trained in program evaluation to judge the quality of athletic training education programs for schools requesting accreditation. External evaluators can also be useful for reducing bias. It may be difficult or even impossible for athletic trainers to be objective about their own programs. Asking expert third parties who have little to lose or gain through the evaluation process to assess the program will help lend credibility to the evaluation results (Joint Committee on Standards for Educational Evaluation, 1981).

Before the external evaluator arrives, the institution must commit itself to allowing reasonable access to the people and information the evaluator will need to make accurate judgments and to generate useful suggestions for improvement. A competent external evaluator will want to have access to all the evidence listed in Figure 2.9. In addition, a good external evaluator will interview the athletic trainers, team physicians, athletic administrators,

summative evaluation *An assessment designed primarily to describe the effectiveness or accomplishments of a program or employee to determine appropriate actions.*

formative evaluation *An assessment designed primarily to improve a program.*

external evaluators *Experts not affiliated with the organization who are retained to assess the various programs within the organization.*

coaches, student athletic trainers, and athletes to gain a broad-based perspective of the quality of the sports medicine program. After the site visit, the evaluator should prepare a report that lists perceived strengths and weaknesses of the sports medicine program and specific steps that could be taken to improve the program.

How often should the sports medicine program be evaluated? Although there is no universal answer, some guidelines should apply regardless of the setting in which the sports medicine clinic is housed.

- Collect and collate evaluation evidence continuously. If data is only collected immediately preceding the evaluation, there may not be sufficient time to complete the task. Gathering the evidence is the most time-consuming aspect of program evaluation.

- Perform a "mini evaluation" once every year. There are two advantages to this approach: It will force you to compile evidence of program effectiveness for a reasonable time frame, and it will identify program weaknesses that require immediate attention.

- Conduct a complete evaluation of the sports medicine program every three to five years. This schedule will allow the athletic trainer to examine strategic issues, such as mission congruence and program goals and objectives, which shouldn't change very often.

As you may recall, part of the mission statement for the Memorial Hospital Sports Medicine Outreach Program specified that the program would be evaluated on an ongoing basis to insure quality care for the high school student-athletes being served. One of the ways Janet could evaluate the effectiveness of the program would be to design and go through a self-study process every three to five years (see Figure 2.10). The self-study should critically examine all the major elements of the program. It should result in a report to the primary stakeholders of the sports medicine program (Morris & Fitz-Gibbon, 1978). Reports from external evaluators and condensed transcripts of documentary evidence should be included as appendixes.

∎ Applications to Athletic Training: Theory Into Practice

The following two case studies will help you apply this chapter's concepts to real-life situations. The questions at the end of the case studies have many possible correct solutions. Use these studies as homework or exam questions or to stimulate class discussion.

CASE STUDY 1

The chairperson of the Department of Physical Education and Athletics met Susan, the college's athletic trainer, in the hallway. After exchanging the news of the day, the chairperson said, "By the way, I've been working on the NCAA self-study, and one of the sections deals with drug education programs and policies. I know we are just a small college that doesn't have many problems with drugs, but I can't send this thing over to the president without addressing this issue, especially in light of the emphasis the NCAA

Sports Medicine Outreach Program Self-Study

Instructions

The self-study for the sports medicine program shall consist of four areas: general considerations, patients, staff, and program. The athletic trainer in charge of the program shall answer the questions below and prepare a report with supporting evidence to be submitted to the Director of Rehabilitation Services and the Vice President for Patient Services. In addition, the Director of Rehabilitation Services, in consultation with the athletic trainer, shall select an appropriate external evaluator. The external evaluator's report shall be included in the self-study as an appendix.

General considerations

1. What is the mission of the program? Is the mission statement consistent with the mission of Memorial Hospital? Is the mission statement consistent with national standards for the delivery of sports medicine services?
2. Does the program work well in the context of the Department of Rehabilitation Services? How does the program take advantage of available resources? Do the program's staff members work well together? Do they work well with the rest of the hospital staff?
3. Who provides leadership for the program? Are the program leaders effective?
4. What are the priorities of the program? Are they appropriate? Do they mesh well with the priorities of Memorial Hospital? Do the priorities of individual staff members mesh well with the priorities of the sports medicine program?

Patients

1. Do patients achieve the short- and long-term goals established at the beginning of their treatment programs? Do patients have easy and quick access to evaluation and treatment services? Do the students of the Ashton County high schools use the program? If not, why not? Are the program's patient loads consistent with national averages?
2. Does the program help reduce the incidence of injury in the Ashton County high schools? If not, what factors account for this? In what ways can the program be improved so as to reduce the incidence of injury?
3. Are the students of the Ashton County high schools better educated with respect to healthy lifestyles than students elsewhere? What efforts have been made to educate students regarding healthy lifestyles? What additional efforts should be/could be made in this area?

Staff

1. How effective are staff members as providers of sports medicine services? Are some staff members ineffective? What can be done to resolve the problem?
2. Do staff members possess the standard credentials for delivery of sports medicine services? Do they engage in programs of continuing education?
3. Are staff members considered experts in their fields? Can they boast of professional accomplishments consistent with experts of regional or national reputation?
4. Are staff members performing in a manner consistent with their position descriptions and codes of professional conduct?
5. Is the size of the staff appropriate for the tasks it must accomplish? Could the same job be done with the same quality with fewer staff members?

Program

1. Is each component of the sports medicine program effective? Which components are the strongest? Which are the weakest? How could the weak components be strengthened?
2. Is each component of the sports medicine program necessary? If not, should some components be eliminated? Are there additional components that should be added to the program? Who would they serve? What is the desired effect of any new component?
3. Is the sports medicine program cost-effective? Does the income it generates support its budget? Is it efficient? How could it become more efficient?

Figure 2.10 Self-study form for a hospital-based sports medicine clinic.

places on it. Would you be willing to organize a program so we can at least meet the NCAA guidelines?''

''What would you want such a program to include?'' asked Susan. ''This could potentially be a huge project.''

''You're the expert,'' replied the chairperson. ''Let me know what you come up with.''

Susan had strong opinions on the use and abuse of alcohol and other drugs. Several of her family members had been negatively affected by their use. She had plenty of examples of how alcohol had impacted her students. She decided that if she was going to take on this program, she wasn't going to allow any half-measures. She knew that for a problem as complex as drug and alcohol use among college students, she was going to have to develop a comprehensive program to be successful.

After checking with several other athletic trainers who had developed programs for their schools, Susan began writing a proposal for the program. She decided to include the following elements:

- *A standards-setting workshop led by a trained facilitator to help the coaches and team captains develop their own rules and sanctions for alcohol and other drug use*
- *A policy statement that addressed the college's concern over the drug and alcohol issue with procedures to provide an action plan to deal with the problem*
- *A series of educational seminars and workshops for the student-athletes that would form the bulk of the drug and alcohol education program*
- *A research study to find out the extent of the problem on campus and to determine the effectiveness of the program*

The entire program would cost approximately $3,000 for the first 18 months. Since the department wouldn't allocate any funds for the project, Susan wrote a grant proposal to a local community foundation that covered the cost. Susan was pleased and confident. After 6 months of planning, the program was finally ready to go.

QUESTIONS FOR ANALYSIS

1. Based on what you know of Susan's planning effort, how successful is the drug and alcohol education program likely to be? How would you have planned for this program?

2. Who are the inside interests in this case? Who are the outside interests? How are they likely to be affected by this program? How should they be involved in planning it?

3. How much support do you think Susan will be able to develop for the program? What strategies should she use to develop support?

4. How should Susan evaluate the effectiveness of the program? What elements should be included in the evaluation plan?

5. How should the policy that Susan wants to see adopted be written? Develop an example of a process and a procedure that might support such a policy.

6. If you were in Susan's position, would you have handled anything differently? What alternative actions would you have taken?

Dan was halfway through his first year as the chairperson of the Department of Athletic Training Studies at a midsize university. The department he led offered a CAHEA-accredited undergraduate major in athletic training. The department was housed in the College of Allied Health and had graduated an average of 10 students per year for the past 8 years. The department was staffed by two full-time faculty members and three adjunct members who had release time from the athletic department.

Dan received a memo from the Dean of Allied Health informing him that it was his department's turn for a departmental review. In keeping with the new policy of allowing greater administrative freedom to department chairpersons, Dan would be allowed to collect and present the evidence he thought the Provost and the Dean's Council should use to judge the effectiveness of the department. Dan was told he would have to submit his report in 5 months.

A few days later Dan was having lunch in the faculty cafeteria when the Dean of Allied Health walked over. "Dan," the dean said, "you should know that the Dean's Council has been given instructions to reduce our budget by 10% next year. After discussing the problem, we all agreed that the only way to do it without weakening all the programs is to eliminate one of them. I wanted you to know that, unofficially, your department is one that is being considered in the cutback. No decision will be made until after the departmental reviews come in."

QUESTIONS FOR ANALYSIS

1. What evidence should Dan present when preparing the report for the departmental review? What plan for collecting the evidence would you develop if you were in Dan's position?

2. Which aspects of the evidence should Dan highlight considering the uncertain future of his department? How could he best feature this evidence for maximum impact?

3. Would an external evaluator be useful in this situation? What qualities of the external evaluator would help lend credibility to the report?

4. Besides the departmental self-study, what other steps could Dan take to safeguard the future of the department? What are the likely effects of these actions? Could any of these actions have negative consequences?

▌ Summary

Change is a pervasive aspect of organizational life that affects sports medicine programs. The development of vision and mission statements can help the sports medicine program develop a philosophical infrastructure that will allow it to adapt appropriately to change. A vision statement should identify the service provider, the service to be provided, the recipients of the service, and the expected quality of the service. The mission statement is a broadly defined, enduring statement of purpose that defines the scope of operations of the sports medicine program. The mission statement should direct the athletic trainer toward accomplishing specific tasks, motivate and inspire, and guide the development of goals and objectives.

Planning is a set of activities the athletic trainer should use to bring about a desired future state for the sports medicine program. Strategic plans are broadly written guides for developing specific program goals and objectives. The development of a strategic plan involves identifying the needs of both outside and inside interests; gathering information that identifies the historical and present status of the program; and analyzing the strengths and weaknesses of, the threats to, and the opportunities for the sports medicine program. Operational plans are explicit steps that guide the actions of the athletic trainer so specific tasks can be accomplished. A policy is an operational plan for expressing the organization's intended behavior relative to a specific program subfunction. Policies require the approval of persons in legal authority, such as boards of trustees or owners. Processes are a collection of incremental and mutually dependent steps designed to direct the most important tasks of the sports medicine program. Procedures provide athletic trainers with specific direction for various processes. Operational planning can be enhanced through the use of techniques such as PERT and Gannt charts. Planning will be ineffective unless support can be developed for the plan by identifying and influencing allies, opponents, bedfellows, and adversaries.

Athletic trainers should evaluate the effectiveness of the sports medicine program to ensure that the program will continue to improve and to document program quality. Formative program evaluation identifies strengths and weaknesses and provides alternatives for improvement. Summative evaluation judges the quality of the program. Program evaluation is most valid when it compares program clients and persons without access to the program using the scientific method. This is often difficult, expensive, and impractical. As much comparative data as possible should be used to evaluate the program. The use of an external auditor can facilitate unbiased assessments. A periodic self-study process that involves collecting evidence of program quality and answering questions crucial to program development is recommended.

∎ Annotated Bibliography

Ackoff, R.L. (1970). *A concept of corporate planning*. New York: Wiley-Interscience.

> Ackoff attempts to explain why managers should plan, how they should plan, and who should plan. Although written for persons in the business world, the concepts are easily transferred to sports medicine settings.

Ammer, C., & Ammer, D.S. (1984). *Dictionary of business and economics* (2nd ed.). New York: The Free Press.

> Most citations in this comprehensive dictionary of business and economic terms and phrases are accompanied by a brief explanation and example.

Block, P. (1987). *The empowered manager: Positive political skills at work.* San Francisco: Jossey-Bass.

This book tries to persuade managers that the creative use of political power in the organization can be a positive force in accomplishing the organizational mission.

Castetter, W.B. (1986). *The personnel function in educational administration* (4th ed.). New York: Macmillan.

This comprehensive text helps administrators apply conceptual models to become more effective human resource managers. Pages 65 to 75 offer an excellent argument for the importance of planning that can be applied in a wide variety of settings.

Fitz-Gibbon, C.T., & Morris, L.L. (1987). *How to design a program evaluation.* Newbury Park, CA: Sage.

Although this book has a "how to" title, it is a fairly technical treatment of the basic principles and approaches to program evaluation. Athletic trainers can gain insight into how to evaluate their sports medicine programs from this book, but they are cautioned to read chapter 1 carefully.

Garofalo, M.J. (1989). How strategies can get lost in the translation. *Business Month,* **134**(10), 82-83.

A useful article that offers strategies for helping senior managers assist middle managers in implementing organizational goals.

Gibson, C.K., Newton, D.J., & Cochran, D.S. (1990). An empirical investigation of the nature of hospital mission statements. *Health Care Management Review,* **15**(3), 35-45.

This article presents a background discussion of the definitions and underlying theory of a mission statement. In addition, the authors analyze their survey of 700 hospital managers' perceptions of hospital mission statements.

Joint Committee on Standards for Educational Evaluation. (1981). *Standards for evaluations of educational programs, projects, and materials.* New York: McGraw-Hill.

This book describes 30 standards designed to improve the utility, feasibility, propriety, and accuracy of program evaluation. The standards were developed primarily for use in education, so they are most applicable to undergraduate and graduate athletic training education programs. Most of the standards, however, could easily be used to develop and improve program evaluation systems in other sports medicine settings.

Morris, L.L., & Fitz-Gibbon, C.T. (1978). *How to present an evaluation report.* Newbury Park, CA: Sage.

An excellent guide on how to write and discuss an evaluation report. Athletic trainers will find many useful suggestions that will improve their ability to defend the strengths of their sports medicine programs.

Pearce, J.A. (1982). The company mission as a strategic tool. *Sloan Management Review*, **23**(2), 15-23.

This article provides a useful "how to" approach for those organizations that wish to define or modify their mission statement.

Penton/IPC Education Division. (1982). *Fundamentals of PERT*. Cleveland, OH: Author.

A programmed learning course designed to develop skill in using the Program Evaluation and Review Technique (PERT) planning system. This is a self-paced course that takes approximately 3 hours to complete. It is fairly elementary and is a good way for athletic trainers to learn this planning technique.

Randolph, W.A., & Posner, B.Z. (1988). What every manager needs to know about project management. *Sloan Management Review*, **29**(4), 65-73.

This paper provides 10 suggestions for improving the athletic trainer's managerial skills in the following areas: defining goals, establishing schedules and checkpoints, planning resources, motivating staff, communicating, and managing conflict.

The Software Encyclopedia (1990). New York: R.R. Bowker.

A compendium of thousands of computer programs for many types of computers. This useful reference gives the attributes and characteristics of each program it indexes.

Steiner, G.A. (1979). *Strategic planning*. New York: The Free Press.

Steiner offers a compelling argument for strategic planning in all types of organizations. The book has many practical suggestions for organizing the planning effort and implementing the plan once it has been developed.

Stoner, J.A.F. (1982). *Management* (2nd ed.). Englewood Cliffs, NJ: Prentice Hall.

A comprehensive textbook emphasizing the scientific approach to management. Chapters 4 and 7 are particularly appropriate for athletic trainers interested in program planning theory and methodology.

Want, J.H. (1986). Corporate mission. *Management Review*, **75**(8), 46-50.

A broad-based article about the importance of the mission statement to organizational success. Want suggests an approach to developing a mission statement.

Worthen, B.R., & Sanders, J.R. (1973). *Educational evaluation: Theory and practice*. Worthington, OH: Charles A. Jones.

Written primarily for those interested in evaluating educational programs and projects, this book offers many practical suggestions for the athletic trainer. Chapter 3 is the most useful for athletic trainers who are developing an evaluation model for their sports medicine programs.

"By working faithfully eight hours a day, you may eventually get to be a boss and work twelve hours a day."

Robert Frost

Who Athletic Trainers Work With: Human Resource Management

STUDENT OBJECTIVES

▌ Understand the different forms of organizational culture that can exist in the sports medicine program.

▌ Be able to formally define the relationships of the persons working in the sports medicine program by developing an organizational chart.

▌ Understand the strengths and weaknesses of the different organizational systems.

▌ Understand the components of staff selection.

▌ Be able to develop a position description and a position vacancy notice.

▌ Understand the recruitment and hiring process, especially as affected by discrimination and bias based on race, gender, disability, religion, or national origin.

▌ Understand the differences between the three major supervisory models.

▌ Understand the purposes, methods, and standards for the evaluation of athletic trainer performance.

OPENING CASE

David Lewis had just completed his 10th year as the head athletic trainer at a major NCAA Division I university. David liked his job, and the feedback he received from most of the coaches and athletic administrators was positive. In short, David was content.

David was concerned about one aspect of the job, however: Problems had developed with Judy Armstrong, one of his assistants. Although the coaches and athletes she worked with thought she was doing a good job, Judy seemed to have difficulty working with the other athletic trainers on the staff. She was perceived as argumentative, inflexible, and arrogant. David decided on a face-to-face meeting to confront the problem.

David was not prepared for Judy's assessment of her problems with the rest of the staff. "David," she began, "I'm not the problem around here—you are! I'm no different in most respects from any of the other staff athletic trainers except that I'm not willing to keep my mouth shut and put up with all the garbage that goes on around here. For instance, none of us knows where our job responsibilities begin and end. Oh sure, we know what sports we're supposed to work with, but beyond that who is responsible for the duties that overlap from team to team? Where is it spelled out? There are eight assistant trainers here at the university, not counting graduate assistants. We are constantly stepping on each other's toes because we don't know what our own jobs are, let alone what the other person's is. And another thing. Where do I stand relative to the other trainers? I've been here 3 years and my performance has never been evaluated! I might be able to put up with the lousy hours and the miserable pay if I just got some positive reinforcement for the good things I do from time to time. Think about it, Dave. The average employment length for assistant athletic trainers since you came is about 2 years. Why do you think everybody leaves so fast if this is such a great place? Don't pin this on me, because I'm not the problem!"

Although the meeting with Judy had put David in an angry and defensive mood, he sensed a kernel of truth in her arguments. He was not a strong personnel administrator and he knew it. In fact, he hated most of the administrative duties that his position required of him. The assistant trainer turnover problem had nagged at him for years. Suddenly, the contentment that David had with his job had vanished. He was frustrated.

The problems with personnel administration that led to David and Judy's confrontation are typical of many sports medicine programs. Athletic trainers are professionals who are, in general, oriented toward providing clinical services. Most have never had any training in how to manage human resources. Some athletic trainers excel at this aspect of administration without any formal understanding of human resource systems, but they are the exceptions. The most complicated tools the athletic trainer will ever work with are people. Without a system for managing these assets, the sports medicine program is unlikely to accomplish its mission. This chapter will make the athletic trainer better acquainted with the human resource function of the sports medicine program and provide the skills to carry it out.

▌ Organizational Culture

The first decision the athletic trainer in charge of a staff will make, consciously or unconsciously, will be what kind of organizational culture the program will have. *Organizational culture* includes the basic values, behavioral norms, assumptions, and beliefs present in an organization (Owens, 1987). The sports medicine program's organizational culture will define, to a large extent, what it means to be an athletic trainer in that setting. It will influence the level of commitment and loyalty of the athletic trainers working in the program.

Bennis and Nanus (1985) have described three general categories of organizational cultures (which they refer to as "social architecture") that the athletic trainer should consider as part of sports medicine human resource management: collegial, personalistic, and formalistic.

organizational culture The values, beliefs, assumptions, and norms that form the infrastructure of the organizational ethos.

The Collegial Culture

The *collegial* sports medicine program is one in which the emphasis is on consensus, teamwork, and participation in most decisions by all members of the staff, who tend to view each other as peers. The head of the department allows and encourages everyone to offer input so the decision-making process is consensual. Although this type of organizational culture appears ideal, it is inappropriate in some settings. For example, when quick decisions are required, the consensus-oriented style of the collegial culture is inappropriate because formal authority is watered down among the members of the staff. If the staff is small, on the other hand, the collegial culture is probably both appropriate and useful.

collegial culture A type of organizational culture characterized by consensus, teamwork, and participatory decision making.

The Personalistic Culture

The sports medicine program that Dave "leads" has a *personalistic* organizational culture. It places little emphasis on policy and procedure. Each member of the staff makes her or his own decisions. Teamwork and group consensus are not high priorities. Although program leaders may be available for advice and counsel, the staff athletic trainers' problems are perceived to be *their* problems, not the program's. The personalistic organizational culture is a form of controlled anarchy.

personalistic culture A type of organizational culture characterized by autonomy in decision making and problem solving.

The Formalistic Culture

The sports medicine program with a clear chain of command and well-defined lines of authority operates in a *formalistic* culture. The formalistic culture is typical of bureaucratic programs in which there is a heavy emphasis on policy, procedure, and rules. It discourages risk taking and deviation from the established source of authority. Although this may seem undesirable for a sports medicine program, there are certain advantages to the formalistic

formalistic culture A type of organizational culture characterized by a clear chain of command and well-defined lines of formal authority.

style. First, decisions can be made more rapidly since various members of the staff have formal authority. Second, established policies and procedures can provide direction to staff athletic trainers and continuity in quality of service for clients. Finally, programs with large staffs may benefit from a formalistic culture because it divides and defines responsibilities and thereby enhances internal organization.

∎ Organizational Structures

organizational structure
A model that defines the relationships between the members of an organization.

Every sports medicine organization has a structure. The ***organizational structure*** of the sports medicine program plays an important role in how well staff members accomplish the program's mission. Each athletic trainer in the program has a different job to perform. Although there may be overlapping duties and similarities from one athletic trainer to another, each is responsible for distinct duties. The only exception to this rule, of course, is the sports medicine program staffed by only one athletic trainer, which is not uncommon at most high schools and many small colleges. Organizational structure need not be a concern for athletic trainers in these environments.

span of control   *The number of subordinates supervised by a particular individual in an organizational setting.*

When designing the organizational structure of the sports medicine program athletic trainers must consider the desired span of control. ***Span of control*** refers to the number of subordinates who report to a given supervisor. Although management researchers disagree on the precise formula for establishing a span of control, most agree that supervision of employees, including athletic trainers, is easier and more effective if supervisors are directly involved with three to six subordinates (Ouchi & Dowling, 1974).

organizational chart   *A graphic representation of an organization's structure, usually arranged by function or service or in a matrix format.*

Organizational structures are typically depicted in organizational charts. The ***organizational chart*** is a graphic illustration that shows the formal relationship between the various athletic trainers and other health care workers in the sports medicine program. Organizational charts are useful because they show members of the sports medicine program their roles in relation to the overall program. In the case illustrated above, Judy would probably have better understood the role David expected her to play if he had taken the time to develop an organizational chart for the university's sports medicine program. This task is especially important for newly hired athletic trainers because they lack a historical perspective for "how things are done around here."

Trainers can develop an organizational chart by function, by service, or in a matrix form.

Function-Oriented Organizational Chart

The organizational chart based on function is probably the most common in sports medicine settings. It makes supervision easier because it requires supervisors to specialize along lines of expertise (see Figure 3.1). Functional organizational structures are especially well suited to sports medicine clinics or universities with large staffs because they facilitate allocation of staff members to projects for which they have special skills and knowledge.

Functional organizational structures also have several disadvantages. They can make it difficult to make rapid decisions because requests often have to make their way up the chain of command. They can also make it difficult

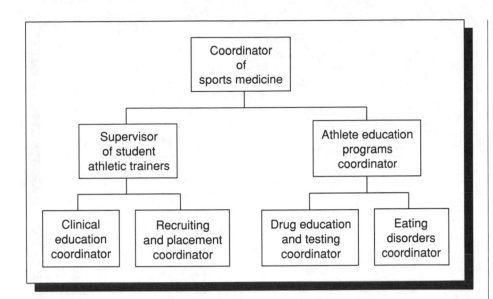

Figure 3.1 Sports medicine organizational chart: division by function.

to establish accountability for particular areas of responsibility. Consider the structure depicted in Figure 3.1. If student athletic trainers are consistently failing the NATA certification examination, who should be held accountable? Is the athletic trainer in charge of clinical education at fault or is the recruiting and placement coordinator guilty of bringing poor students into the program? Finally, the functional approach to organizing the sports medicine program can isolate staff members because it places little emphasis on sharing ideas or teamwork to accomplish program goals (see Figure 3.2).

Advantages	Disadvantages
• Suited to a stable environment.	• Slow response time in large programs.
• Fosters development of expertise.	• Bottlenecks due to sequential task performance.
• Allows specialization.	
• Requires minimal internal coordination.	• Less innovative; narrow perspective.
• Requires fewer interpersonal skills.	• May create conflicts over program priorities and staff responsibilities.
	• Little emphasis on sharing ideas and teamwork.

Figure 3.2 Advantages and disadvantages of a functional structure. *Note.* From James A.F. Stoner, *Management*, 2nd ed. Copyright © 1982, p. 268. Adapted by permission of Prentice Hall, Englewood Cliffs, New Jersey.

Service-Oriented Organizational Chart

Another way to define the structure of the sports medicine program is to organize the staff according to the services they provide. Figure 3.3 provides an example from a large university that operates a sports medicine clinic in addition to the traditional sports medicine services provided by athletic department trainers. Except for the box for the coordinator's position, the boxes in this chart represent athletic trainers who have responsibilities to

Figure 3.3 Sports medicine organizational chart: division by service.

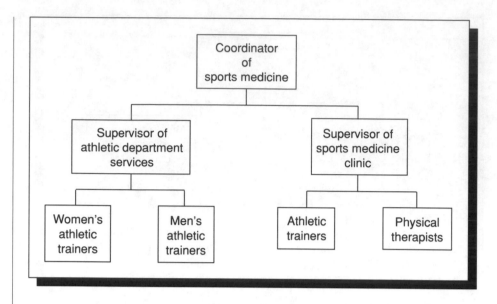

certain client groups. This type of organizational chart is especially appropriate for programs that serve a diverse clientele.

Like its function-oriented counterpart, the service-oriented organizational chart has both advantages and disadvantages (see Figure 3.4). One of the advantages of this system is that it facilitates coordination of services to any one client group because of the relatively strict division of responsibility. Accountability is easier to obtain because athletic trainers work with well-defined client groups. Finally, the chief decision maker can usually act more quickly and easily because intermediate supervisors have more authority to make their own decisions.

Figure 3.4 Advantages and disadvantages of service-oriented organizational structures. *Note.* From James A.F. Stoner, *Management*, 2nd ed. Copyright © 1982, p. 271. Adapted by permission of Prentice Hall, Englewood Cliffs, New Jersey.

Advantages	Disadvantages
• Suited to fast change.	• Fosters politics in resource allocation.
• Allows for high service visibility.	• Inhibits coordination of activities.
• Allows full-time concentration on tasks.	• Restricts problem solving to task needs.
• Clearly defines responsibilities.	• Permits in-depth competencies to decline.
• Permits parallel processing of multiple tasks.	• Creates conflicts between tasks and priorities.
	• Can inflate personnel costs.

Among the disadvantages of this system are problems balancing power and authority. When service groups are tightly defined, the athletic trainers working with a particular client group may tend to place the interests of that unit over the mission of the total program. This can result in power struggles between the members of the various program units. Another disadvantage with the service-oriented organizational structure is that it sometimes inflates personnel costs. Strictly delimiting service groups means that the expertise of an athletic trainer working in one unit is often unavailable to an athletic trainer working in another. Consequently, additional athletic trainers are required to balance the expertise between units. Supervisory expenses go up proportionally.

Matrix Organization Chart

Many athletic trainers will be tempted to structure their sports medicine programs in terms of function or service. Unfortunately, most traditional sports medicine programs will not match these models. Athletic trainers should consider an alternative to function or service paradigms: the matrix structure. The **matrix structure** combines the strongest features of the service and function models (Kolodny, 1979).

In matrix structures, trainers and other members of the sports medicine team report to two or more "bosses," depending on the project they are working on. The organizational chart for a matrix organization has both horizontal and vertical elements. If David accepts Judy's advice and develops an organizational chart for the university's sports medicine program, he might design a structure similar to the one in Figure 3.5. The vertical elements

matrix structure *A type of chart that describes an organizational structure in terms of both functions and services.*

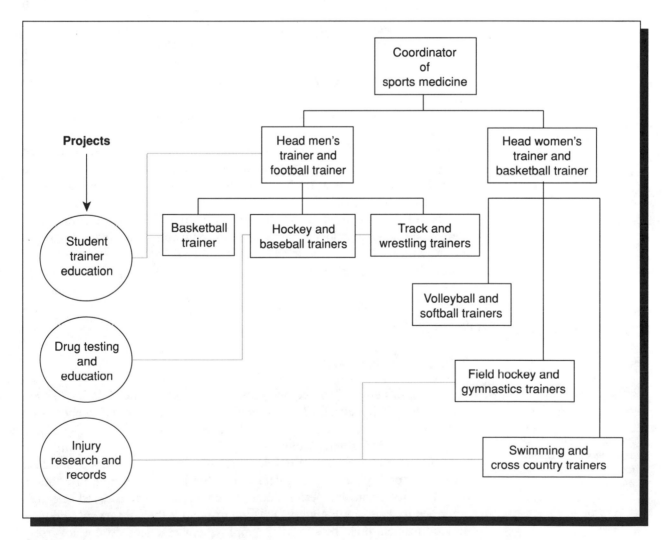

∎ **Figure 3.5**   A matrix organization structure.

show the chain of command in the program. The horizontal elements depict project teams that take advantage of the athletic trainers' specialization in certain areas. Not everyone has to be placed on a project team. Some athletic trainers will lack expertise in some areas. Others will be new to the organization and may need time to become acclimated. In educational settings like David's, some of the athletic trainers may have release time to teach sports medicine courses, making it difficult for them to be assigned to project teams.

The advantages of the matrix system as a model for deploying athletic trainers include the ability to efficiently use the staff's expertise (see Figure 3.6). In addition, the matrix structure reduces coordination problems and

Figure 3.6 Advantages and disadvantages of the matrix organizational structure. *Note.* From James A.F. Stoner, *Management*, 2nd ed. Copyright © 1982, p. 274. Adapted by permission of Prentice Hall, Englewood Cliffs, New Jersey.

Advantages	Disadvantages
• Gives flexibility to the organization.	• Risks creating a feeling of anarchy.
• Stimulates interdisciplinary cooperation.	• Encourages power struggles.
• Involves, motivates, and challenges people.	• May lead to more discussion than action.
• Develops athletic trainers' skills.	• Requires high level of interpersonal skill.
• Frees program coordinator for planning.	• Can be time-consuming to implement.

enhances economic efficiency by assigning only the necessary number of athletic trainers to any given project.

There are also disadvantages to the matrix model. Athletic trainers need a high level of interpersonal communication skill to work effectively with various co-workers on different tasks. For example, in the opening case study, Judy finds that, like most athletic trainers, she must accomplish a number of tasks with other staff members. Because her interpersonal skills were not highly developed, her frustration showed in an inability to get along with her fellow athletic trainers. Another disadvantage of the matrix system is that athletic trainers can become frustrated and morale can suffer when people are switched between projects or when one project ends and another begins. Since many projects have a finite life span, this is a common problem.

▌ Staff Selection

staff selection Any procedure used as a basis for any employment decision, including recruitment, hiring, promotion, demotion, retention, and performance evaluation.

The basis for human resource management in sports medicine is *staff selection*. Although the term *staff selection* may imply only identifying and hiring new athletic trainers, it has a much broader meaning in law. The Equal Employment Opportunity Commission's *Uniform Guidelines on Employee Selection Procedures* (1979) defines *staff selection* as any procedure used as a basis for any employment decision. Athletic trainer hiring, promotion, demotion, retention, and performance evaluation are all considered selection activities by law (see Figure 3.7). To comply with the *Uniform Guidelines*, athletic trainers must be sure their employment practices do not adversely impact any group protected under the law. The only exception to these rules

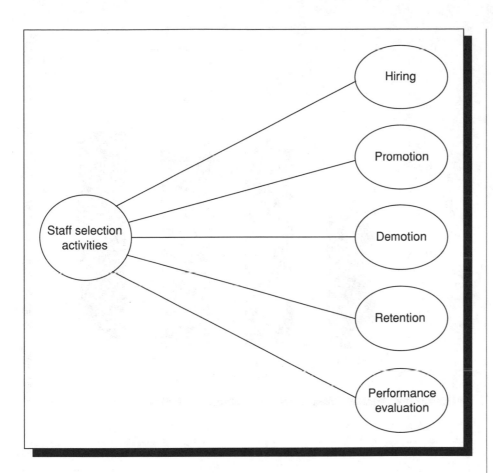

Figure 3.7   Staff selection activities in sports medicine.

occurs when an organization can prove that it discriminates as a result of "business necessity." The following sections provide practical suggestions for athletic trainers with staff-selection responsibilities.

Position Description

A formal document that contains information about the required qualifications for and the work content, accountability, and scope of a job is known as a *position description*. The position description is an important communication link between the athletic trainer and the supervisor that creates a common understanding of the role the athletic trainer should play in the program. Although many supervisors assume their staffs agree with them about the duties for which they are responsible, Myers (1985) concluded that fewer than 50% of the employees he surveyed agreed with their supervisors on the standards and responsibilities of their jobs. When position descriptions are poorly written or absent altogether, athletic trainers are unlikely to be able to meet the undefined expectations of their supervisors. Unfortunately, many athletic trainers do not have position descriptions (Ray, 1991) (see Figure 3.8). In addition, many athletic trainers' position descriptions are poorly written, couched in trait-oriented language, or lacking weights for various job descriptors.

The athletic trainer's position description should be divided into two sections: the job specification and the job description (see Figure 3.9). The

position description   A formal document that describes the qualifications for and work content, accountability, and scope of a job.

▌ Figure 3.8 Position description frequency among athletic trainers. *Note.* The data are from ''Performance evaluation in athletic training: Perceptions of athletic trainers and their supervisors'' by R.R. Ray, 1991, *Dissertations Abstracts International,* **51,** 5053. (Doctoral dissertation, Western Michigan University, 1990)

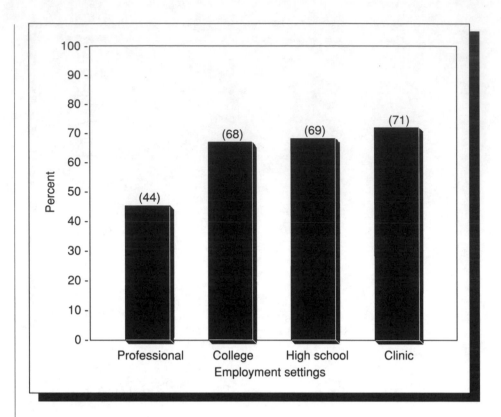

▌ Figure 3.9 Position description components.

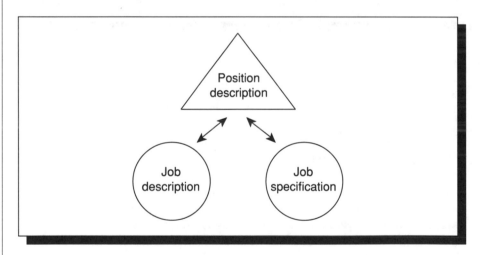

job specification *A written description of the requirements or qualifications a person should possess in order to fill a particular role in an organization.*

job description *A written description of the specific responsibilities a position holder will be accountable for in an organization.*

job specification describes the qualifications an athletic trainer should have to fill the role (Haddad, 1985). The *job description* lists the responsibilities for which the athletic trainer will be held accountable (U.S. Small Business Administration, 1980). Each responsibility should be assigned a weight so the athletic trainer will understand which duties are considered the most important (Fowler & Bushardt, 1986).

Athletic trainers who write position descriptions struggle with several important questions. Should the items be specific or general? Should the document describe what ought to be or what is? Although no definitive answers to these questions would meet the needs of every situation, general guidelines do exist. It is generally useful to be as specific as possible when delineating the duties and responsibilities of the athletic trainer. This is important because it provides clear direction for the athletic trainer. To avoid allowing employees to perform only minimal job responsibilities, Sikula (1976) suggests adding a general concluding statement near the end, such as ". . . and any other duties related to the performance of this job as assigned by the Coordinator of Sports Medicine."

The question of whether the job description should be normative or descriptive is not easy to answer. Ideally, the athletic trainer should have some input into the design of her own position description. She probably knows the most about the job and its responsibilities (Aldrich, 1985). Unfortunately, when incumbents write their own job descriptions, they tend to be narrowly focused and to ignore tasks the incumbent does not enjoy, no matter how important they are to accomplishing the mission of the sports medicine program. For this reason, the program head should perform a final check on all position descriptions. The combination of input from the supervisor and from the subordinate into the position description will be more likely to result in a balance between the needs of the employee and those of the sports medicine program. Position descriptions for new athletic trainers should be written as normatively as possible so the new employee can begin to adapt to the new work setting. In any case, the position description should only reflect the characteristics of the job, not ambiguous personal characteristics like loyalty, initiative, and trust.

Finally, no matter which approach is used, the position description should be reviewed and modified as needed at least once a year to reflect changes in the athletic trainer's qualifications or the work environment (Bruce, 1986). For an example of what Judy's position description might look like, see Figure 3.10.

Recruitment and Hiring

Attracting and retaining qualified, competent staff members is crucial to the overall success of the sports medicine program. **Recruitment** of athletic trainers and other allied health care professionals should be viewed from two perspectives: the long-range need for human resources within the sports medicine program (see Figure 3.11) and the immediate staffing needs.

The long-term staffing plan will depend, to a significant degree, on the strategic plan of the sports medicine program. How is our client base likely to change? How will the accomplishment of our goals and objectives affect our need for staffing? The long-range recruiting plan should consider a number of factors, including the likelihood of promotion or transfer of present staff members, upcoming retirement plans, and the projected availability of athletic trainers and other allied health care workers in the labor pool. All these factors are important. For example, if the program structure will support an additional athletic trainer but the pool of qualified applicants is inadequate, the human resources plan for the sports medicine unit may need to be revised. Each of these factors should be evaluated annually so future staffing needs can be met.

The other perspective in the recruitment process is the immediate need for staffing the sports medicine program. Immediate staffing needs typically arise as a result of four changes in the makeup of the present staff: radical

recruitment The process of planning for human resources needs and identifying potential candidates to meet those needs.

POSITION DESCRIPTION

Job title: Assistant Athletic Trainer   Date: July 1, 1992
Department: Intercollegiate Athletics   Status: Salaried Nonfaculty
Incumbent: Judy Armstrong   Supervisor: Linda Black, Head Women's Trainer
Written by: David Lewis, Coordinator of Sports Medicine, & Judy Armstrong
Approved by: James Wilson, Director of Intercollegiate Athletics

Job Specification

Factor	*Job Specification*	*Person Specification*
Education	Requires minimum of bachelor's degree.	Must have a bachelor's degree.
Certification	Requires credentials consistent with Ohio law and recognized national standards.	Must be NATA certified, hold a valid Ohio license, and be certified in CPR.
Working conditions	Requires travel over weekends & holidays, 50-70 hours of work per week, and exposure to all kinds of weather.	Must have flexible schedule and be in good physical condition.
Physical demands	Requires lifting of injured athletes, manual dexterity, and administration of CPR.	Must be able to lift heavy weights and have functional use of all four extremities.

Job Description

Job Responsibilities

*Relative Importance
(1 = low   5 = high)*

Coordinates and delivers athletic training services to members of the field hockey and gymnastics teams including, but not limited to, coordination of physical exams, evaluation and treatment of injuries at practices and games, design and supervision of rehabilitation programs, counseling within the limits of expertise, and prepractice/game taping.   5

Refers injured athletes to appropriate physicians according to guidelines in the *Standard Operating Procedures.*   5

Submits injured athlete status reports to coaches by 11:00 a.m. of the day following the injury.   4

Maintains computerized injury/treatment data base according to guidelines in the *Standard Operating Procedures.*   3

Coordinates NCAA Injury Surveillance program by conducting in-service training for student trainers, collecting and checking the accuracy of individual and weekly injury report forms, and mailing completed forms to the NCAA by Monday of each week.   3

Prepares annual injury and treatment report for all sports by June 1.   3

Exhibits behaviors in strict compliance with the NATA *Code of Professional Practice.*   5

Performs other duties not specifically stated herein but deemed essential to the operation of the sports medicine program as assigned by the Coordinator or the Head Women's Trainer.   Varies

▌ **Figure 3.10**   Sample position description.

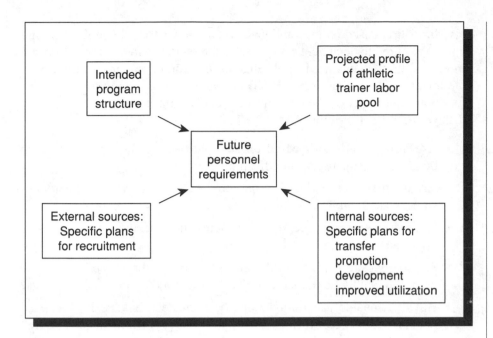

Figure 3.11 Long-range recruiting considerations. *Note.* Adapted with the permission of Macmillan Publishing Company from *The Personnel Function in Educational Administration*, Fourth Edition by William B. Castetter. Copyright © 1986 by William B. Castetter.

program changes, termination (for either personal or professional reasons), retirement, and death. Each of these actions can result in the immediate need to fill a vacant position (see Figure 3.12).

Many institutions that employ athletic trainers have specific procedures in place for recruiting and hiring all personnel. In these institutions, the athletic trainer in charge of staffing the sports medicine program has little choice but to become well informed about the policies and procedures and to scrupulously adhere to them. Most institutional recruitment and hiring policies and procedures are designed to prevent the more blatant forms of

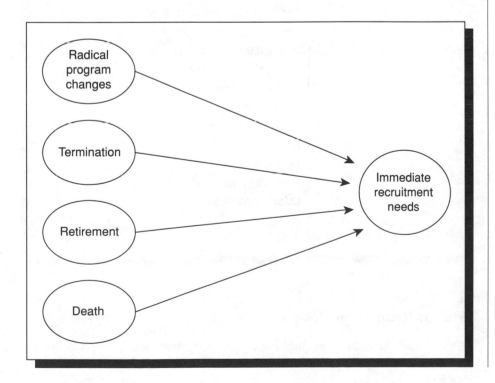

Figure 3.12 Factors influencing immediate recruitment needs.

discrimination based on race and gender. In many cases, the athletic trainer will be required to document every step of the recruitment and hiring process to ensure that all qualified applicants were afforded equal opportunity in the hiring process. McCarthy (1983) has suggested that employers ask the following questions of their recruitment and hiring practices to determine if they could be discriminatory:

- Are hiring restrictions based on sex, national origin, age, or religion bona fide occupational qualifications?

- Are the prerequisites listed in the job specifications valid indicators of success as an athletic trainer?

- Is there a legitimate necessity for policies and procedures that adversely affect any given class of employee?

- Are the questions asked in the hiring interview directly related to the prospective athletic trainer's ability to perform the job responsibilities?

- Have reasonable accommodations been made to enable handicapped persons or persons of various religious beliefs to perform the job required of an athletic trainer?

- What precautions have been taken to ensure that present recruitment and hiring policies and procedures do not perpetuate past discriminatory practices?

Although the recruitment and hiring process for the sports medicine program will vary among organizations, several steps are common to most settings (see Figure 3.13).

Figure 3.13 Common steps for recruiting and hiring sports medicine personnel.

Step number	Recruiting and hiring process
1	Request for position
2	Position request approval
3	Position vacancy notice
4	Application collection
5	Telephone interviews
6	Reference checks
7	On-site interview
8	Recommendation and approval for hiring
9	Offer of contract
10	Hiring

Step 1: Request for Position

Athletic administrators, general managers, principals, and clinic administrators will not consider filling a vacancy or adding a new position unless the athletic trainer makes a specific request. Some organizations require that a specific form be completed as part of the request process. Others require a position description. Obviously, requests for additional personnel are generally screened more cautiously than requests for position replacements. Such requests should be detailed enough to document need based on both present and forecasted program conditions.

Step 2: Position Request Approval

After the athletic trainer in charge has submitted the request to the appropriate administrative officer, the request will probably be approved, denied, or held up pending further study. Athletic trainers should try to anticipate the data administrators will need in order to make a decision.

Step 3: Position Vacancy Notice

Once the request for position is approved, the athletic trainer may be required to advertise the position vacancy to satisfy collective bargaining agreements and state and federal guidelines. Position vacancies should be posted both internally, so present sports medicine staff who wish to apply for the positions may do so, and externally. Position vacancy notices may be posted externally in any of the following locations:

- Local newspapers
- Athletic trainer job placement services[1]
- National Athletic Trainers Association job hot line
- *NCAA News*
- *Chronicle of Higher Education*
- Publications of the American Alliance for Health, Physical Education, Recreation and Dance
- Publications of the American Physical Therapy Association

Finally, many athletic trainers find it useful to send a copy of the position vacancy notice to program directors of NATA-approved athletic training education programs and to the head athletic trainers of schools that offer internships for their student athletic trainers.

The position vacancy notice should not be a carbon copy of the position description, but it should include a summary of the major responsibilities, a list of prerequisite qualifications, and a brief description of the major attributes of the institution or organization. In addition, the position vacancy notice should have the name, address, and telephone number of the person responsible for coordinating the hiring effort for the sports medicine program along with a list of required application documents. Typical application documents include a resume or curriculum vitae, letter of application, letters of reference, and transcripts. Many institutions require notice of

[1]Athletic Training Services, P.O. Box 158, Mt. Pleasant, MI 48804-0158   517-772-5888.

Position Vacancy

Ohio Technological University
Assistant Athletic Trainer

OTU is seeking applications for the position of assistant athletic trainer in the Department of Intercollegiate Athletics. Primary responsibilities include the delivery of athletic training services for the field hockey and gymnastics teams, although occasional work with other teams will be required. This position also includes responsibility for coordinating the sports medicine program's injury research and records program, including maintenance of the computer data base and coordination of student athletic trainers involved in NCAA injury surveillance data collection.

Minimum qualifications include a bachelor's degree, NATA certification, an Ohio athletic training license, and current American Red Cross CPR certification.

Salary is negotiable and will be commensurate with experience. This position is a 10-month, renewable-term, salaried nonfaculty contract.

Ohio Technological University has an enrollment of 25,000 students and is located in an urban center of over 250,000. OTU offers 41 undergraduate majors and 15 graduate degree programs. The university is a member of the NCAA Division I and offers eight sports for men and eight for women. OTU is an equal opportunity, affirmative action employer. Women and members of minority groups are encouraged to apply.

Interested persons should send a letter of application, resume, three letters of reference, and undergraduate transcript by June 1 to

David Lewis
Coordinator of Sports Medicine
Ohio Technological University
Urban Center, OH 40000
(217) 555-5555

Figure 3.14   Sample position vacancy notice.

---

nondiscrimination near the bottom of all position vacancy notices (see Figure 3.14).

Step 4: Application Collection

The next step in the process is to receive and screen applications for the position. A common practice is to appoint a committee of interested persons with a legitimate stake in hiring the athletic trainer to screen applications. The operation of search committees varies widely. Some operate on consensus while others follow strict parliamentary procedure and vote on the suitability of various candidates for the position.

In any case, incoming applications should be sorted into three groups: unqualified applicants, qualified applicants with complete application files, and apparently qualified applicants with incomplete application files. As the application deadline approaches, the committee should send a letter to apparently qualified applicants with incomplete files requesting an immediate response if they wish to remain under consideration for the position. A copy of all correspondence with applicants should be kept on file as evidence of good faith hiring practices on the part of the institution or organization.

Step 5: Telephone Interviews

After the qualified applicants have been identified, members of the search committee should interview especially promising candidates by telephone. Telephone interviews prior to on-site interviews are important to weed out unsuitable applicants and provide additional information not readily communicated in application letters or resumes. Telephone interviewers should be friendly and informative, but they should avoid making statements the candidate may interpret as promises or verbal contracts that may be binding upon the institution. Questions asked in the telephone interview should elicit additional information unavailable in the application documents. Each candidate should be asked the same questions in the same order to ensure reliability. Questions should always focus on candidates' job-related behavior and should not focus on personal characteristics (Drake, 1982). Examples of questions that are illegal in some states include these:

- What is your religion?
- Sean McLeary. Is that Irish?
- Are you married?
- Do you have children? Do you plan to have children?
- Do you belong to any social clubs or fraternities?
- Do you have AIDS? Are you HIV-positive?
- Do you have a photo of yourself we could staple to your application?

❚ The telephone interview is an important preliminary step in the hiring process.

Step 6: Reference Checks

After the applicant pool has been further narrowed as a result of the telephone interviewing, the search committee should begin checking references. This is an important aspect of the recruitment and hiring process, because it allows the athletic trainer to validate the information supplied by the candidate. Some application materials need not be checked. Notarized transcripts, diplomas, and certificates are usually, but not always, valid. Expiration dates and signatures should be checked.

The most valuable information source is usually the applicant's previous employers or, for entry level applicants, internship supervisors. An applicant's performance in similar employment settings is the best predictive factor of how the person will perform the new job. Notes of all conversations should be kept in the applicant's file for future reference by other members of the search committee.

Step 7: On-Site Interview

On-site interviews are costly and time consuming. Only those applicants who are obviously well qualified for the job should be interviewed on-site. Candidates about whom the search committee has serious reservations should not be interviewed. The on-site interview is important for both the candidate and the organization. It allows the candidate to become familiar with the work setting and it allows the search committee to see the candidate in the work setting.

The on-site visit can be organized in many ways. Most visits should include a number of interviews with institutional stakeholders such as coaches, student-athletes, athletic administrators, owners, team physicians, and other athletic trainers. Time should be set aside for the candidate to ask questions about the job. Candidates should have an opportunity to tour the facilities and inspect their potential work sites. The visit should typically be one or two days in length, depending on the level of responsibility of the position and the number of people who need to be involved in the interview process. If David Lewis, the athletic trainer in the opening case, was conducting an on-site interview for a candidate in the Ohio Technological University sports medicine program, the visit might be structured like the one in Figure 3.15.

Step 8: Recommendation and Approval for Hiring

After the candidates have been interviewed on-site, the search committee must make a recommendation for hiring to the appropriate person in the organization with formal authority to approve such an act. The recommendation for hiring should be accompanied by supporting documentation so the decision maker will have the necessary information to make a final choice. Search committee members should be sure they make a final recommendation for hiring based solely on the qualifications of the candidate and not on personal characteristics unrelated to the job.

Step 9: Offer of Contract

After the most outstanding candidate has been selected, whoever is authorized to negotiate a contract with the candidate should make contact by telephone and verbally extend an offer of employment. If terms of employment can

---

Itinerary for the visit of

John Olmstead
Candidate for the position of head men's trainer

Monday, June 11

    10:00 a.m.—Arrive at Urban Center Airport, met by David Lewis.
    10:30 a.m.—Meet with Linda Black, head women's trainer, Fieldhouse Training Room.
    11:45 a.m.—Lunch with Student Trainers Club representatives Jim Gleason and Elaine Williams.
    1:30 p.m.—Meet with James Wilson, director of intercollegiate athletics, Central Administration Building.
    2:45 p.m.—Meet with Dr. Reid Chesterfield, team physician, Student Health Service.
    3:30 p.m.—Meet with Greg Campbell, head football coach, Memorial Stadium.
    4:15 p.m.—Meet with Lucy Sneller, director of human resources, Central Administration Building.
    5:00 p.m.—Check into Campus Inn.
    6:30 p.m.—Dinner with David Lewis, coordinator of sports medicine, and Rick Ellis, assistant athletic
               trainer, Campus Inn Grill.

Tuesday, June 12

    7:30 a.m.—Breakfast with Tom Hernandez, head men's basketball coach, University Club.
    8:30 a.m.—Meet with members of the search committee, Fieldhouse conference room.
    11:00 a.m.—Fly home. Jim Gleason will accompany to the airport.
    11:00 a.m.—Search committee meeting, Fieldhouse conference room.

▌ **Figure 3.15** Sample on-site interview itinerary.

be agreed to over the telephone, the authorized institutional representative should prepare a formal employment contract consistent with institutional rules, collective bargaining agreements, and state and federal law. The contract should include the length of employment, salary and benefits, position title, and job responsibilities as specified in the position description. In addition, a clause stating that the athletic trainer agrees to abide by the terms and conditions delineated in the institution's employee handbook should be included. Two copies of the signed contract should be sent to the athletic trainer with instructions to sign and return one of the copies by a given date, usually within 10 to 14 days.

Step 10: Hiring

Once a written employment contract has been signed, a letter should be sent to the other applicants thanking them for their interest in the position and informing them that the position has been filled. This is an important courtesy that too many institutions, unfortunately, ignore. Another step that some institutions take at the end of the hiring process is to distribute a press release to the media announcing the addition of the new athletic trainer to the sports medicine staff. This can not only be a valuable public relations tool for the sports medicine program, but also make the new athletic trainer's induction into a relatively unfamiliar work setting more comfortable.

▌ Staff Supervision

The concept of management as defined in Chapter 1 includes the notion that managers coordinate the activities of a group of people toward a common

supervision *A process whereby authority holders observe the work activities of an employee to improve the outcomes of the employee's work or the employee's professional development.*

goal. They accomplish this partly through the use of supervision. *Supervision* is a process whereby authority holders observe the work activities of an employee to improve the outcomes of the employee's work or the professional development of the employee. Supervision is different from summative evaluation. The purpose of summative evaluation is to place a value on the quality of an employee for the purpose of determining appropriate employment actions including retention, promotion, demotion, transfer, discharge, and compensation level. In the opening case, you may recall that Judy was upset that David had never evaluated her performance during the three years she had worked for him. Judy lacked both summative evaluation and supervision. She didn't know if she was meeting the expectations of the program. She became frustrated because David didn't appear to care about her, her work, or her development as a professional.

Supervision is one of the most difficult managerial functions for the athletic trainer to master for several reasons. First, unless the employees the athletic trainer supervises are perfect in every way, supervision requires some degree of confrontation. Second, almost every supervisional problem is unique in some way. Responding to the employment-related problems of athletic trainers requires creativity and emotional investment in the staff and their development. Finally, effective supervision requires the athletic trainer to consider the opinions and perspectives of others. Athletic trainer-supervisors should develop strategies to reduce the level of bias they bring to situations so the needs of both the sports medicine program and its employees can be met.

Athletic trainers can use many different supervisory models. Tanner and Tanner (1987) have described four: inspection, production, clinical, and developmental. This discussion will combine the inspection and production models because their differences are minor.

Inspection-Production Supervision

inspection-production *A supervisory model that emphasizes the use of formal authority and managerial prerogatives in order to improve employee efficiency and efficacy.*

The primary characteristic of the *inspection-production* model of supervision is an emphasis on authoritative managerial efficiency. Athletic trainers who prefer this approach to supervision insist on strict observance of program policies and procedures. This model views services of the sports medicine program as products and the athletic trainer employees as the raw materials used to develop those products. In the inspection-production mode, supervising athletic trainers require all employees of the sports medicine program to develop a comprehensive list of goals for the year. Then they carefully check progress toward accomplishing these goals during the course of the year. This model's overriding emphasis is on accomplishment of program goals and objectives and on attainment of the program mission.

The advantage of the inspection-production model is that it can be effective in helping the sports medicine program accomplish its goals. It sets well-defined limits on job-related behavior for all employees and consequently enhances common understanding of the athletic trainers' roles. This approach to supervision is usually associated with formalistic bureaucratic organizations with many levels of supervisory management.

There are several disadvantages to using the inspection-production system of supervision in service-oriented enterprises, including sports medicine programs. This model was originally developed and implemented in industrial settings where inputs and outputs could easily be measured. Inputs and outputs are not easily measured in most sports medicine settings. Although some measures of program success or failure should be developed, interpretation of them will vary widely depending on the audience.

Another problem with this model is the nature of the work that athletic trainers do. Most trainers perform a wide variety of jobs, and not all of them are easily observed or quantified. For example, if David Lewis wanted to be sure Judy Armstrong was meeting the program standard for taping effectiveness and efficiency, he could simply observe her as she prepared a team for a practice or game. But how would David Lewis inspect the effectiveness and efficiency of Judy Armstrong's counseling skills? Her rehabilitation skills? Finally, the inspection-production method of supervision can cause professional employees like athletic trainers to feel unappreciated and unfulfilled. Since the dominant ethos is program goal accomplishment and not professional development, athletic trainers will rarely appreciate what little developmental feedback they receive. They will tend to view such feedback in negative terms.

Clinical Supervision

Clinical supervision is the process, borrowed from education, of direct observation of the athletic trainer at work and the subsequent development of plans to remediate deficiencies in performance (Acheson & Gall, 1987). It requires the supervisor to observe a sample of the athletic trainer's performance, to analyze the strengths and weaknesses of the performance, and to collaboratively develop a structure for helping the trainer overcome such weaknesses. This type of supervision may be particularly appropriate for student interns, although it is useful for professional staff as well. Among the many supervisory techniques that can be applied within the clinical supervision model, one of the most promising for athletic trainers is work sampling (Hagerty, Chang, & Spengler, 1985). Work sampling identifies the type of work athletic trainers do and the amount of time they spend doing it. Hence, it can be an effective tool for both clinical supervision and job analysis. Work sampling consists of logging the activities of athletic trainers at randomly selected times and analyzing the data to judge the nature and quality of the work being performed. Appropriate activities facilitate the goals and objectives of the sports medicine program. Inappropriate activities duplicate efforts, are extraneous to the purposes of the program, fulfill purely personal or social wants, or allocate too much time to tasks that are not suited to the athletic trainer's qualifications.

Among the advantages of clinical supervision is its emphasis on collegial working relationships and cooperative planning. The clinical model of supervision promotes the professional status of the athletic trainer and involves the athletic trainer in as much of the supervisory process as possible. The role of the supervising athletic trainer is consultative rather than authoritative.

The primary disadvantage of the clinical system of supervision for athletic training is that the supervising athletic trainer must devote large blocks of time to supervising individual employees. Because clinical supervision requires direct observation of an athletic trainer's performance and most supervising athletic trainers have significant responsibilities in the treatment

clinical supervision *The process of direct observation of an employee's work, with emphasis on measurement of specific behaviors, and the subsequent development of plans to remediate deficiencies in performance.*

of injured clients, it becomes very difficult to find the time to implement a truly clinical system of supervision. Another problem with clinical supervision is that it requires training to properly interpret observed supervision data.

❚ Video analysis of clinical tasks can be an effective supervisory technique.

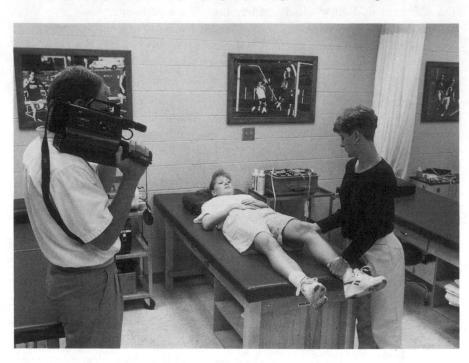

Developmental Supervision

developmental supervision
A supervisory model that emphasizes collaboration between supervisors and those supervised to help them solve problems and develop professionally.

Developmental supervision is the process of collaboration between the supervising athletic trainer and employees through which employees develop professionally while meeting the needs of the sports medicine program. The overriding theme of developmental supervision is participative management—employees discuss common problems and suggest and implement creative solutions. The system is intended to improve both the sports medicine program and its employees by increasing involvement in problem solving by all employees. It emphasizes the interdependence of the goals of the program and those of the athletic trainers.

The primary advantage of the developmental model is its emphasis on personal growth and its integration of athletic trainer and sports medicine program goals. The developmental system tends to build an organizational culture that places a high level of importance on meeting the needs of athletic trainers to improve program quality. This results in athletic trainers who are generally happy and content in their professional development.

Unfortunately, well-developed, happy employees are not a guarantee of overall program success. Collegiality and collaboration are desirable only when they bring different perspectives and new ways of thinking to difficult problems. Heavy emphasis on collaboration can actually delay problem solving because of the need to preserve the collegial organizational climate.

Which supervisory model is best? Is one model more appropriate for a university setting? For a sports medicine clinic setting? These are difficult questions to answer because these three supervisory models have never been empirically investigated in sports medicine settings. We can intuitively draw a few tentative conclusions, however. First, most sports medicine programs should probably integrate elements of each model into their supervisory plans. Whenever collaborative problem solving can be used it should be because it results in better-informed solutions in which athletic trainers have a greater sense of ownership. When questions arise about the effectiveness of an athletic trainer, direct observation of her work and suggestions for improvement by the supervising athletic trainer would probably be useful. There will be times, however, when the supervisor will have to take other actions. If an employee has not responded well to attempts at collaborative problem solving or suggestions from the supervisor, there may be no alternative but for the supervising athletic trainer to impose a solution to correct the actions of the employee.

∎ Performance Evaluation

Performance evaluation is the process of placing a value on the quality of the athletic trainer's work. Performance evaluation is important for at least two reasons. First, it can help the supervising athletic trainer make valid and reliable distinctions between athletic trainers who are performing at or above program expectations and those whose work is unsatisfactory. Second, a properly implemented system of performance evaluation helps the athletic trainers being evaluated identify areas of weakness and eliminate or reduce them.

performance evaluation
The process of placing a value on the quality of an employee's work.

Many readers may be disappointed that there are no performance evaluation instruments in this book. The reason is that any performance evaluation instrument not based on a specific athletic trainer's weighted job description and not designed for a particular purpose is useless. Performance evaluation is *not* the annual completion of a form. Performance evaluation is a process carried out throughout the entire year that involves mutually establishing goals, creating performance standards for accomplishing those goals, measuring the level of accomplishment, mutually understanding how well the athletic trainer met his goals, and mutually developing plans to remediate performance deficiencies and continue professional development. Measuring performance often requires the input of the athletic trainer being evaluated, the athletic trainer's peers, the supervisor, the clients, and the consulting physicians. Any performance evaluation instrument not built on these principles would be so riddled with caveats as to render it meaningless.

Status of Performance Evaluation in Athletic Training

Of the few printed resources for athletic trainers on performance evaluation, most are outdated and advocate a trait-oriented approach (Parks, 1977; Penman & Adams, 1980). Trait-oriented evaluation systems place a value on athletic trainers' performance by assessing human qualities. For example, if David Lewis were to evaluate Judy Armstrong's performance using a trait-oriented approach, he would be likely to label her as "aggressive," "unfriendly," and "difficult to get along with." Unfortunately, none of these terms refers to the quality of her work. Although trait-oriented systems are the easiest to implement, they usually lack validity and reliability (Dobbins & Russell, 1986; Huber, Podsakoff, & Todor, 1986). For example,

Cascio and Bernardin (1981) reported a survey of 47 administrators that identified 75 different definitions of *dependability*.

Unfortunately, the performance of athletic trainers in many settings is not formally evaluated annually (see Figure 3.16). For example, in Ray's 1990

❙ Figure 3.16   Incidence of athletic trainer performance evaluation by employment setting. *Note.* The data are from ''Performance evaluation in athletic training: Perceptions of athletic trainers and their supervisors'' by R.R. Ray, 1991, *Dissertations Abstracts International*, **51**, 5053. (Doctoral dissertation, Western Michigan University, 1990)

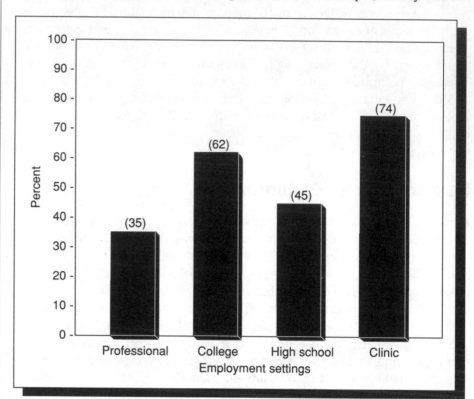

study of performance evaluation in all athletic training settings, only 35% of athletic trainers employed in the professional athletics setting reported being evaluated on an annual basis. Of those athletic trainers that are evaluated regularly, most perceive their performance evaluations differently from their supervisors. For example, athletic trainers and their supervisors had different perceptions on whether the NATA's *Competencies in Athletic Training* and *Standards of Practice for Athletic Training* were used as a basis for evaluating athletic trainer job performance. One of the most likely reasons for this discrepancy is that a significant number of athletic trainers are evaluated by nonmedical supervisors who are not very familiar with the athletic trainer's job responsibilities. In addition, only about half of these supervisors have had any formal training in how to conduct a performance evaluation or interpret the data derived from the evaluation (see Figure 3.17). Another reason that athletic trainers and their supervisors have differing opinions on the nature of performance evaluation is that many athletic trainers, even if they are formally evaluated, never receive feedback regarding their performance from their supervisors (see Figure 3.18). This lack of communication is an important reason for the lack of understanding between athletic trainers and their supervisors.

Performance Evaluation Methods

Practitioners of performance evaluation disagree about which methods are most effective for rating employee job performance (Reinhardt, 1985). The

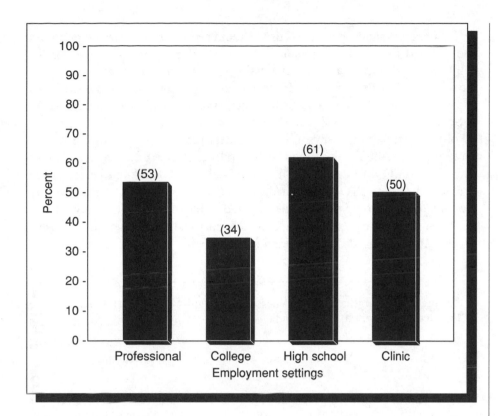

▌Figure 3.17 Percentage of supervisors of athletic trainers who have been formally trained in performance evaluation. *Note.* The data are from "Performance evaluation in athletic training: Perceptions of athletic trainers and their supervisors" by R.R. Ray, 1991, *Dissertations Abstracts International*, **51**, 5053. (Doctoral dissertation, Western Michigan University, 1990)

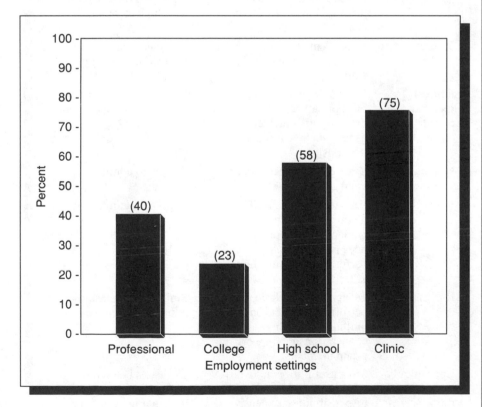

▌Figure 3.18 Percentage of athletic trainers who receive feedback regarding their performance from their supervisors. *Note.* The data are from "Performance evaluation in athletic training: Perceptions of athletic trainers and their supervisors" by R.R. Ray, 1991, *Dissertations Abstracts International*, **51**, 5053. (Doctoral dissertation, Western Michigan University, 1990)

performance evaluation methods used should be appropriate for the purposes and defined uses of the evaluation (Schneier, Beatty, & Baird, 1986). No single method of performance evaluation will match every setting or meet the need of every organization. Table 3.1 contains a summary of the strengths and weaknesses of the most common performance evaluation methods.

Seven performance evaluation methods are used most often: management by objectives, written essays, critical incident reports, graphic rating scales, forced choice rating, ranking, and behaviorally anchored rating scales. Fowler and Bushardt (1986) developed a method called task-oriented performance evaluation system (TOPES) that they alleged to be a simple, job-specific method of measuring performance-related behavior. Unfortunately, it has not been field tested extensively or validated for different settings or uses. Work sampling as described previously can also be used as a form of

Table 3.1　Strengths and Weaknesses of the Most Commonly Used Performance Evaluation Methods

Method	Weaknesses	Strengths
Management by objectives	Tends to emphasize job characteristics that can be measured over those that cannot.	Employee is able to have input into the standards by which he or she is evaluated.
Written essay	Dependent on subjective data; validity dependent on writer's skill and judgment.	Evaluator can write a detailed profile of the employee's work.
Critical incident report	Can be subject to writer bias; often based on subjective data; negative incidents usually receive more notice than positive.	More detail regarding the employee's work can be provided.
Graphic rating scale	Scale elements often not valid or job-related.	Simple to administer; low cost.
Forced choice rating	Fails to provide specific feedback; not useful in human resource planning; does not relate job performance to selection criteria.	Simple to administer; low cost.
Ranking	Difficult to discriminate performance levels on multitask jobs; discourages cooperation among work group members.	Simplifies the task of allocating rewards.
Behaviorally anchored rating scales	Most useful for employees with identical job responsibilities; expensive and time-consuming to develop; difficult to update as job responsibilities change.	Evaluates behaviors rather than traits; specific to single job category.

performance evaluation. Keaveny and McGann (1980), in their research into performance appraisal format and its influence on role clarity and evaluation criteria, determined that behaviorally anchored rating scales were superior to graphic rating scales to help professionals understand the performance area being rated, the perceived performance level for each rating area, and the behavior changes that would be necessary to improve ratings for each performance area.

Performance Evaluation Standards

The Personnel Evaluation Standards (Joint Committee on Standards for Educational Evaluation, 1988) are likely to influence the practice of performance evaluation in athletic training. This publication provides widely accepted evaluation principles that educational professionals can use to improve their personnel evaluation systems. These standards may be adopted by policy boards as the official standards for judging performance evaluation systems. As these standards will improve the validity and reliability of performance evaluation systems, if they are widely adopted, they will certainly benefit athletic trainers who work in educational institutions. Although *The Personnel Evaluation Standards* were written for educational settings, they are rooted in valid and reliable evaluation principles and could be applied in noneducational settings. Athletic trainers employed in professional athletics, sports medicine clinics, and industry will benefit from the application of these standards because validity and reliability of performance evaluation is important in their job settings as well (see Figure 3.19).

> • Legal and fair   • Practical
> • Useful   • Accurate

❚ Figure 3.19 Elements of standards-based performance evaluation for athletic trainers.

The Joint Committee on Standards for Educational Evaluation (1988) has identified 21 standards in four broad categories: propriety standards, utility standards, feasibility standards, and accuracy standards.

Propriety Standards

The following five *propriety standards* help ensure that performance evaluation is legal and fair.

propriety standards Performance evaluation standards intended to help ensure that the process is legal and fair.

Service Orientation: Performance evaluation systems for athletic trainers should meet the needs of the persons they are intended to help, including athletic trainers, their clients, and their employing institutions. If any of these groups is neglected, the system should be reconfigured accordingly.

Formal Evaluation Guidelines: The procedures by which the athletic trainer's performance is evaluated should be recorded as written institutional policy and made available to athletic trainers so they are aware of the process.

Conflict of Interest: Evaluation procedures should ensure that potential conflicts of interest are ameliorated. For example, if Judy Armstrong and her supervisor, Linda Black, were both candidates for the same job promotion, Linda would have a conflict of interest when evaluating Judy's performance. Formal evaluation procedures should specify how to avoid such conflicts.

Access to Personnel Evaluation Reports: Only those persons who have a legitimate "need to know" should be allowed access to the athletic trainer's performance evaluation records. Each athletic trainer should be informed of who will have access to the information and under what circumstances such access will be granted.

Interactions With Evaluatees: Athletic trainers should be treated with respect and dignity when being evaluated. When supervisors are judgmental, they are less likely to enhance trust in the performance evaluation system. They can promote trust by taking a counseling attitude (Dorfman, Stephan, & Loveland, 1986).

Utility Standards

utility standards   Performance evaluation standards intended to ensure that employee appraisal is useful to workers, employers, and others who need to use the information.

The following five **utility standards** ensure that the athletic trainer's performance evaluation is useful (Joint Committee on Standards for Educational Evaluation, 1988).

Constructive Orientation: If performance evaluation is to be useful, both athletic trainers and their supervisors must perceive that evaluation procedures actually result in improvements in professional development and accountability. If either perceives evaluation as a meaningless waste of time, the information obtained is unlikely to be useful. Performance evaluation should help athletic trainers improve their performance.

Defined Uses: Performance evaluation data should only be used for the purposes for which it was collected. Athletic trainers should be informed of these uses prior to data collection. The data may not be valid if used for other purposes. Athletic trainers are also likely to lose trust in the system if the information is used for unstated purposes.

Evaluator Credibility: The persons who evaluate the athletic trainer's performance should have institutional authority and be knowledgeable of athletic training duties. In addition, they should be trained in the theory and practice of performance evaluation methods. Team physician and peer athletic trainer input can improve the credibility of evaluation because they are often more knowledgeable about athletic training job responsibilities than coaches or athletic administrators.

Functional Reporting: If performance evaluation is to be perceived as useful, athletic trainers should receive both formal and informal feedback on job performance. This feedback should be job related and timely, and it should contain specific suggestions for improving performance.

Follow-Up and Impact: All recommendations from the performance evaluation should be implemented so professional development can occur. An important component of the follow-up process involves forming a plan for professional improvement that focuses on identified weaknesses in the athletic trainer's performance. This plan should be developed jointly by the athletic trainer and his or her supervisor.

Feasibility Standards

The following three *feasibility standards* foster practicality in performance evaluation (Joint Committee on Standards for Educational Evaluation, 1988).

Practical Procedures: Performance evaluation procedures should intrude as little as possible into the athletic trainer's normal job-related activities. Athletic trainers will view evaluation procedures that require them to redirect significant amounts of energy and attention away from clients as impractical.

Political Viability: All the users of the athletic trainer performance evaluation system should have input into its development so it will be accepted and used as intended. Evaluation systems designed without input from athletic trainers are unlikely to be effective for professional development—they may be viewed as bureaucratic tools that interfere with the athletic trainers' jobs.

Fiscal Viability: Institutions should recognize that effective athletic trainer performance evaluation systems require resources of both time and money. Administrators who develop budgets should build the costs of evaluating performance into the overall institutional budget.

feasibility standards Performance evaluation standards intended to help foster practicality in the employee appraisal process.

Accuracy Standards

The following eight performance evaluation standards are intended to improve the validity and reliability of the athletic trainer's performance evaluation and thereby lend *accuracy* to the system (Joint Committee on Standards for Educational Evaluation, 1988).

accuracy standards Performance evaluation standards intended to improve the validity and reliability of the employee appraisal process.

Defined Role: Athletic trainers should be evaluated using job-related criteria for the specific roles for which they are responsible. This standard is especially important for athletic trainers because of the wide variety of roles they often assume in addition to their athletic training duties. If evaluation data is collected and interpreted without regard to role definition, it is likely to lack validity for evaluating job-related performance behaviors. Developing a weighted position description is an important first step in defining the athletic trainer's role.

Work Environment: Specific aspects of the athletic trainer's work environment should be recorded during the performance evaluation process so individual differences in working conditions can be considered in the final evaluation. For example, if Judy Armstrong is working with a new coach, it should be taken into consideration during her performance evaluation since it is a factor beyond her control that may drastically alter the nature of her job.

Documentation of Procedures: The procedures that are actually followed during the evaluation process should be recorded so athletic trainers and other users of the information can compare actual with intended evaluation procedures.

Valid Measurement: Procedures developed or adopted for evaluating athletic trainers' performance should measure the job-related behaviors they are actually intended to measure so accurate conclusions about performance can be drawn. Institutions should be able to defend the accuracy of the procedures.

Reliable Measurement: Institutions should ensure that methods used to evaluate performance are consistent across time and for different evaluators. Using multiple evaluators trained to follow specific evaluation procedures is a good way to build reliability into the evaluation system.

Systematic Data Control: Information collected during performance evaluation should be recorded and stored so it can easily be retrieved in the future and so that future interpretations are similar to those conclusions drawn immediately after the athletic trainer's performance evaluation. If data are misplaced or lost, future evaluators may draw erroneous conclusions because they will lack a complete perspective.

Bias Control: All possible biasing factors should be eliminated from athletic trainer performance evaluation so accurate conclusions can be reached. Using multiple evaluators is an effective technique to help reduce bias. Evaluating only job-related behaviors also controls bias. Personal traits unrelated to the actual job performance expected of athletic trainers should not be considered in the performance evaluation. Rigorous adherence to the other accuracy standards will help reduce performance evaluation bias.

Monitoring Evaluation Systems: Since the circumstances related to the athletic trainer's job may change over time, the systems used to evaluate performance should be modified as well. Institutional policies should require periodic evaluation and modification of athletic trainer performance evaluation systems.

▌ Applications to Athletic Training: Theory Into Practice

Use the following two case studies to help you apply the concepts in this chapter to real-life situations. The questions at the conclusion of the studies are open ended, with many possible solutions. Use the case studies as homework, exam questions, or to spur class discussion.

CASE STUDY 1

The new manager of the Wellness Center, a physician-owned sports medicine and rehabilitation clinic, instituted a policy requiring all supervisors to evaluate their employees and recommend salary increases. This new program was an attempt to implement a merit pay system at the center. In the past, everyone had received an across-the-board increase without regard to how they had performed during the past year.

Sandra Hotchkiss supervised the center's six certified athletic trainers. Upon receiving the memo mandating the new policy, Sandra decided she would simply write a narrative describing each of the athletic trainers. She felt such a narrative would be a useful guide for the new manager in awarding pay increases since it would provide her with in-depth analysis of the strengths and weaknesses of each athletic trainer. The following are examples of the evaluations she submitted.

Brian Robinson

Brian Robinson is one of the best athletic trainers employed by the center. He is thoughtful, works well with the patients, has a cheerful personality, and gets along great with the staff. Brian has received positive feedback from the athletic director at South High School, where he is assigned during the fall and spring. The athletes and parents seem to like him and there haven't been any problems that I am aware of, although I have only been out there a couple of times. My recommendation is that Brian be given a 5% salary increase.

Juan Diaz

Although I think Juan is basically a pretty good athletic trainer, he has had several problems over the past year. Juan seemed to be in the middle of a couple of controversies at Martin Luther King High. I know King is an inner city school and Juan has a lot of tough problems to overcome down there, but I just wish he could deal more effectively with them so we wouldn't have to spend time on them at the center. Juan hasn't been very effective in getting many referrals to the center from his high school. As I mentioned earlier, although I think Juan does a good job as an athletic trainer, I can't recommend anything higher than a 3% increase for him this year.

Sandra was surprised 3 weeks later when, on the day after the salary increases were announced, Juan stormed into her office and informed her that he was going to sue both her and the center for discrimination based on negligent evaluation.

QUESTIONS FOR ANALYSIS

1. What were the strengths and weaknesses of the performance evaluation system initiated by Sandra Hotchkiss?

2. How could the center's new manager have approached the problem more constructively and effectively? How would this have affected Sandra? How would it have affected Brian, Juan, and the other athletic trainers?

3. Describe the performance evaluation system you would have implemented if you were in Sandra's position. What concerns, if any, would you express to the new manager regarding the new policy?

CASE STUDY 2

John Freeman had just bought the local professional football franchise. He had made his fortune in the fast-food restaurant business, starting off with one small fried chicken restaurant and building it into a multimillion dollar chain with restaurants all over the world. At his first meeting with the club's staff, John announced that he was bringing in a consultant to do a management audit of every department. He explained that sound management was the cornerstone of his success in business and in life. He expected each member of the staff to adopt that philosophy. Sound management, in his opinion, was the key to success in any business—and professional football was a business!

A few weeks later, Rick Condelato and the rest of the sports medicine staff spent the better part of two days answering questions and explaining the club's sports medicine operation to the management consultant. The consultant asked about policies and procedures. He examined the record-keeping system. He investigated the supply and equipment purchasing routines. He became familiar with how Rick selected student athletic trainers for summer training camp. As far as Rick could tell, no stone was left unturned.

About a month later, the management consultant and John Freeman, the new owner, walked into the training room and told Rick they wanted to discuss the results of the recent management audit with him. "Rick," the consultant began, "For the most part, you are managing this part of the club's operations fairly effectively. You only buy what you need and you don't pay more than you have to. The procedures you have implemented are consistent with club policy, and they seem to be efficient and effective. But in talking with your assistants, the assistant coaches, and some of the players, I have determined that you don't do a very good job of utilizing your staff to its fullest potential. The information they provided leads me to believe that you don't delegate authority enough. You try to do too much by yourself. Take a look at the organizational chart I developed of your operation as it presently exists [see Figure 3.20]."

▌**Figure 3.20**   Organizational chart for Rick's sports medicine program.

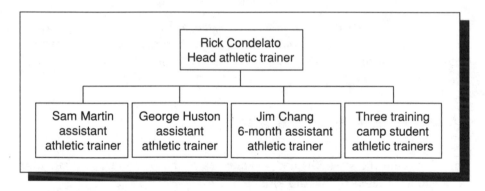

"Rick," said John Freeman, "I want you to reorganize your staff so you can work more efficiently. From what everybody tells me, you're obviously a good man and although I expect maximum effort, I don't want you to get burned out simply because you haven't organized your staff well enough. I expect to see your reorganization report on my desk by Monday of next week."*

QUESTIONS FOR ANALYSIS

1. What is wrong with the current organizational structure in Rick's program? What problems are likely to arise based on the present structure?

2. How could Rick reorganize to reduce the amount of work he is responsible for and still accomplish everything that needs to be done?

3. If you were in Rick's position, what organizational structure would you devise to meet the mandate of the new club owner?

4. What strategies should Rick employ to make sure that his assistants develop ownership in the new organizational structure?

▮ Summary

Most athletic trainers have never had any formal education or training in the management of human resources. This is ironic because people are the most important assets of any sports medicine program.

Organizational culture includes the basic values, behavioral norms, assumptions, and beliefs of the sports medicine program. The type of organizational culture will have an effect on human resource management. The three major types of organizational cultures are the collegial, personalistic, and formalistic cultures.

The relationships between the various members of the sports medicine program is best described through the use of an organizational chart. Athletic trainers can describe these relationships in one of three ways: by function, by service, or in a matrix format.

Staff selection is a commonly misunderstood term. It is defined by the *Uniform Guidelines on Employee Selection Procedures* as any procedure used as a basis for an employment decision. Hiring, promotion, demotion, performance evaluation, retention, and discharge are all examples of selection activities as defined by federal law.

A position description is a formal document that describes the qualification requirements, work content, accountability, and scope of a person's job. The weighted position description is an important first step in helping athletic trainers understand the expectations of their employers. The position description is generally comprised of two sections: the job specification and the job description.

Recruitment and hiring is one of the most visible, expensive, and time-consuming aspects of the human resources function in sports medicine. Recruitment activities should be viewed in terms of long- and short-term needs. The prime directive in recruiting and hiring is that all qualified applicants should receive equal consideration. Athletic trainers and other sports medicine personnel must be hired on the basis of their qualifications and not on the basis of race, gender, religion, or national origin. The recruitment and hiring process usually follows the following 10 steps: request for position, position request approval, position vacancy notice, application collection, telephone interviews, reference checks, on-site interviews, recommendation and approval for hiring, offer of contract, and hiring.

Supervision of sports medicine employees is an important managerial function of many athletic trainers. Supervision should help improve the performance and the professional development of the employees of the sports medicine program. The three major types of supervisory models include inspection-production, clinical, and developmental.

Performance evaluation is the process of placing a value on the quality of an athletic trainer's work. In some settings, the majority of athletic trainers are not formally evaluated and lack position descriptions. Much of the performance evaluation literature intended for athletic trainers is based on a trait-oriented approach. Trait-oriented evaluation is usually biased and rarely useful for improving performance. Athletic trainers should acquaint themselves with the 21 performance evaluation standards developed by the Joint Committee on Standards for Educational Evaluation. They are intended to guide the development of performance evaluation systems and to offer improvements in four major areas: propriety, accuracy, utility, and feasibility.

▌ Annotated Bibliography

Acheson, K.A., & Gall, M.D. (1987). *Techniques in the clinical supervision of teachers* (2nd ed.). New York: Longman.

This how-to book is intended to help those who supervise teachers apply clinical supervision methods more effectively. It describes over 30 supervisory techniques, many of which have potential application in sports medicine.

Aldrich, J.W. (1985). Staffing concepts and principles. In W. Tracey (Ed.), *Human resources management and development handbook* (pp. 165-173). New York: AMACOM.

Athletic trainers will find the most useful section of this article to be the part on long-term and short-term personnel recruitment. Information about orientation and induction also applies to sports medicine.

Bennis, W., & Nanus, B. (1985). *Leaders*. New York: Harper & Row.

This book, intended for a popular audience, brings together the authors' considerable experience in the study of leadership. It is very readable, and most athletic trainers would find the authors' suggestions about leadership valuable.

Bruce, S.D. (1986). *Prewritten job descriptions*. Madison, CT: Business and Legal Reports.

This is an excellent resource for athletic trainers who need to develop position descriptions for themselves or for those they supervise. In addition to a section on how to write position descriptions, the book offers hundreds of prewritten position descriptions that can be used as examples.

Cascio, W.F., & Bernardin, H.J. (1981). Implications of performance appraisal litigation for personnel decisions. *Personnel Psychology*, **34**, 211-226.

This article reviews case law on performance evaluation. The authors list eight prescriptions for avoiding legal action for performance evaluation malfeasance.

Dobbins, G.H., & Russell, J.M. (1986). The biasing effects of subordinate likableness on the leaders' responses to poor performers: A laboratory and a field study. *Personnel Psychology*, **39**, 759-777.

This study determined that supervisors who like the people they supervise are less likely to take punitive action against them if they perform poorly than supervisors who don't like their subordinates. The authors conclude that personal qualities of subordinates do have a biasing effect so performance evaluation should only attempt to measure job-related behavior.

Dorfman, P.W., Stephan, W.G., & Loveland, J. (1986). Performance appraisal behaviors: Supervisor perceptions and subordinate reactions. *Personnel Psychology*, **39**, 579-597.

The authors found that supportive behavior by supervisors in the performance evaluation conference improved employee motivation; discussion of pay and job advancement improved employee job satisfaction; and suggestions of improvement for poor performers had not influenced job performance 1 year later.

Drake, J.D. (1982). *Interviewing for managers*. New York: AMACOM.

This book offers practical suggestions to assist athletic trainers in hiring. The primary focus of the book is on interviewing techniques and interpreting interview data. A chapter on fair employment practices in interviewing is especially useful.

Equal Employment Opportunity Commission. (1979). *Uniform guidelines on employee selection procedures*. Washington, DC: Bureau of National Affairs.

This pamphlet contains both the *Uniform Guidelines* and a helpful analysis of laws about staff selection.

Fowler, A.R., & Bushardt, S.C. (1986). T.O.P.E.S.: Developing a task oriented performance evaluation system. *Advanced Management Journal*, **51**(4), 4-8.

The authors propose a performance evaluation system based on job analysis and weight of job-related tasks.

Haddad, S.A. (1985). Compensation and benefits. In W. Tracey (Ed.), *Human resources management and development handbook* (pp. 638-660). New York: AMACOM.

This article presents a comprehensive treatment of alternative compensation and benefit strategies commonly used in human resources management, but the most useful section for athletic trainers is the discussion of job description development and job analysis.

Hagerty, B.K., Chang, R.S., & Spengler, C.D. (1985). Work sampling: Analyzing nursing staff productivity. *Journal of Nursing Administration*, **15**(9), 9-14.

Hagerty and her colleagues describe the work sampling technique. They offer suggestions for planning, implementing, and analyzing the results of work sampling studies in medical and allied health settings.

Huber, V.L., Podsakoff, P.M., & Todor, W.D. (1986). An investigation of biasing factors in the attributions of subordinates and their supervisors. *Journal of Business Research*, **14**, 83-97.

The authors of this investigation determined that both supervisors and their supervisees attribute job success more to ''internal'' factors such as ability and motivation than ''external'' factors such as luck or task difficulty. They suggest that both groups have a self-serving bias that tends to cloud accurate perception of causative factors for good and poor performance.

Joint Committee on Standards for Educational Evaluation. (1988). *The personnel evaluation standards*. Beverly Hills, CA: Sage.

The standards for personnel evaluation described in this book were developed by representatives of 14 major professional educational associations. Anyone involved in evaluating athletic trainer performance should become familiar with them.

Keaveny, T.J., & McGann, A.F. (1980). Performance appraisal format: Role clarity and evaluation criteria. *Research in Higher Education*, **13**(3), 225-232.

The authors conclude that behaviorally anchored rating scales are the most effective performance evaluation method to clarify roles among supervisees.

Kolodny, H.F. (1979). Evolution to a matrix organization. *Academy of Management Review*, **4**(4), 543-553.

This paper presents the author's theories of how an organization evolves from a function or service model to a matrix model. Kolodny explains the stages of evolution and the organizational characteristics needed to make the transition.

McCarthy, M.M. (1983). Discrimination in employment. In J. Beckham & P. Zirkel (Eds.), *Legal issues in public school employment* (pp. 46-47). Bloomington, IN: Phi Delta Kappan.

This chapter focuses primarily on the effect of Title VII legislation as it applies to employment discrimination against employees of public schools. Much of the information could be applied in other settings as well.

Myers, O.J. (1985). Myths concerning employees' performance appraisal. *Supervision*, **47**(12), 14-16.

This article discusses four common performance evaluation misconceptions and offers practical suggestions for supervisors to overcome problems with evaluations.

Ouchi, W.G., & Dowling, J.B. (1974). Defining the span of control. *Administrative Science Quarterly*, **19**, 357-365.

This paper describes the results of an empirical investigation into the effectiveness of four different definitions of span of control.

Owens, R.G. (1987). *Organizational behavior in education* (3rd ed.). Englewood Cliffs, NJ: Prentice Hall.

This book is a comprehensive examination of the factors that influence the behavior of persons working in education. Although written for educators, most of the principles can be widely applied in other settings as well.

Parks, J. (1977). Athletic trainer evaluation. *Athletic Training*, **12**(2), 92-93.

This article provides a trait-oriented evaluation instrument alleged to be useful in determining the strengths and weaknesses of an athletic trainer. No information on the validity or reliability of the instrument is provided.

Penman, K.A., & Adams, S.H. (1980). *Assessing athletic and physical education programs.* Boston: Allyn & Bacon.

A manual with reproducible forms to assist the athletic administrator in evaluating athletic programs and personnel. The section on evaluating the athletic trainer is based on a trait-oriented approach not recommended by most evaluation experts.

Ray, R.R. (1991). Performance evaluation in athletic training: Perceptions of athletic trainers and their supervisors. *Dissertation Abstracts International,* **51,** 5053. (Doctoral dissertation, Western Michigan University, 1990)

The results of an empirical investigation into the status of performance evaluation of athletic trainers. Differences between employment settings and differences between athletic trainers and their supervisors were examined. Chapter 2 contains a very thorough review of the performance evaluation literature.

Reinhardt, C. (1985). The state of performance appraisal: A literature review. *Human Resource Planning,* **8**(2), 105-110.

This is a comprehensive review of the performance evaluation literature. The author divides the review into areas of agreement and disagreement among performance evaluation researchers so the reader can more easily discern the status of the research in this area.

Schneier, C.E., Beatty, R.W., & Baird, L.S. (1986). How to construct a successful performance appraisal system. *Training and Development Journal,* **40**(4), 38-42.

As its title suggests, this article describes the basic elements of an effective performance evaluation system. The authors point out many common pitfalls of performance evaluation that athletic trainers would be wise to avoid.

Sikula, A.F. (1976). *Personnel administration and human resources management.* New York: Wiley & Sons.

Sikula's text is intended as an introductory textbook for students of human resources management. Chapters 5 and 6 are especially appropriate for athletic trainers in most sports medicine settings.

Tanner, D., & Tanner, L. (1987). *Supervision in education.* New York: Macmillan.

Tanner and Tanner offer a somewhat theoretical but complete treatment of supervision as practiced in education. They give the reader a useful historical perspective of the subject. Athletic trainers should pay special attention to chapter 6, which compares and contrasts the various models of supervision.

U.S. Small Business Administration (1980). *Job analysis, job specifications, and job descriptions.* Washington, DC: U.S. Government Printing Office.

An excellent self-instructional booklet that will help athletic trainers devise accurate position descriptions. Several examples of job analyses, specifications, and descriptions are included.

"We haven't got the money, so we've got to think!"

Ernest Rutherford

What Athletic Trainers Use: Financial Resource Management

STUDENT OBJECTIVES

▮ Understand sports medicine budgeting, purchasing, and inventory control.

▮ Be able to develop a budget, implement a purchasing plan, and manage a sports medicine inventory.

▮ Be able to analyze existing sports medicine budgets, purchasing plans, and inventory management techniques to determine their strengths and weaknesses.

OPENING CASE

Stan Curtis was a certified athletic trainer for a large metropolitan school system in Grant, California. Stan's job was to provide athletic training services for school district athletes in a centralized training room located in a municipal stadium where the schools of the district played football, soccer, baseball, and softball, and ran track meets. In addition, Stan supervised the certified athletic trainers who worked at the six high schools of the district. Every aspect of running the district's sport medicine program, from budgeting and purchasing to maintaining an inventory for each school, fell into Stan's sphere of responsibility.

One day in early June Stan received a phone call from his boss, the director of cocurricular activities. "Stan, I'm not going to be able to approve those purchase orders you sent over the other day," she said. The recent defeat of our tax referendum has really screwed up the district's finances. I don't think any of your trainers are going to lose their jobs because they're all tenured and have been in the system for quite a while, but your supply budget is definitely going to feel the pinch. Not only are you going to have to reduce it by 30% immediately, but from now on you're going to have to justify every line item. I'm sorry about all this, Stan, but I've got my orders and there isn't anything I can do about it. I'll send those POs back to you today."

Stan was troubled. He didn't know how he was going to be able to cut 30% of his budget and still provide the same services at the same level of quality. In the past the budgeting process had been fairly simple. He had simply checked with the athletic trainers at the school to find out what they would need for the upcoming year. If it sounded reasonable and the whole thing fit within the amount he had to work with, he ordered the supplies and that was that. He knew his athletic trainers were going to be furious about this. Budgeting was about to become a whole new ball game.

The common denominator in almost every management problem is related to money or the lack of it. Money is the engine that drives athletic enterprises, regardless of the level of competition. Sports medicine programs associated with athletic programs are subject to all the economic pressures they experience, whether the setting is a high school, college, university, professional team, or hospital. For athletic trainers working in independent sports medicine clinics, the need for sound financial management practices is even more acute because these operations are usually impacted more rapidly during an economic downturn. The effects of poor financial management are generally compounded when the resource pool is shallow. The amount of money an athletic trainer will have to operate a sports medicine program in an educational setting varies greatly depending on the level of competition engaged in by the institution's teams (Rankin, 1992). The purpose of this chapter is to help athletic trainers become more astute stewards of their institutions' financial resources by presenting the theory and application of various techniques for budgeting, purchasing, and inventory control. Although these three topics are presented as distinct and separate processes, they are closely related to each other in a financial planning network (see Figure 4.1).

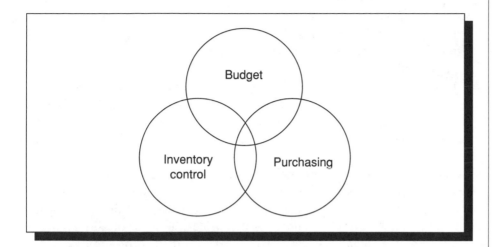

■ Figure 4.1 Interrelationship of financial activities of the sports medicine program.

Although the ideas discussed in this chapter are applicable in almost any setting, athletic trainers should realize that certain types of sports medicine clinics, as small businesses, require more financial planning than this book can suggest. Athletic trainers who manage independently owned and operated sports medicine clinics should seek the counsel of experienced management consultants, attorneys, and accountants. In addition, the U.S. Small Business Administration publishes a management series that can help these athletic trainers become more familiar with the wide variety of issues facing owners of small businesses of all types.[1]

■ Budgeting

Budgeting financial resources is a process organizational leaders ask program heads to accomplish. Athletic trainers and others responsible for planning and delivering sports medicine services must develop skills in planning and implementing budgets so needed services are delivered in an effective, timely manner and allocation of financial resources is consistent with the strategic plans of both the institution and the sports medicine program.

A **budget** is a plan for the coordination of resources and expenditures (Horine, 1991). A budget also serves as a tool for estimating receipts and disbursements over a period of time (Mayo, 1978). Beyond its practical uses as a restraint on resource waste and as a predictive tool for the financial health of the sports medicine program, a budget is a quantitative expression of the athletic trainer's management plan. As such, it is both a strategic plan for how the sports medicine unit will function over a given period of time and an operational plan for how it will accomplish its goals.

budget A type of operational plan for the coordination of resources and expenditures.

---

[1]Available from the Superintendent of Documents, U.S. Government Printing Office, Washington, DC 20402.

Although many practitioners think of budgeting as a task that begins and ends in a narrow time frame during a particular part of the year, the wise athletic trainer should see budgeting as a continuous process of prioritizing, planning, documenting, and evaluating the goals of the sports medicine unit and translating these goals into concrete plans for how to expend available resources. As athletic seasons stretch over all 12 months and new programs of all types are added to the athletic trainer's responsibilities, the budgeting process requires constant attention to fund status and ongoing evaluation for the next budget cycle.

Jones and Trentin (1971) have suggested that budgets should be used as the primary tools for planning and controlling the program. This helps us differentiate between the concepts of budgeting and forecasting. As mentioned in Chapter 2, forecasting is the process of predicting future conditions on the basis of various statistics and indicators that describe the past and present situation. Forecasting is typically accomplished by only a few people near the top of the organizational chart. Because budgeting is a type of planning, however, it requires input from the grass roots of the sports medicine program. An effective budget will consider the input of all employees about using the financial resources to meet documented program needs as opposed to simply allocating funds according to past traditions.

Types of Budgets

Most sports medicine budget planning is based on three models: the spending ceiling, spending reduction, and zero-based models. But there are at least nine different types of budgets (Ray, 1990).

Spending Ceiling

spending ceiling model   A type of expenditure budgeting that requires justification only for those expenses that exceed those of the previous budget cycle. Also known as the incremental model.

The **spending ceiling model**, also known as the *incremental model* (Wildavsky, 1975), is the budgeting method most often employed by sport medicine program directors in educational institutions. This is the model Stan used to determine his budget in the opening case. This method requires justification only for expenditures that exceed those of the previous budget cycle. Budget increases are most often linked to the inflation rate, which presents problems for sports medicine programs because prices for medical goods and services have risen faster than inflation (see Figure 4.2). Sports medicine program directors who use this method are often able to balance financial resources and expenditures for 2 to 3 years, but typically fall behind after that because of the difference between the inflation rate and the cost of medical goods and services.

Spending Reduction

spending reduction model   A type of budgeting used during periods of financial retrenchment that requires reallocation of institutional funds, resulting in reduced spending levels for some programs.

The second common budgeting model is the **spending reduction model**, which is typically employed in institutions in financial crisis. This is the model that Stan will be forced to adopt as a result of the financial problems in his school district. Under the spending reduction model, department heads, including directors of sports medicine programs, are required to reduce their budgets to preserve institutional funds. This budget method requires the most

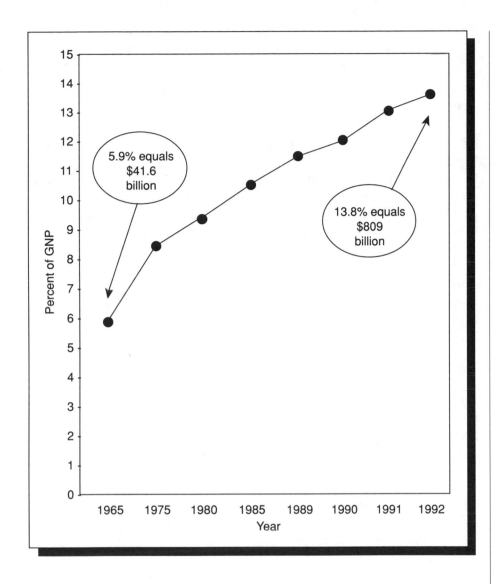

Figure 4.2 Health care costs as a percentage of GNP. *Note.* From "U.S. Grapples with Health Care Costs" by H.B. Saftlas, 1992, *Industry Surveys*, August 20, 1992, p. H-15. Copyright 1992 by Standard and Poor's Corporation. Adapted by permission.

imagination and creativity of all the budget models for obvious reasons. Because financial resources tend to be reduced periodically in most sports medicine settings, the wise athletic trainer should identify those goods and services that could be cut without seriously impacting the program. If a financial crisis does arise, the athletic trainer will be prepared.

Zero-Based Budgeting

Zero-based budgeting is an administrative method that requires unit directors to justify every expense without reference to previous spending patterns. This method requires close attention to documentation of actual program needs. Stan is being forced to adopt a combination of the spending reduction and zero-based methods in the opening case. Although it requires more effort on the part of the athletic trainer, zero-based budgeting can be an excellent tool for developing priorities in the sports medicine program. Zero-based budgeting requires athletic trainers to evaluate each subfunction of the sports medicine program and to rank it according to its importance to the accomplishment of the overall mission. The director should include a rationale for

zero-based budgeting A budgeting model that requires justification for every budget line item without reference to previous spending patterns.

each item included in the budget request, explaining why the expense is necessary and what alternatives there are to funding it.

PPBES

Planning, Programming, Budgeting, and Evaluation System (PPBES)   A long-term budgeting process based on strategic planning and program evaluation.

PPBES stands for *Planning, Programming, Budgeting, and Evaluation System*, a complicated budgeting technique designed for long-term budgeting based on strategic planning and program evaluation. PPBES is different from traditional forms of budgeting in that it requires the athletic trainer to focus on program outputs, such as goal and objective attainment, as opposed to program inputs such as salaries, supplies, and equipment (Young, 1976). It is similar to zero-based budgeting in that each item must be justified, but unlike the zero-based approach, PPBES ties expenditures to long-term accomplishment of specific program goals and objectives. PPBES is an inappropriate budgeting method for most sports medicine programs in schools or clinics. It is most appropriate for large government-sponsored programs.

Fixed Budgeting

fixed budgeting model   A budgeting method whereby expenditures and revenues are projected on a monthly basis, thereby providing an estimate of cash flow.

Fixed budgeting is a process that is appropriate for sports medicine programs in financially stable environments. It requires the athletic trainer to project both expenditures and program income, if any, on a month-by-month basis to determine total program costs and revenues for the fiscal year. This is useful because it can help the athletic trainer determine what the cash flow of the operation is likely to be at various points in the year. This type of budgeting is probably most appropriate for large, well-established sports medicine clinics during periods of relative economic certainty. It is rarely used in school sports medicine programs because most of these programs are not income oriented.

Variable Budgeting

variable budgeting system   A budgeting method that requires that monthly expenditures be adjusted so they do not exceed revenues.

Unfortunately, the athletic trainer who coordinates the activities of a sports medicine clinic will rarely be able to predict the monthly balance of expenditures to revenues with perfect accuracy. The *variable budgeting system* requires that expenditures for any given time period bc adjusted according to revenues for the same time period. For example, assume that the clinic director budgeted for expenses in June of $25,000, anticipating that revenues would be approximately $50,000. Under the variable budgeting system, if the actual revenues were only $40,000, the clinic director would be required to reduce expenditures by 20% for that month. As with fixed budgeting, this method is rarely used in school-based programs.

Lump Sum Budgeting

When the parent organization provides the athletic trainer with a fixed sum of money and the authority to spend that money any way the athletic trainer sees fit, the sports medicine program is operating under *lump sum budgeting*. Most athletic trainers who use lump sum budgeting like it because it gives them the freedom to spend money where they think it is needed the most. Lump sum budgeting requires that athletic trainers be held accountable after the fact. Lump sum budgeting can operate in either a spending ceiling or spending reduction mode.

lump sum budgeting A method that allocates a fixed amount of money for an entire program without specifying how the money will be spent.

Line Item Budgeting

Line item budgeting requires that athletic trainers list anticipated expenditures for specific categories of program subfunctions. Typical line items for a sports medicine program include expendable supplies, equipment repair, team physician services, and insurance (see Table 4.1). Line item budgeting

line item budgeting A method that allocates a fixed amount of money for each subfunction of a program.

Table 4.1 Sample Line-Item Budget for a School-Based Sports Medicine Program

Budget comparison report

Acct no: 213702		Dept: Sports medicine		Responsible person: Stan Curtis	
Object code	Account description	89/90 expense	90/91 budget	91/92 request	Percent change
3110	Travel	229.25	300.00	300.00	0
3205	Supplies	7632.32	9000.00	9475.75	5.3
3305	Printing	89.28	100.00	100.00	0
3315	Speakers	0	1500.00	1500.00	0
3320	Stipends	5997.96	6300.00	6300.00	0
3360	Postage	257.65	300.00	300.00	0
3530	Repairs	313.15	500.00	500.00	0
3850	Periodicals	150.00	150.00	150.00	0
4035	Insurance	200.00	250.00	300.00	16.7
4100	Dues	90.00	100.00	100.00	0
Department total		14959.61	18500.00	19025.75	2.8

allows the parent organization to retain a higher level of control over the sports medicine program because money budgeted for one line usually cannot be spent on another line without permission. The advantage of line item budgeting is that it is easy to understand and prepare. The disadvantage of this method is that the athletic trainer has limited flexibility in responding to midyear financial crises because funds dedicated to one use cannot be easily transferred to another use.

Performance Budgeting

Performance budgeting breaks the functions of the sports medicine program into discrete activities and appropriates funds necessary to accomplish these

performance budgeting A method that allocates funds for discrete activities.

activities. Examples of activities typically associated with a school sports medicine program include prepractice and pregame team preparation, rehabilitation, injury treatment, administration, patient education, and emergency first aid (see Figure 4.3). Expenses for each of these activities can be calculated and used to determine the overall budget. This method is similar

Figure 4.3 Performance budget activities.

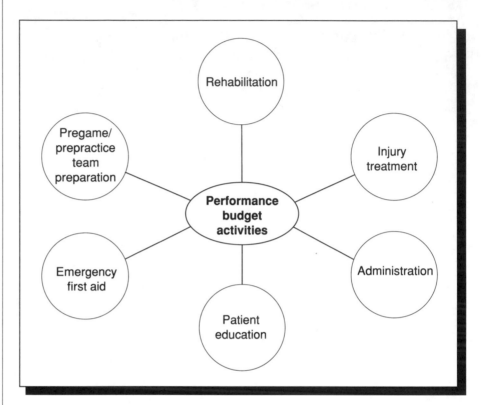

to line item budgeting in that "mini-budgets" are developed for separate categories of expenditures. Performance budgeting is not commonly used in sports medicine programs because of the expense and difficulty of analyzing specific activity costs.

Planning the Budget

The process of budget planning differs depending on institutional budgeting cycles and rules and the type of budgeting system being used. Before the budget crisis Stan now faces, he probably used a spending ceiling or incremental budget model like the one that follows.

The first step in planning a budget for a sports medicine program is for the athletic trainer and the division head (i.e., athletic director, chair of the physical education department, general manager, principal, etc.) to agree which fund will provide the various items the athletic trainer needs. Protective pads, for instance, can fall into the sports medicine or equipment budgets. Costs associated with physical examinations can be covered by the health services budget. Expenditures for travel to professional meetings can be included in the parent department's travel budget instead of the sports medicine budget. These decisions will depend on both the working relationship and the financial philosophies of the individuals involved.

Which fund these expenditures fall under will have an impact on who controls the funds. If Stan's travel to professional conferences is covered under the director of cocurricular activity's overall travel budget, Stan will probably be required to justify each meeting he wishes to attend. In addition, he will likely be subject to all the restrictions on travel that apply to other district employees who report to the same director.

Another important decision that must be made involves whether the purchase of certain injury protection equipment should be covered by the sports medicine budget or by the budget of the team that will be using the equipment. If an item is clearly intended for use by one team, it makes sense to include that item in the team's budget rather than that of the sports medicine program. If such items are placed in the budget of the sports medicine program, other teams may develop false expectations of the sports medicine staff. For example, if Stan purchases lateral knee braces to be used specifically by injured football players, then other coaches may expect Stan to purchase knee braces or similar devices for their athletes. This is probably an expense the sports medicine program will not be able to continue to support. A more rational approach would be for the football coaches to include the expense of the knee braces in their own budgets. Only in this way will Stan be able to avoid setting a precedent he won't be able to afford for long.

The first year a budget is planned for the sports medicine unit is often the most difficult because of the lack of precedent upon which to base financial plans. The process of budgeting for the first year of operation most closely approximates the zero-based budgeting model because a rationale for each purchase must be developed without reference to established spending patterns. The presence of such spending patterns facilitates subsequent budget planning, which then approximates the spending ceiling or incremental model. Budget planning for sports medicine goods and services can be enhanced by following these steps:

- Keep a running inventory of all consumable and nonconsumable supplies.
- When budget submission time comes, calculate the amount of each type of consumable supply that has been used. Project and estimate how much more of the supply will be needed to complete the fiscal year, taking into account the different needs of the sports seasons yet to come.
- Based on estimates of how much of each type of supply will be needed to complete the fiscal year, and taking into account any changes that will take place during the next fiscal year (e.g., new varsity sports, longer seasons, etc.) estimate the amount of each type of supply that will be needed for the next fiscal year.
- Consult with several vendors to obtain estimates of how much prices are expected to rise for the next fiscal year. With this information, develop anticipated prices for all the consumable supplies that will be needed for the next fiscal year.

Capital Improvements

Budget planning for nonconsumable capital improvements is often more difficult than for consumable supplies that are typically reordered every year. Therapeutic modalities, ice machines, and rehabilitation equipment are examples of nonconsumable capital improvements. They are very expensive and many sports medicine directors are not able to include them in their annual supply budgets. Planning for acquisition, repair, and replacement of such items requires careful coordination between directors of sports medicine units and higher level decision makers. Because the capital budget is often unrecoverable once spent, it is essential that purchases of this type be screened by multiple levels of authority and that such purchases are consistent with the accomplishment of the sports medicine program's mission (Jones & Trentin, 1971). The following suggestions will help budget planners meet the needs of the sports medicine program in this area:

- Treat equipment repair as a consumable supply and include it as a line item in the annual operating budget. If the institution will agree to "roll over" the unused balance of this account from year to year, it can serve as a fund for sports medicine equipment purchases.

- Develop priority lists for capital equipment requests complete with documentation of need. Suggest possible funding alternatives to decision makers.

- Make institutional fund raisers aware of the priority list and the documentation of need so they can keep these needs in mind when soliciting funds from contributors.

- Consider writing grant requests from funding agencies or engaging in research projects funded by industry. For example, Hope College became a testing site for a new analgesic cream, which brought the sports medicine unit over $25,000. This money is now used to fund equipment purchases for the sports medicine program.

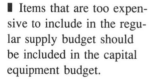

▌ Items that are too expensive to include in the regular supply budget should be included in the capital equipment budget.

Budget Evaluation

Most directors of sports medicine units either ignore budget evaluation completely or perform it reluctantly. Evaluation of the budget is, however, very important in the overall budgeting process because it allows administrators to reach informed judgments on how well the financial resources of the institution are being expended. The following three relatively simple steps can help athletic trainers evaluate how well the budget process is working.

Maintain Dual Accounting Systems

In addition to the accounting done in the sports medicine unit, request the computer outputs from the institution's business office to make sure expenditures are being charged to the proper funds.

Evaluate Service Contracts

Service contracts, such as for ambulance service, insurance, team physicians, and student athletic trainers should be evaluated each year to make sure that pay rates are competitive for the amount of work being done. Keep a running log of all activities of each contractor including the number of hours worked and the type of work actually performed.

Compile Statistical Information

Periodic statistical reports of how consumable and nonconsumable supplies and equipment are being used can help the athletic trainer justify financial resource deployment. For example, treatment records are an excellent source of information on how often and on whom therapeutic modalities are being used. Many computer software packages can help develop statistical reports.

▌ Purchasing

Once the sports medicine budget has been approved, the process of budget implementation can begin. *Purchasing* is the process that athletic trainers use to implement the budget plan. Methods of purchasing supplies, equipment, and services are critical to the cost-effective operation of the sports medicine program. Creative purchasing strategies have been shown to reduce expenditures for sports medicine supplies by up to 40% (Ray, 1991). Six basic steps in purchasing (Wright, 1983) include requisition, request for quotation, negotiation, purchase order, receiving, and accounts payable (see Figure 4.4).

purchasing The process of acquiring goods and services.

Requisition

The first step in the purchasing process is completing and submitting a *requisition* for needed supplies, equipment, or services (Wright, 1983). This step can either be formal or informal depending on the authority level of the athletic trainer in the overall institutional bureaucracy. The requisition is simply a written request to expend institutional funds for needed resources (see Figure 4.5).

requisition A type of formal or informal communication, usually written, used for requesting authorization for purchasing goods or services.

Figure 4.4   Six steps in the purchasing process.

Step number	Purchasing process
1	Requisition
2	Request for quotation
3	Negotiation
4	Purchase order
5	Receiving
6	Accounts payable

request for quotation (RFQ)   A document that provides vendors with the specifications for bidding for the sale of goods and services.

bidding   A process whereby vendors provide cost quotations for goods and services they wish to sell.

Request for Quotation

A *request for quotation (RFQ)* is a document that accompanies a bid sheet and provides instructions for vendors to bid on the supplies, equipment, and services needed by the sports medicine program (see Figure 4.6). The use of RFQs is known as *bidding* and is the most effective way to reduce costs for expendable sports medicine supplies (see Figure 4.7). The following questions should be considered before supply bids are distributed to vendors:

Grant Public Schools   Purchase requisition

Suggested vendor		Previous supplier? Yes ☐ No ☐	Date	
Ship to:		Attn:	Date needed	
Quantity	Description		Unit	Total
Requested by:	Requested for:	Acct. no.	Approved by:	
For purchasing department use only				
Date ordered	P.O. No.	Ordered from:	Ship via:	

Figure 4.5   Sample purchase requisition form.

Question	Consideration
• Will brand names be specified or are generic products acceptable?	• Products for which a brand name is required should have a "no substitute" notation clearly marked on the bid sheet.
• How many and which vendors will be invited to bid?	• The suggested minimum is three. Vendors who have a reputation for excellent service should be considered over those who do not.
• Will the institution or the vendor be responsible for paying shipping costs?	• Most suppliers of consumable products are willing to pay shipping if specified on the bid.
• What types of products will be purchased via bidding?	• Consumable supplies and some types of durable equipment are good candidates for bidding. Most services should be bid only with great caution because the quality of service may be reflected in lower prices.
• When should RFQs be sent to vendors?	• This depends on the institution's purchasing process. If athletic trainers are required to purchase supplies through a central purchasing department, a minimum of 3 months from RFQ to delivery should be allowed.

Negotiations

Negotiations are an important part of the purchasing process since their effective use can help safeguard the interests of the sports medicine program. Athletic trainers should negotiate for the following three categories of purchases.

negotiation   The process of bargaining.

Large Capital Improvements

These are the expensive, durable equipment items that often make up the bulk of the rehabilitation and therapeutic modality inventory for the sports medicine program. Purchases are infrequent and costly.

Medium-Priced Annual Rebuys

These are usually purchases of services that require annual renegotiation. Examples include salaries, physician consulting fees, ambulance services, and athletic medical insurance.

Lower Cost Consumable Supplies

These items constitute the bulk of the sports medicine supply budget. Although some supplies will have to be reordered throughout the year, careful

Grant Public Schools   Department of Sports Medicine

Request for Quotation
(This is not an order)

Submit Bid To: Stan Curtis, Head Athletic Trainer
                  Grant Public Schools
                  Municipal Stadium
                  Grant, CA 98201

If additional information is required, contact Stan Curtis at (415) 555-7708.

Date Mailed: April 11, 1992   Closing Date: May 2, 1992

Goods must be able to be delivered before: August 1, 1992   Billing not before: July 1, 1992

In order to receive consideration, one copy of this "Request for Quotation," with your bid properly filled in, must be signed and returned by the specified closing date.

All prices and conditions, including freight charges, must be shown. Additions or conditions not shown on this bid will not be allowed.

Contracts or purchase orders resulting from this quotation may not be assigned without the consent of the Head Athletic Trainer, Grant Public Schools.

The seller agrees to protect the purchaser from all damages arising out of alleged infringements of patents.

Unless otherwise specified, the right is reserved to accept or reject all or any part of your proposal.

Delivered F.O.B. to specific address in Grant, California 98201. Seller assumes all freight and delivery expenses.

If given an order for item(s) specified on the attached "Grant Public Schools Sports Medicine Bid Request" bidder agrees to furnish the items at the price(s) specified and under the conditions indicated.

Bidder to complete:
_____

Bidder's name and address: Prices will be good for _____ days.

_____   Delivery will be made _____ days after receipt of
                                               order.
_____

_____   Signed by _____

Telephone Number: Printed name _____

1-800- _____ and/or   Title_____ Date_____

Area Code (_____)_____

▌ Figure 4.6   Sample request for quotation form to accompany bid sheet.

planning will allow the athletic trainer to place only one major supply order for the entire year. This will help the athletic trainer's negotiating position because of the discounts normally associated with quantity purchasing.

The following five elements can be negotiated for purchases in each of the three categories (Barlow, 1982; see Figure 4.8).

Price: Price is the most obvious point for negotiation in purchasing sports medicine goods and services. The use of the RFQ is the first step in price negotiation for consumable supplies, but it isn't the only option available. Vendors are often willing to negotiate price reductions after submitting the

Grant Public Schools Sports Medicine Bid Request

Please complete and return within three weeks of receipt to Stan Curtis, Head Athletic Trainer, Grant Public Schools, Grant, CA 98201.
Phone (415) 555-7708 or fax (415) 555-7922

All bid prices should include the following factors:
—Cost of shipping to Grant, CA
—Billing no sooner than 7/1/92

*If listing a substitute item, please specify brand name, packaging quantities, and product codes. If no brand is specified in the *Item* column, please specify the brand you are bidding in the *Substitute* column.

Item	*Substitute	Quantity	Bid price/unit	Total
1.5-inch J & J Coach Tape (no substitute)		110 cases		
3-inch elastic tape (Elastikon or substitute)		10 cases		
2-inch elastic tape (Conform or substitute)		10 cases		
3-inch underwrap		5 cases		
6-inch elastic wraps (irregular if available)		20 dozen		
3-inch elastic wraps (irregular if available)		4 dozen		
1/8-inch adhesive felt (6" × 36")		20 pieces		
1/8-inch adhesive foam (5" × 72")		10 pieces		

❚ Figure 4.7 Sample bid sheet to accompany request for quotation.

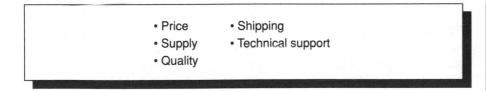

- Price
- Supply
- Quality
- Shipping
- Technical support

❚ Figure 4.8 Negotiable points in sports medicine purchasing.

RFQ. However if athletic trainers use excessive price negotiation after vendors have returned the RFQ, a poor working relationship and higher prices in subsequent years are likely to result. Price negotiation is usually the most effective when purchasing services.

Supply: Among the most common points for negotiation between athletic trainers and vendors are delivery and payment schedules for purchased goods.

Because many educational institutions have fiscal years that begin on July 1, it has become common practice for athletic trainers to order supplies for the next school year in May, take possession in June, and defer billing until after July 1. This allows the athletic trainer time to restock and prepare for the fall seasons during one fiscal year while paying for the supplies during the subsequent year. Negotiation over delivery and billing is even more important for sports medicine clinics, where fluctuations of cash flow have a greater impact.

Quality: Athletic trainers typically negotiate for the quality of the goods they purchase by specifying brand names or generics on the bid sheet. Another item of negotiation that is particularly applicable to large capital improvement items is the warranty. Although every product should be accompanied by an *implied warranty*, the athletic trainer is free to negotiate an *express warranty* that affirms the performance characteristics of the product.

Shipping: The two primary points for negotiation about shipping purchased goods are payment of shipping costs and the freight-on-board (f.o.b.) point. The wise athletic trainer will include a statement in the RFQ stipulating that the vendor will assume all costs associated with shipping and handling the product. This is a common practice that clarifies the cost of supplies for athletic trainers by allowing vendors to factor the costs of shipping into their bids. The *f.o.b. point* specifies the place at which title for the sports medicine supplies will pass from the vendor to the purchaser. Generally athletic trainers should specify their institutions or clinics as the f.o.b. point to provide greater protection against loss or damage during shipping.

Support: Negotiation for technical support is especially important for high-technology capital improvement items. Computers and isokinetic testing and rehabilitation devices are two typical examples of the type of equipment purchase for which athletic trainers may require technical support. The cost of this support is often negotiable and will become an important factor in the overall cost during the life of the equipment.

Purchase Order

A *purchase order* is a document that formalizes the terms of the purchase and transmits the intentions of the buyer to purchase goods or services from the vendor (see Figure 4.9). It should be completed and transmitted only after the RFQs have been received from the vendors. An important decision is whether to award purchase orders to vendors based on the low bid for the entire supply order or to make the award based on the low bid for each individual item. Athletic trainers will save the most money if they make the award based on each item. There are drawbacks to this method, however. Most vendors have a minimum order policy. A vendor awarded a purchase order for $4.95 out of a possible $10,000 RFQ will be unlikely to negotiate favorable terms in the future. One possible solution is to award purchase orders only for amounts over a certain critical level, usually around $200. This breaks the total supply order into packages that will save the athletic trainer money while insuring a reasonable profit margin for the most competitive vendors.

implied warranty   An unstated understanding that a vendor will "make good" if a product is faulty.

express warranty   An explicit statement specifying the conditions, circumstances, and terms under which a vendor will replace or repair a product if found to be faulty.

freight-on-board (f.o.b.) point   The point at which the title for shipped goods passes from vendor to purchaser.

purchase order   A document that formalizes the terms of a purchase and transmits the intentions of the buyer to purchase goods or services from a vendor.

Vendor's copy

Grant Public Schools

Purchase order

This number must appear on all invoices! ↑

To:

↓ Ship to Grant Public Schools, Grant, CA

☐ Memorial Stadium, 225 Stadium Dr.

☐ Central Administration, 321 Pine St.

☐ Physical Plant, 5436 Elm Ave.

Bill to: Grant Public Schools
Grant, CA 98201

Account number	Order date	Ship via:		
Quantity	Description		Unit price	Amount
Please send duplicate invoices	Approved by			

Figure 4.9 Sample purchase order form.

Receiving

Receiving is the process of accepting delivery on goods purchased from vendors. When goods are received they should immediately be checked to make sure that the packing slip matches the contents of the shipping container and to determine if all the goods specified in the purchase order have been received. All goods should be inspected for damage. If any damage is discovered, it should be reported to the vendor immediately. Most vendors have a policy of replacing damaged goods only if reported within a given time period.

receiving   The process of accepting delivery on goods purchased from a vendor.

Accounts Payable

Payment for sports medicine supplies and equipment is usually due within a specified time period after the receipt of the goods or the invoice, whichever arrives last. Athletic trainers who work in educational, professional, or industrial settings should submit invoices to their respective business offices as soon as they are received to take advantage of early payment discounts offered by most vendors. Those athletic trainers who work in independent sports medicine clinics should evaluate the terms of the early payment discount. If the finance charge is lower than the current cost of money, it would make sense to stretch the payments as far as possible into the payment term.

Alternative Purchasing Strategies

Besides the traditional method of bidding for sports medicine supply purchases, athletic trainers should also consider two other potential sources of cost savings: pooled buying consortia and the use of alumni and booster organizations.

Pooled Buying Consortia

*pooled buying consortium
A group of similar institutions that merge resources to purchase goods in large quantities to receive volume discounts.*

A *pooled buying consortium* can be an effective method for purchasing certain types of sports medicine supplies. Schools that are members of an athletic conference should consider pooling their adhesive tape orders, for example, to receive a quantity discount. This method can be effective for many different types of supplies including bandages, ice bags, paper cups, elastic wraps, and crutches, among others. Pooled buying consortia have been used for many years by coaches and athletic directors to purchase balls and other athletic equipment for less than it would cost to purchase such supplies individually.

Alumni or Booster Organizations

Alumni and booster organizations can be very helpful in offsetting the costs of large capital expenses that would normally lie outside the normal budget of the sports medicine program. Treatment and rehabilitation devices are expensive items that booster clubs are often willing to purchase for the sports medicine program. Athletic trainers are cautioned, however, to work in conjunction with the institutional development officer when making such requests of booster clubs. Many institutions have policies designed to insure that all philanthropy is channeled through the development office to maximize the ability of the institution to obtain such gifts.

Capital Equipment—Buy or Lease?

Once a decision has been made to acquire an expensive piece of equipment, the athletic trainer and the organization's business manager must decide whether to purchase the equipment or lease it. Many expensive rehabilitation devices and other therapeutic modalities can be leased rather than purchased. Obviously, there are advantages and disadvantages to both methods (see Figure 4.10). The primary advantage of purchasing over leasing is cost. This

❚ Figure 4.10   Relative merits of leasing.

Advantages	Disadvantages
• Possible tax advantages	• Higher overall costs
• Decreased risk of obsolescence	• No ownership
• Lower initial costs	• Higher effective interest rate than traditional financing

is especially true if the equipment is being purchased outright as opposed to being financed. The other advantage of purchasing is that the sports medicine program owns the equipment. This can become a disadvantage, however, if the equipment is based on high technology that becomes obsolete before the equipment is fully depreciated (Kess & Westlin, 1987). One of the advantages of leasing is that it allows the institution to use its capital in other ways than encumbering large amounts in equipment purchases. There can also be some tax advantages for sports medicine clinics when they lease their equipment as opposed to buying it.

■ Inventory Management

The U.S. Small Business Administration (1980) defines *inventory management* in the following terms:

- *Acquiring an adequate supply and variety of inventory to meet production and sales needs*
- *Providing safety stocks to meet unexpected demand or delays in inventory replenishment*
- *Investing in inventory wisely so that excessive capital is not tied up, excessive space is not required, or unnecessary borrowing and interest expense is not required*
- *Maintaining accurate and up-to-date records to help identify and prevent shortages and to serve as a data base for decisions (pp. 2-3)*

Inventory management is one of the most important aspects of increased efficiency in the sports medicine program. It is equally important for large and small operations. Large operations, such as professional athletic teams and universities with NCAA Division I football programs, have big investments in sports medicine supplies, which ought to be managed wisely and prudently. Larger programs are more likely to operate multiple facilities, making the control and distribution of sports medicine supplies more difficult and requiring more attention to inventory techniques.

Inventory control is important for small programs as well because errors in inventory and supply management result in more financial hardship for programs with smaller budgets. Another problem faced by athletic trainers in smaller programs is that coaches, athletic administrators, and physical education teachers often have access to the training room and the sports medicine supplies in it.

The following suggestions should help athletic trainers improve their ability to track the location and rate of use of their supplies.

Inventory Regularly

Compile a complete inventory of expendable supplies at least once a month. Institutions that operate multiple training rooms should inventory the stock in each facility every week. The inventory reports for these satellites should be compiled in the primary training room and used to develop the monthly inventory report.

inventory management
The process of controlling equipment and supply stocks so that services can be provided without interruption while the use of institutional resources is maximized.

■ Inventory control is an important aspect of financial management in the sports medicine program.

Centralize Storage

Wherever possible, centralize the storage of sports medicine supplies to make them easier to manage. If supplies need to be stockpiled in several locations, send the smallest amount that will suffice for a reasonable time period, preferably one week. This system requires athletic trainers to be more attentive to inventory levels and will help prevent sudden or unexpected shortages.

Automate the Inventory Process

Develop and implement a continuous monitoring system that allows for a quick check of inventory levels at any time. One effective method utilizes a computerized inventory record based on standard spreadsheet software. When supplies are removed from the central storage site, the trainer fills out a small form indicating the date, type, and amount of supply being taken and the amount remaining after the withdrawal (see Figure 4.11). At the end of each day a student athletic trainer or secretary enters the information on the forms into the computer record. This allows the athletic trainer to track the status of the inventory on a daily basis.

Restrict Access

Unauthorized access to the training room and the supply room where sports medicine supplies are kept is the primary cause of inventory control breakdown. Institutions should develop policies and procedures that specify who will have access to the sports medicine facility and under what circumstances they will have such access. I strongly recommend that as few people as possible have keys to the facility—access should be limited to only those

Sports Medicine
Supply Check-Out Form

Date ______________________________

Supply type ______________________________

Quantity ______________________________

Supply destination ______________________________

Amount remaining
in storage ______________________________

Person taking
the supplies ______________________________

Person recording the
withdrawal into the computer ______________________________

Figure 4.11 Sample inventory control form.

persons with a legitimate need to use it and responsibility for its operation. Policies should clearly state the responsibilities of anyone issued keys to the facility.

Reminder System

Each type of supply should be marked with a sign that reads "Reorder when *X* amount remains" to remind athletic trainers to reorder supplies when they reach a critically low level.

Applications to Athletic Training: Theory Into Practice

Apply the concepts discussed in this chapter to the following two case studies to help you prepare for such situations you might face in actual practice. The questions at the end of the studies are open ended—many possible correct solutions exist. Use the case studies as homework, test questions, or in class discussion.

Case Study 1

Tammy Jenkins had just arrived at Los Ranchos College after being appointed the school's first certified athletic trainer. It was mid-June and Tammy knew she had quite a bit to do to get ready for the arrival of the fall sports athletes in August. She decided to start by approaching the athletic director.

"Coach," Tammy began, "I need to order the sports medicine supplies as soon as possible if we expect to be ready to go in August. I need to know a few things. First, how much money do I have to work with? Second, are there any specific purchasing procedures I need to follow? I'd really like to get busy with this today if I could."

The athletic director informed Tammy that she didn't have a specific budget for sports medicine supplies. In the past, sports medicine supplies were paid for out of the general athletics budget, which he controlled. "You just put your list together and I'll take a look at it," he told her. "Oh, I almost forgot," the athletic director continued, "I wanted to make sure we at least had the tape here in time, so I went ahead and ordered it. It should be delivered some time in July."

Although Tammy was uncomfortable about not having a specific budget, she knew she wouldn't be able to change everything right away. She spent the rest of the day compiling an inventory of the supplies on hand. That evening she put together a list of the supplies she thought she would need to get through the first year along with an estimate of each item's cost.

When she presented it to the athletic director the next day, he told her she would need to cut the proposal by 25%. "I think this list is fairly modest," Tammy said. "I'm not sure I can cut that much out of it." After further discussion, the athletic director told Tammy that the cost of the tape, when added to the total cost of her supply list, was just more than he could afford. When Tammy asked how much he had paid for the tape, she was astonished to find out that it was 100% higher than the price she paid at the school where she used to work. "Where did you order the tape from?" asked Tammy. "We get all our supplies from Acme Sporting Goods downtown. We always have. Anything you need—just call them and they'll take good care of you. The owner is a big supporter of the college," replied the athletic director. Tammy suddenly realized that she had her work cut out for her!

QUESTIONS FOR ANALYSIS

1. What budgeting system does the Los Ranchos College sports medicine program use? Is it optimal for the conditions? What system would you implement? Why?

2. Why was Tammy so distressed when she found out how the tape had been purchased? What is the likely effect of this purchasing system on Tammy's program? How should the purchasing system be altered?

3. If Tammy changed from direct purchasing at Acme Sporting Goods to a system of competitive bidding, what would be the likely result?

4. What can Tammy do to lower her costs for sports medicine supplies while maintaining the supportive relationship the college enjoys with the owner of Acme Sporting Goods?

5. If you were in Tammy's position, would you have taken the same approach to purchasing supplies? If not, what would you have done differently? Why?

CASE STUDY 2

Diversified Physical Therapy Services is a large rehabilitation services corporation that operates a string of clinics in a 10-county area in eastern Iowa. In addition to the clinics, DPTS also supplies rehabilitation professionals to 12 hospitals. DPTS recently acquired contracts at 15 high schools to supply sports medicine services. The contracts provide an athletic trainer for each school for 1,000 hours per year. As an additional service, DPTS *purchases all the sports medicine supplies for the schools up to a maximum of $2,500 per school.*

At a recent meeting of the DPTS partners, one of the owners expressed concern over the plan to provide the schools with sports medicine supplies. Although he liked the idea in general, he was concerned about waste and cost-effectiveness. He also pointed out to the other partners that if each school used less than their $2,500 allotment, the company would be coming out ahead.

The DPTS partners decided to create a central storage site for all 15 high schools. The athletic trainers would be allowed to take what they needed for a two-week period. When those supplies were exhausted, they would have to come to the central storage site, which was housed in a clinic in the geographic center of the schools' service area, and check out enough for another two weeks. The business manager in the clinic where the supplies were stored would be responsible for auditing supply requisitions to ensure that each school remained below the $2,500 limit.

QUESTIONS FOR ANALYSIS

1. What are the strengths of the central supply plan adopted by DPTS? What are the weaknesses?

2. What alternatives are there to the central supply plan? Would they be superior? If so, why?

3. What are the strengths and weaknesses of the plan to provide up to $2,500 in supplies to each school? Is this a service that most schools would want? Why or why not?

∎ Summary

The need for sound financial management of sports medicine resources is commonly recognized. A budget is a plan for the coordination of resources and expenditures. It helps ensure that needed services are delivered effectively and on time and that financial resources are expended in accordance with the institutional mission. There are at least nine different types of budgeting systems: spending ceiling (or incremental), spending reduction, zero-based, PPBES, fixed, variable, lump sum, line item, and performance. Careful consideration of which funds will support the various activities of the sports medicine program enhances budget development. Budgeting for the first year of the sports medicine program is the most difficult because of a lack of previous spending patterns. Budgeting for capital improvements is more difficult than for consumable supplies because of the expense involved. Budget evaluation is an important but often neglected activity that will help athletic trainers make more informed decisions on how to expend program resources.

Purchasing is the process of budget implementation. The six most common steps in the purchase of sports medicine supplies include requisition, request for quotation, negotiation, purchase order, receiving, and accounts payable.

Athletic trainers should attempt to negotiate with vendors over price, supply, quality, shipping, and technical support. Alternatives to purchasing via bidding include pooled buying consortia and the use of alumni and booster organizations. Athletic trainers should consider the relative merits of leasing over buying when shopping for expensive capital equipment.

Inventory management is an important aspect of administration for athletic trainers. Mistakes in inventory management can have drastic consequences for both large and small programs. Athletic trainers should be aware at all times of the status of their supply inventory so they are able to deliver sports medicine services in a timely manner.

Note. Brief sections of this chapter appeared previously in *Athletic Business*, **15**(1), copyright 1991 by Richard Ray and *Athletic Business* magazine; and in *College Athletic Management*, **2**(1), copyright 1989 by College Athletic Administrator, Inc. Reprinted by permission.

∎ Annotated Bibliography

Barlow, C.W. (1982). *Negotiating skills for the purchasing agent*. New York: American Management Association Membership Publications Division.

This useful pamphlet will help athletic trainers improve their negotiating skills not only in purchasing, but also in other aspects of their jobs. Chapters 1 and 3 are especially relevant.

Horine, L. (1991). *Administration of physical education and sport programs* (2nd ed.). Dubuque, IA: Brown.

Although there are several excellent chapters in this book, chapter 8 ("Financial Management in Physical Education and Sport") and chapter 9 ("Purchasing, Maintenance, and Security Management in Sport") are especially applicable to athletic trainers. Horine's discussion of several purchasing strategies in chapter 9 would be useful for athletic trainers in any employment setting.

Jones, R.L., & Trentin, H.G. (1971). *Budgeting: Key to planning and control* (2nd ed.). New York: American Management Associations.

This book provides an in-depth treatment of the business and industry budgeting process. Although few of its examples apply to sports medicine, the book contains a good treatment of budgeting concepts.

Kess, S., & Westlin, B. (1987). *Business strategies*. Chicago: Commerce Clearinghouse.

On pages 2251 to 2257 the authors discuss the relative merits of leasing versus buying equipment and facilities. The section entitled "Making the Lease-or-Buy Decision" will help athletic trainers understand the complexities of this issue.

Mayo, H.B. (1978). *Basic finance*. Philadelphia: Saunders.

In part 2 Mayo presents a broad variety of financial concepts that will help athletic trainers, especially those that manage sports medicine clinics, become better businesspersons.

Rankin, J.M. (1992). Financial resources for conducting athletic training programs in the collegiate and high school settings. *Journal of Athletic Training*, **27**, 344-349.

Rankin surveyed high school and college athletic trainers and documented the difference in funds allocated for the health care of their athletes: NCAA Division I colleges spent an average of $925 per athlete whereas high schools spent only about $95.

Ray, R.R. (1990). An injury-free budget. *College Athletic Management*, **2**(1), 42-45.

This article discusses budget concepts, planning, implementation, and evaluation in sports medicine settings.

Ray, R.R. (1991). Training room efficiency. *Athletic Business*, **15**(1), 46-49.

Information in this article will help athletic trainers become more efficient in purchasing and keeping an inventory of their sports medicine supplies. The article also discusses standard operating procedures and their application in sports medicine.

U.S. Small Business Administration. (1980). *Business basics: Inventory management*. Washington, DC: U.S. Government Printing Office.

This self-instructional booklet published by the U.S. government is designed to help small business owners improve their inventory management skills. The information can be applied in a wide variety of sports medicine settings.

Wildavsky, A. (1975). *Budgeting: A comparative theory of budgetary processes*. Boston: Little, Brown.

The author examines several different budgeting methods, with a particular emphasis on public sector and very large program budgeting.

Wright, B.J. (1983). *Automated purchasing: Key to new potential*. New York: American Management Association Membership Publication Division.

The most useful part of this book for athletic trainers is chapter 2, ''Overview of the Purchasing System.'' It describes in detail the steps to follow when purchasing consumable supplies and capital equipment improvements.

Young, H.C. (1976). *PPBS: Planning, programming, budgeting systems in academic libraries*. Detroit, MI: Gale Research Company.

Although written for those with an interest in the budgeting process as it applies to libraries, the first chapter of this book provides a good introduction to the PPBES system and compares it with other budgetary methods.

5

"No architecture is so haughty as that which is simple."

John Ruskin

Where Athletic Trainers Work: Facility Design and Planning

STUDENT OBJECTIVES

▌ Understand and defend the importance of the design phase in planning and constructing new sports medicine facilities.

▌ Understand the facility design and construction process in sports medicine settings.

▌ Understand the common design elements found in a well-planned sports medicine facility.

▌ Describe the sports medicine facility in terms of its specialized function areas.

OPENING CASE

After meeting with the university president, the whole staff was excited about beginning the planning for a new athletic building. The president informed everyone that the board of trustees had approved the project. The athletic director, the chair of the physical education department, and the vice president for finance were appointed to the planning committee for the new building. After the meeting the athletic director asked Kelly McCarthy, the director of sports medicine, to submit his ideas for the sports medicine facility in the new complex. Although Kelly was enthusiastic about the prospect of a new facility, he was a little nervous about having to design the new sports medicine center because he had never done anything like this before.

Kelly spent a few weeks toying with some ideas for the new sports medicine center before he finally drew a rough sketch and submitted it to the athletic director. The athletic director thanked him and filed the sketch away in a drawer labeled ''New Building.'' Kelly didn't hear from the athletic director about the new sports medicine center again, so he assumed his ideas had been accepted.

Six months later construction began. Four months after the ground breaking, Kelly and the rest of the athletic department staff were given a ''hard-hat tour'' of the site to view the progress on the project. When they reached the area that was to contain the new sports medicine facility, Kelly was astonished at how small it seemed in comparison to the sketch he had submitted. When he asked the construction manager about its size, he was told that the planning committee had to shave off a few feet to accommodate the conference and media area in the adjacent basketball coaches' dressing room. Kelly was assured that the sports medicine facility would look much bigger after the ''finish work'' was completed.

When the building finally opened, Kelly and his staff moved into a sports medicine facility that, although brighter and newer than the old facility had been, was neither bigger nor more functional. He had essentially traded one undersized facility for another.

Kelly McCarthy's experience with planning a new athletic building is common among athletic trainers. The opportunity to be involved in the planning, design, and construction of a sports medicine facility usually comes only once during the careers of most athletic trainers, who typically have little or no experience in facility planning. Most buildings are designed and constructed to provide service for decades, so decisions made during the planning, design, and construction phase of the sports medicine facility are, for all practical purposes, permanent. Hence, it is understandable but very unfortunate when expensive and uncorrectable mistakes are made. This chapter will help athletic trainers understand the basic processes of planning, designing, and constructing a sports medicine center.

∎ Conceptual Development

The most important phase in constructing a new sports medicine center is developing an appropriate concept for its design. Whether the facility is intended to serve a school, professional, or private sports medicine clinic client, the conceptual development process is essentially the same despite the important differences in layout and funding strategy between these facilities.

At least two arguments support paying careful attention to the conceptual development of the design of the sports medicine center. First, this is the only stage of the project that involves review by those people who will actually use the facility. After the project has begun there will be many reviews, but they will primarily be carried out by construction professionals and municipal employees such as plumbing and electrical inspectors. The athletic trainer is empowered during the design phase of a facility construction project. In the opening scenario, Kelly McCarthy made a poor decision by assuming that because he did not receive any feedback from the planning committee his recommendations would be implemented as submitted. Obviously, Kelly should have checked often to be sure that his ideas were being implemented. The construction of a new building is a political act that involves making choices about how limited resources will be utilized. The time for athletic trainers to exercise their influence is during the design phase.

The second argument for paying attention to design development relates to permanency and cost. Buildings are intended to last a very long time. Once the foundation is poured and bricks and mortar are in place, changes based on new thinking about the way the sports medicine facility should be designed become very expensive to implement. Although the owners of privately based sports medicine clinics can always sell the building in the future if they become dissatisfied with its design, school and university officials generally do not have this option because most campus-based sports medicine centers are part of large, multipurpose buildings.

The Design Process

Most athletic trainers will never be involved in the selection of an architect. As mentioned before, however, many will be responsible at some point in their careers for input into the design of new sports medicine centers. Understanding the processes normally used by institutions during the design and construction phases of a new building can help athletic trainers to avoid the kinds of mistakes made by Kelly McCarthy in the opening case (see Figure 5.1).

The Planning Committee

The *planning committee* is a group of individuals appointed to work with the architect to develop the design of a new building. Planning committees should include people representing the various activities that will take place in the building. Fletcher and Ranck (1991) suggest that the members of the planning committee be appointed by the chief executive officer of the institution and include employees who will be responsible for operating, maintaining, and using the building. They also recommend that in school and university settings at least one person from administration, the business office, and the physical plant be assigned to the planning committee. Theunissen (1978) suggests that the most appropriate person to act as chair of the planning committee is the person who leads the department or discipline

planning committee A group of institutional employees who work with an architect to develop the design of a building.

▌ Figure 5.1 Phases of design and construction of the sports medicine center.

Step number	Design and construction process
1	Conduct a needs assessment
2	Seek approval for the project
3	Select a construction process model
4	Select an architect
5	Develop schematics
6	Secure the required funding
7	Bid the construction
8	Analyze bids and take action
9	Begin construction
10	Monitor construction

most responsible for the use of the new facility. In many, if not most, cases this person will not be an athletic trainer. Hence, athletic trainers must effectively communicate their needs so they can be incorporated into the overall design.

The planning committee should reflect a balance between primary decision makers, secondary decision makers, and definers (Dougherty & Bonanno, 1985). Among the ***primary decision makers*** are institutional members with formal authority over large units or subunits of the organization—the people in a position to see "the big picture." ***Secondary decision makers*** are typically professional staff members who deliver the program. In a school sports medicine setting, they include athletic trainers, team physicians, and

primary decision makers
Institutional members who have formal authority over large units or subunits of an organization.

secondary decision makers
Professional staff members primarily responsible for delivering a program within an organization.

▌ The sports facility should be designed by an architect assisted by a planning committee.

selected faculty members. **Definers** are the people who will actually use the facility. In a sports medicine setting, definers would be patients, students, and athletes. Athletic trainers from other institutions may also act as definers by giving advice and asking questions that may not have occurred to the primary and secondary decision makers.

Step 1: Conduct a Needs Assessment

The first step in designing a new sports medicine facility is a comprehensive assessment of future program needs. Information from the **needs assessment**, combined with a statement of present operating status, is called the **program statement**. The program statement is an important document because it helps the architect determine space requirements for the new facility (Dibner, 1982). The process of needs assessment may seem tedious, but without it a competent job of planning for future space needs cannot be accomplished. One of the many mistakes Kelly McCarthy made in the opening case was that he sketched out a design for the new sports medicine center without taking into account future growth patterns. The needs assessment is usually conducted at the departmental or program level and involves asking and answering a series of questions (see Table 5.1). If the administrator of the

defiiners People who use or receive the services of a program.

needs assessment A process of evaluating the present status and future requirements of a program.

program statement A document, prepared by the users, the architect, or both, that specifies the anticipated space requirements based on known work patterns provided by the users.

Table 5.1 Sports Medicine Facility Needs Assessment Concerns

Questions	Where to look for answers
What is the present clinic caseload? How is it likely to change?	Annual reports, interviews with staff and administrators
Is the present facility adequate? Why or why not?	Building codes, national design standards, literature review, peer consultation
Is the present facility suitable to implement the strategic plan?	Program and institutional facility strategic plans
Which program problems are related to facilities?	Critical incident reports, interviews with staff, accreditation reports

---

sports medicine program has been doing a good job of programmatic self-study, the needs assessment will be much easier to complete (see Figure 2.10).

Step 2: Seek Approval for the Project

Once the needs assessment has been completed, assuming it justifies the need for a new sports medicine facility, the people with financial control of the institution must be convinced that the project is necessary. This step is important whether the sports medicine program is in a school, professional, or private clinic setting. Every organization has a person or a group of people who must ultimately decide whether to spend the vast sums required for new construction. The athletic trainer must be willing to document the need for such facilities in great detail. Even after such documentation is presented, however, the athletic trainer should not be too disappointed if it takes months, or more realistically, years for such a project to be approved.

Step 3: Select a Construction Process Model

lump sum bidding A process whereby general contractors provide cost quotations for the right to construct or renovate a building.

There are three common ways to proceed when constructing new facilities. *Lump sum bidding* is the most traditional method, often used for governmental units like public schools and colleges. In lump sum bidding, the architect submits schematic drawings to several general contractors. The contractors study the plans and quote a cost based on the instructions provided by the architect. Since some contractors may intentionally underbid a project to secure a contract, it is wise to screen the contractors in advance and send bids only to those with proven records. It is also prudent to visit at least one building constructed by each of the contractors to determine the quality of their work (see Figure 5.2).

I Figure 5.2 Advantages and disadvantages of lump sum bidding.

Advantages	Disadvantages
• Lowest possible price	• Contractors may underbid
• Ensures fairness	• Less control for owner
• Complies with state and federal statutes	• Contractor may cut corners

construction management A method that involves the general contractor as part of the design team from the beginning of the building process.

Another construction model that may be used is termed *construction management*. The construction management approach utilizes the general contractor as part of the design team. This method has the advantage of having the general contractor on board from the beginning of the project, rather than bringing the contractor on near the end of the design phase. The construction manager can advise on building materials, schedules, cost analysis, and necessary subcontractors. The drawbacks to using the construction management approach include the manager's fee, which can approach 5% of the total project cost, and the fact that as a member of the design team staff, the manager will not exert direct authority over the work of the subcontractors (Snider, 1982) (see Figure 5.3).

I Figure 5.3 Advantages and disadvantages of construction management.

Advantages	Disadvantages
• Construction manager part of design team	• Construction manager's fee
• More advice on materials, costs, and schedules	• No direct control over subcontractors

design/build A method that uses only one firm to both design and construct a new building.

The third construction process method is known as *design/build*. This system utilizes only one firm to both design and build the new sports medicine center. As with the other construction models, there are both advantages and disadvantages to the design/build concept. The obvious advantage is that the owners have only one firm with which to communicate. They can take any problems that arise to a single source for redress, allowing for more rapid, and potentially cost-saving, approaches to solving problems that arise during the construction phase of the project.

The streamlined approach utilized in design/build is also its weakness, however. It involves fewer checks and balances between the various firms normally involved in a construction project. The integrity of the entire project rests on the abilities of one firm—specifically on the abilities of a few people in one firm. This is a good reason to screen design/build proposals even more carefully than a more traditional construction process model (see Figure 5.4).

Advantages	Disadvantages
• Easier communication	• Fewer checks and balances
• Ability to "fast track" problems	• Greatest potential for "major" problems

▌ Figure 5.4 Advantages and disadvantages of design/build.

Step 4: Select an Architect

An architect is retained by the owner of a clinic or the chief executive officer of an institution to operationalize the sports medicine program through building designs. In addition, the architect should be available to provide advice and guidance from the very beginning of the project until the keys to the new facility are handed over to the users. Several possible methods can be used for selecting an architect (Dibner, 1982). The first and easiest way to select an architect is to contract with a firm recommended by friends or colleagues. For obvious reasons, this may not serve the sports medicine program well. A better method is to develop a list of architectural firms with a variety of different attributes—big and small, local and distant, and so on. Interview each firm on the list to determine whether it would be suitable for and interested in taking on the project. A site visit to at least one project each firm has completed is recommended. A third method for selecting an architect is to commission a design competition. This method is typically used only on very large projects because it is costly both in money and time (see Figure 5.5).

Whichever method is used to select an architect to design the new sports medicine center, a good match between the client and the architect must be obtained. Forseth (1986) recommends that architects for sports medicine facilities be selected on the basis of their openness to suggestions and their previous experience in designing similar facilities. *Athletic Business* (1992) magazine publishes a directory of architects that have experience in designing athletic facilities. Many of these architects have designed sports medicine facilities as a part of these larger projects.

Step 5: Develop Schematics

Once the program statement mentioned previously has been developed, the architect will develop *schematic drawings* that describe the relationships between the principal functions of the sports medicine center. One of Kelly McCarthy's errors in the opening case was that he never met with the

schematic drawings A graphic representation, derived from the program statement, that illustrates the relationships between the principal functions of a building.

Figure 5.5 Three methods for selecting an architect.

architect to develop the schematic drawings that were eventually submitted. Had he done so, the architect probably would have been able to help him think in detail about traffic patterns and space requirements—two of the major elements that should be addressed in the schematic drawings.

Determining Space Needs: Several authors have suggested methods to help athletic trainers determine how much space will be needed when planning for a new sports medicine center. Penman (1977) has suggested that the minimum amount of space required for a "bare bones" training room stocked with only one treatment table, one taping table, some counter space and miscellaneous equipment is 300 square feet. Secor (1984) has expanded on Penman's idea by creating a formula athletic trainers can use to plan for space requirements based on the number of athletes they expect to serve during peak caseloads:

$$\frac{\text{Number of athletes at peak}}{20 \text{ per table per day}} \times 100 \text{ sq ft} = \text{Total square footage}$$

Although the base estimate of 100 square feet per treatment and taping table may provide a useful starting point for determining space needs, athletic trainers charged with the design of the new sports medicine center must take into account that varied functions will take place in the sports medicine center and each of these functions will have different space requirements.

Another factor that will influence the overall space requirements of the sports medicine center is the proportion of work that will be done in each of the various sections. The type of client served by the sports medicine center will largely determine this factor. For example, the hospital-based sports medicine center will probably dedicate a greater proportion of its space to rehabilitation. In contrast, the typical college and high school sports medicine facility will require a larger taping and bandaging section than private or hospital-based sports medicine clinics. Finally, the anticipated growth of the program must be factored into the size estimates that go into the schematic drawings (Cohen & Cohen, 1979). Growth is one of the most difficult forecasts to make, but it is very important—especially considering the exploding demand for access to sports medicine services. In summary, the following factors influence the space requirements of the sports medicine facility:

- Number of clients to be served
- Type of clients to be served
- Amount and kinds of equipment needed
- Number and qualifications of staff
- Projected growth of the program

Traffic Patterns: When working with the architect to develop the schematic drawings, it is essential to determine anticipated ***traffic patterns*** based on the relationship of the subfunctions of the sports medicine center to each other. Muther and Wheeler (1973) suggest that the best way to accomplish this task is to identify each of the subfunctions and to justify the space they will occupy by placing them on a ***relationship chart*** (see Figure 5.6). Once charted, the physical relationship of subfunctions to each other become less conceptual and more concrete.

Once the space relationships have been established, coded, and justified on the relationship chart, the next step is constructing a ***bubble diagram***. The bubble diagram illustrates the spatial relationships between the subfunctions of the sports medicine center based on the "closeness" established in the relationship chart. Although the bubble diagram is by no means a floor plan, it is the first step toward being able to visually understand how all the parts of the sports medicine center will be laid out (see Figure 5.7).

Step 6: Secure the Required Funding

Obviously, all construction projects require a source of funding. A wide variety of funding options are available for sports medicine center construction depending on the type of institution. Private sports medicine clinics generally have fewer options, however, than public sector institutions like public high schools, colleges, and universities. Even professional athletic teams have greater flexibility in financing sports medicine facilities than the private clinic because many of the stadiums that house them are constructed at least in part with public tax dollars. The owners of most private sports medicine clinics will be forced to secure loans from a bank for new construction.

Athletic trainers who approach a financial institution for a loan for construction of a new sports medicine facility should remember that banks are

traffic patterns   *The anticipated flow of people from one area of a building to another.*

relationship chart   *A table used to justify the placement of various rooms within a building.*

bubble diagram   *An abstract, graphic representation of the relationship of one function of a building to another based on the "closeness" established by the relationship chart.*

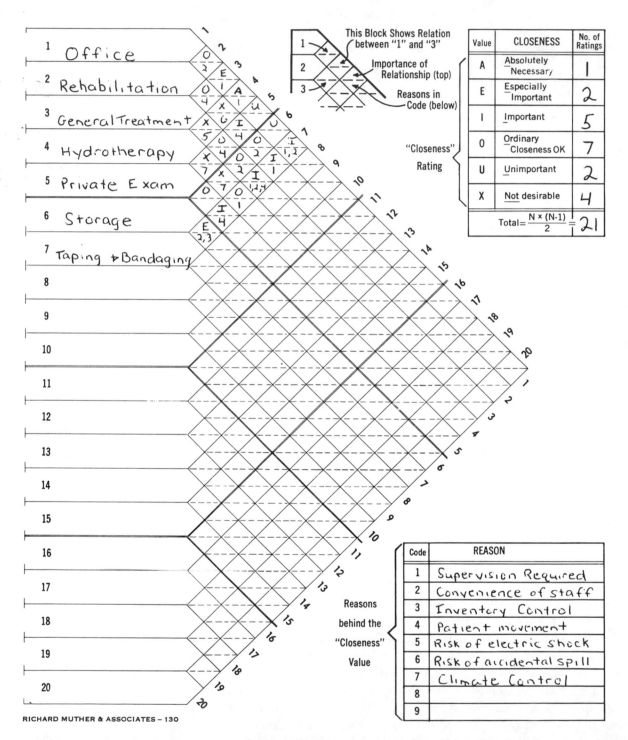

RICHARD MUTHER & ASSOCIATES – 130

■ **Figure 5.6** Example of a relationship chart for planning the closeness of the elements of the sports medicine facility. *Note.* From *Simplified Systematic Layout Planning* by Richard Muther and J.D. Wheeler, 1973, Kansas City: Management & Industrial Research Publications. Extended copyright 1990 by Richard Muther. Adapted courtesy of copyright holder: Richard Muther.

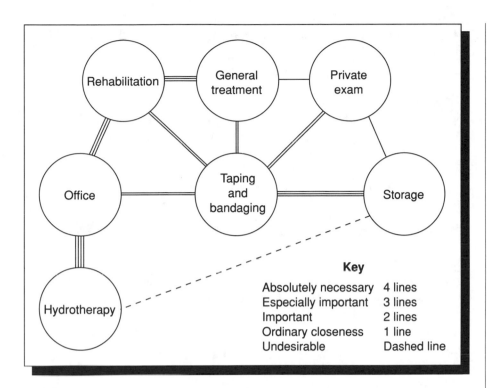

Office

Rehabilitation

General treatment

Private exam

Taping and bandaging

Storage

Hydrotherapy

Key

Absolutely necessary	4 lines
Especially important	3 lines
Important	2 lines
Ordinary closeness	1 line
Undesirable	Dashed line

▌Figure 5.7 Bubble diagram showing accessibility needs within a sports medicine facility.

more likely to make loans for construction of multipurpose buildings. For example, the athletic trainer who wishes to build a sports medicine clinic as part of a larger medical arts building will probably have a better chance of securing a loan than the person who wants to build a health club that offers sports medicine services. The medical arts building can be used for many diverse purposes whereas the health club would probably require extensive remodeling prior to resale should the bank need to foreclose. In general, medical practitioners are perceived by bankers to be good risks.

At least two things are generally required of the athletic trainer who applies for a ***commercial loan*** from a bank for new construction of a private sports medicine facility. The first thing the bank will require, especially if the athletic trainer is the sole proprietor of the clinic, is an assignment of life insurance. This protects the bank against loss in the event the athletic trainer dies before paying off the debt. Second, and most important, the bank will want to see the athletic trainer's ***business plan***. The business plan contains information the bank will need to project whether the clinic is likely to succeed or not. The components of the business plan include:

- a statement of the activities the clinic will engage in;

- a ***market analysis*** detailing the clinic's competitive advantages, analysis of competition, pricing structure, and marketing plan;

- the credentials of the principal owners and operators of the clinic;

- historical and projected financial statements of both cash flow and income;

- a breakdown of costs associated with the project based on the schematics developed by the architect;

commercial loan *An amount of money borrowed from a lending institution for the purpose of establishing, improving, or maintaining a business.*

business plan *A written description of a business' activities, market analysis, historical and projected financial statements, and other associated information. Used by commercial loan officers to assess the viability of a business.*

market analysis *A written description detailing a business' competitive advantages, analysis of competition, pricing structure, and marketing plan.*

- the amount of personal equity being committed by the athletic trainer; and
- the amount of the loan being requested.

Sports medicine facilities in the public sector, including private educational institutions that receive state and federal assistance, can be funded in at least three ways other than by a commercial loan (see Figure 5.8).

Figure 5.8 Methods for funding public sector sports medicine facilities.

• Capital campaigns	• Borrow from endowment
• Bond sales	• Commercial loans

capital campaign A program, usually of fixed length, designed to raise funds for program creation, development, and improvement.

One of the most common methods to raise the funds is by conducting a *capital campaign*. A capital campaign is a major institutional response to several needs intended to be remedied over 3 to 5 years. Capital campaigns are usually authorized and directed by the persons at the very top of the institutional hierarchy. They are intended to secure pledges of financial support from a broad institutional constituency including alumni, faculty and staff, foundations, affiliated institutions such as churches, and friends. Funds for the new sports medicine center will almost always be a small fraction of the overall goal for a capital campaign. Nevertheless, the athletic trainer may be heavily involved in helping secure pledges under the direction and supervision of the institutional development officer.

tax exempt bonds Bonds authorized and sold by governmental agencies to provide funding for construction projects.

Another way public sector institutions and some hospitals secure funding for the construction of sports medicine facilities is through the sale of *tax exempt bonds*. The sale of such bonds is usually authorized either by public vote (as in the case of elementary and high school construction) or by a bonding authority established by the states. Bonds are usually sold in one of two ways: publicly, usually to friends of the institution, or privately to a bank or other financial institution as part of its investment portfolio. A common practice is for similar institutions to pool their projects and sell bonds together under one issue. This is a useful practice because it lowers the overhead costs associated with conducting a bond issue.

endowment That portion of an institution's assets in cash and investments not normally used for operational purposes.

The third common method institutions use to finance new sports medicine facilities is to borrow internally from their *endowments*. An institution's endowment is the sum of its assets in cash and investments. Institutions usually hesitate to borrow from endowments, however, because the interest earned from an endowment can account for a significant percentage of the annual operating budget. If the endowment is quite large, however, and the sports medicine building project is relatively modest in relation to it, this is probably the easiest method of financing such a project.

Step 7: Bid the Construction

construction documents The highly detailed, technical drawings a contractor will use to determine building costs and guide construction.

If you're using the lump sum bidding model, it is now time to bid the construction. Before the actual bids are sent to the contractors who will compete for the job, the architect will develop the *construction documents* (Dibner, 1982). The construction documents are highly detailed, technical drawings that the contractors will need to determine a realistic estimate of construction costs. The construction documents are the drawings that will actually be used to guide construction of the new sports medicine center.

The architect will then prepare and send a packet of ***bidding documents*** to acceptable contractors. The bidding documents include an invitation to bid, the bid form, and special instructions from the architect. The bidders must submit their bids within a specified reasonable amount of time, and all bids are opened at the same time. Normally, administrators hire the contractor who submits the lowest bid. In many states, public institutions are required by law to allow all qualified contractors to bid for new construction projects. In addition, a certain percentage of the construction budget may have to be reserved for general contractors of historically underrepresented minority groups.

bidding documents *The package of materials prepared by the architect and sent to contractors, including the invitation to bid, the bid form, and special bidding instructions.*

Step 8: Analyze Bids and Take Action

Once the sealed bids have been opened, the planning team must carefully analyze each one. First, the athletic trainer–architect team must make sure that the information on the returned bids is consistent with the project as described in the bidding documents. If a contractor changes any item of the project, producing a lower bid, and the change goes unnoticed, legal problems could result. Another reason to carefully screen the bids is to ensure that there is some consistency in the costs quoted by the various contractors. If one contractor's quotation is significantly lower than all the others, the athletic trainer and architect should ask for an explanation. Obviously, the quality of the finished facility will suffer if the contractor cuts corners to secure the contract.

If the returned bids exceed the available funding, four possible courses of action could be pursued (Biehle, 1982). The first is to delay the project while additional funding is raised. If it takes excessive time to raise the funds, the total project cost will probably rise as a result of inflation. The second option is to negotiate a lower price with the contractor. This almost always involves eliminating certain features that were part of the original design or using less expensive building materials. Another option to be considered involves asking the architect to develop an alternative design. This will be expensive, both in time and money. Finally, the project can be abandoned. If this happens, the athletic trainer should realize that there are termination fees written into most architects' contracts in excess of the compensation the architect will be owed for the time and energy already spent on the project. In addition, the architect may retain the rights to the drawings. If the athletic trainer plans to use them for a future project, the right to do so should be negotiated prior to signing the architect's contract.

Step 9: Begin Construction

This step is fairly self-explanatory. Once the contractor's bid has been accepted, the architect will work with the athletic trainer's (or the institution's) attorney to draw up the construction contract. The architect will have access to several standardized contract forms for this purpose.

general contractor The company responsible for coordinating the actual construction of a building.

subcontractor A company hired by the general contractor to complete a portion of the building project. The subcontractor's work is usually devoted to a particular skilled trade, such as plumbing, electricity, and landscaping.

Step 10: Monitor Construction

Several people play important monitoring roles during construction. The first is the *general contractor*, who is responsible for coordinating the work of the various *subcontractors* and for assuring the quality of their workmanship. It is the architect, however, who acts as the representative of the athletic trainer or the institution in making sure that the building is being constructed according to the standards developed by the architect. If the workmanship does not comply with the standards enumerated in the contract and construction documents, the architect has the authority to reject the work (Dibner, 1982).

The athletic trainer and the planning committee have important roles to play during the construction phase. They should be present on the job site as often as possible to make sure the design features agreed upon are being implemented. The frequent presence of the athletic trainer at the construction site can assure that the "little details" are implemented as planned. The athletic trainer should know the sports medicine facility better than anyone else.

If the athletic trainer suspects that the contractor or subcontractor is not properly implementing the architect's design, she or he should quickly inquire into the situation. It is very important, however, that the athletic trainer address all concerns to the architect and not to the contractor or subcontractors. As the agent of the athletic trainer or the institution, the architect will investigate and mediate a solution to the problem.

■ Elements of Sports Medicine Facility Design

An athletic trainer must consider at least seven elements when working with an architect to design a new sports medicine facility: size, location, electrical systems, plumbing systems, ventilation systems, lighting, and specialized function areas (see Figure 5.9). Size and space estimates have been discussed in the section on developing schematics. Now I'll address the other six design elements.

Location

A sports medicine center that is intended to serve the general population should be located near other health care providers. Patients will appreciate, for example, not having to travel far for X-ray or laboratory services. And proximity to referring physicians is a practical feature. The ideal location for a private sports medicine clinic is in a medical office building that houses those other health services—physicians, laboratory, and X-ray.

Having athletic facilities nearby is useful for observing a rehabilitating patient's functional capacity in running or other sports skills. If the clinic sees a lot of student-athletes, a location close to the school makes travel convenient for students.

As I mentioned earlier, school-based sports medicine centers for student-athletes are usually housed in large multipurpose athletic, physical education, or recreation buildings. The placement of the sports medicine center within the facility is an important decision. Most experts agree that it should be as

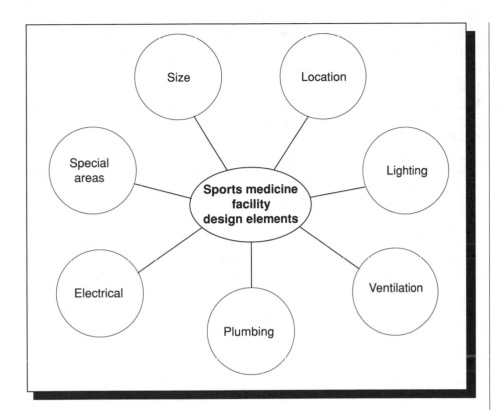

■ **Figure 5.9** Elements in the design of sports medicine facilities.

close as possible to both the men's and women's locker rooms (Fahey, 1986). Although it has been suggested that each locker room have direct access to the sports medicine center, problems of security and privacy may intervene. Athletes should not have to cross through another activity area to reach the sports medicine center.

Another consideration is the position of the sports medicine center relative to outside entrances. An injured athlete should have to walk or be carried through as few doors as possible—ideally, a door should lead directly from the outside playing fields into the sports medicine center. Wherever the center is located, it should have extra-wide doors that will accommodate two people assisting a nonambulating athlete. (Such wide doors will also be able to accommodate a stretcher, spine board, or gurney.)

In a multistory building, a ground floor location is most accessible to clients who ambulate with difficulty. If the sports medicine center cannot be located on the ground floor, it should be close to an elevator.

Having an institution's facilities for health services and sports medicine services adjacent has several advantages. First, cooperation can be enhanced if athletic trainers and other health professionals work together daily. Second, placing these two facilities next to each other means that certain operations can be shared, often resulting in savings of time or money. For example, if health services and sports medicine services are adjacent, medical records can be stored in a single location (the health service file room). Assuming that procedures protecting student confidentiality are upheld, medical records are thus more conveniently available and more complete.

The referral process is also enhanced by proximity between facilities. A student-athlete who reports to the athletic trainer with an illness can be referred without delay to the health service (and the likelihood of compliance is increased). Likewise, if a student who is not an athlete comes to the health service with an orthopedic injury, the athletic training staff is readily available to be consulted. Perhaps the ultimate argument for this arrangement, however, is financial—costs can be lowered because facilities, supplies, and services need not be duplicated. If the health service contains private examination rooms, they don't have to be included in the sports medicine center. Secretarial services can be shared as well as certain types of equipment and supplies, such as cast saws and suture kits. Having health services adjacent to the sports medicine center also eliminates the need for athletic trainers to store or dispense medications; this can more properly be handled by health service personnel.

Although this concept generally functions well on small campuses, larger schools may find it difficult to implement because athletic facilities are typically located on the periphery of campus whereas student health services are more centrally located. But a combined facility should be considered whenever possible in light of the many advantages.

Electrical Systems

Electrical system design is one of the few elements that, if improperly done, could cause injury or death. Three-pronged plugs, grounded electrical outlets, and circuit breakers are useful in preventing damage to electrical equipment, but because electrical shock can cause severe burns or cardiac arrest (see Figure 5.10), all electrical outlets in the sports medicine center should also

Figure 5.10 Effects of 60-cycle electric current on human tissue. *Note.* From "Electrical Safety in the Training Room" by M.M. Porter and J.W. Porter, 1981, *Journal of Athletic Training*, **16**, pp. 263-264. Copyright 1981 by National Athletic Trainers Association. Reprinted by permission.

ground fault interrupter (gfi) *A highly sensitive device designed to discontinue the flow of electricity in an electrical circuit during a power surge.*

```
0-8 milliamps = Safe
8-100 milliamps = Painful
100-200 milliamps = Fibrillation
≥ 200 milliamps = Muscle contraction and tissue burns
```

be equipped with a ***ground fault interrupter (gfi)***, designed to interrupt the flow of electricity if a surge of five milliamps or more is detected (Porter & Porter, 1981). GFIs can be installed either as part of the electrical outlet or as part of the circuit breaker, and they are required equipment in rooms in public and private buildings where water is present.

Another issue in electrical design is the location of electrical outlets. Secor (1984) recommends that electrical outlets be spaced every 4 ft throughout the facility. This spacing gives the athletic trainer the flexibility to move equipment as the program changes. In general, place electrical outlets at least 3 ft from the floor to keep power cords off the floor, which could be dangerous in the event of an accidental spill or flood, and to allow the athletic trainer to move therapeutic modalities more easily, especially if there is limited space between treatment tables.

Many sports medicine centers, especially those located in hospitals, have designed treatment stations with pull-cords that patients can use to shut off electrical power. This is especially useful when patients' electrical stimulation treatments become painful. Rather than wait for the athletic trainer to cross

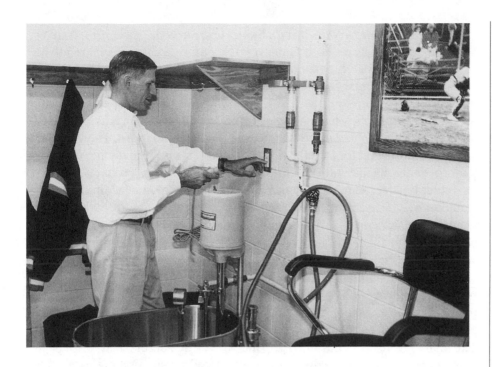

■ Ground fault interruptors should be used wherever the risk for accidental water spillage exists. They must be tested periodically.

the room to adjust the dosage, the patient can simply pull the cord and stop the flow of electricity to the modality. Athletic trainers can also choose to place remote power switches for hydrotherapy units in their offices to prevent accidental shock.

Plumbing Systems

Placement of water outlets and drains is a very important consideration in the design of the sports medicine center. A mistake in the design of the plumbing system is likely to be among the most expensive to correct because it is usually contained inside walls and under floors.

Like the electrical system, plumbing systems should be designed to be easily expandable. As the sports medicine program grows and changes, the need for water or drainage in different parts of the sports medicine facility may change as well. Both hot and cold water outlets should be provided in every section of the sports medicine facility. Some of these outlets should drain into sinks and others should be free standing to fill hydrotherapy tubs. Floor drains should be placed at several strategic points around the facility. The floor should be sloped at least 1 percent toward each of these drains (Penman, 1977).

If the facility is to contain an ice machine, a separate cold water line and floor drain should be provided for it. Whenever possible, each hydrotherapy tank's built-in drain should be connected directly to a dedicated floor drain. The drain faucet of tanks that use a pump drain should be connected to a *standpipe drain* by a hose or similar device to prevent splashing. In every case, a hydrotherapy tank should have an overflow prevention drain.

standpipe drain *A type of drain that is raised above floor level.*

plumbing fixtures *The external hardware used to control the flow and temperature of water.*

mixing valve *A type of plumbing fixture designed to blend hot and cold water, eliminating the need for separate hot and cold water controls.*

foot pedal activator *A water flow device controlled by a foot pedal and used with hand-washing stations.*

A plumbing contractor will be able to offer a wide variety of fixtures. Most ***plumbing fixtures*** used in the sports medicine center can be relatively simple and inexpensive, but athletic trainers may find three exceptions desirable. The first is a ***mixing valve***, which allows a more precise water temperature by manipulating only one valve. Mixing valves are especially useful for filling hydrotherapy tubs. Another plumbing enhancement athletic trainers may choose is a ***foot pedal activator*** for hand-washing stations. These devices are especially useful for athletic trainers who use massage and other activities that cover the hands with lotions, ointments, or similar products. Finally, the athletic trainer may choose to connect hydrotherapy tanks directly to the water source. The advantage of having a dedicated source of hydrotherapy water is that accidental spills are much easier to prevent. On the other hand, using hoses to fill hydrotherapy tanks provides greater flexibility for each water outlet.

It is not uncommon to pay a great deal of attention to designing the plumbing systems and to completely overlook accessories associated with plumbing. For instance, it is often very useful to build in liquid soap dispensers next to hand-washing stations. Paper cup dispensers may be desirable. The planning team could choose paper towel dispensers and wastepaper containers that are recessed into the wall—they're usually more expensive, but they save space and are more aesthetically pleasing. Finally, a drinking fountain will require a dedicated water line and drain and an electrical outlet so the water can be chilled.

Ventilation Systems

Very little has been written concerning ventilation of sports medicine facilities. But if the sports medicine center is improperly ventilated, working conditions can become extremely uncomfortable. The two most important ventilation concerns are temperature and humidity control. Penman and Penman (1982) recommend a maximum of 0.75 ft/sec draft factor with between 8 and 10 changes of air per hour during peak loads. They recommend a humidity level between 40 percent and 50 percent.

thermostat *A device that controls heating and cooling equipment.*

The sports medicine center should have its own ***thermostat***. A common mistake in designing ventilation systems is to use a common temperature control for the sports medicine center and adjacent areas, such as locker rooms and shower areas. The result is that the sports medicine center is almost always too warm to work comfortably. If the sports medicine center has several different rooms, it is probably desirable to have separate thermostats for each of them.

The other major ventilation concern is humidity. Excessive humidity is not only a comfort problem, but also a hygiene problem. Viruses, fungi, and bacteria survive more easily on moist surfaces than dry. Areas where water is used extensively, such as the hydrotherapy section, should be equipped with exhaust fans that are strong enough to keep humidity to reasonable levels.

Whether to provide air conditioning is an important decision because air conditioning is very expensive to install and use. In many areas of the United States, however, the temperature and humidity are so extreme when the sports medicine center is used most heavily that air conditioning is an essential feature. Because air conditioning cools the air by removing moisture, it is an important feature for comfort and hygiene.

Lighting

Illumination is another important, but often overlooked, feature in the overall sports medicine center design. How bright should the sports medicine center be? Arnheim and Prentice (1993) recommend that sports medicine centers be illuminated at 30 footcandles at a height of 4 ft above the floor. Other authors have suggested that a sports medicine facility requires illumination of 50 footcandles 4 ft above the floor (the Athletic Institute, 1979). Common sense dictates that different sections of the sports medicine center have different illumination requirements. Areas devoted to taping, bandaging, and wound care require more lighting than storage or hydrotherapy areas. The areas designated for physician examination and treatment of injured athletes probably require the most intense illumination. Floor lamps can supplement lighting in these areas to provide extra illumination for procedures such as wound debridement and suturing.

In addition to artificial lighting, the sports medicine center can be brightened significantly through the use of ***natural lighting*** from either skylights or windows and light colors on reflective surfaces like ceilings, walls, and floors. Windows have historically been eliminated from school sports medicine centers due to concerns about student-athletes' privacy. The sports medicine center, however, is not a locker room. All athletes should be dressed appropriately when entering the facility, and all athletes should be draped appropriately when receiving treatment.

natural lighting *Outside light used to illuminate indoor spaces, usually through windows or skylights.*

Specialized Function Areas

Seven specialized function areas are common to most sports medicine facilities: office, taping and bandaging, hydrotherapy, general treatment, rehabilitation, storage, and private examination (see Figure 5.11). Many factors determine how much space to devote to each of these functions, including the types and numbers of sports to be served, the number of athletes to be served, the qualifications and expertise of the sports medicine staff, the operational budget, and the type of client to be served.

Office

In most situations, the athletic trainer's office is located within the sports medicine facility. The athletic trainer's office should serve several purposes. First, it should be the central repository for all program records, including athletes' medical files (unless kept in an adjacent health service records room as previously discussed), budget information, correspondence, insurance information, product information, and educational materials for students and clients. The athletic trainer's office can also be used for private examinations and counseling if space is limited or unavailable. Finally, the office serves as an administrative work area for the athletic trainer.

Several design features are important for the athletic trainer's office. First, the athletic trainer should have a clear view of the entire sports medicine

▌**Figure 5.11** Specialized function areas of the sports medicine center.

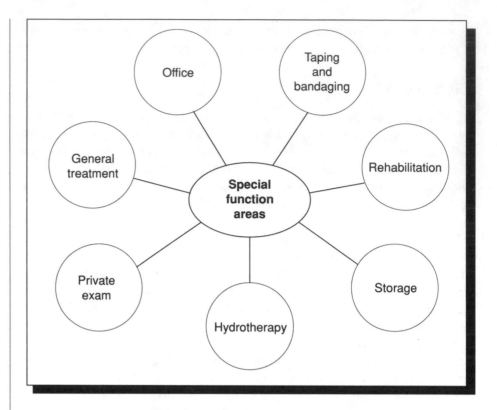

facility from the office—windows should allow supervision of activities at all times. If the office must also be used as a private examination and consultation room, it must be equipped with an exam table and blinds for the windows. Obviously, the office should contain a desk, filing cabinets, bookshelves, and a telephone with a line that is accessible without having to go through a building switchboard operator who may not be on duty after normal business hours. Another useful feature is an extra telephone line for data transfers from a computer. In institutions with centralized mainframe computer operations, a ***data port*** should be included as well. The office should also have enough comfortable seating to accommodate several people at one time for those occasions when the athletic trainer must consult with the athlete, parents, coaches, physicians, and others in groups.

data port *A dedicated phone line used to connect computers in different locations.*

Taping and Bandaging

In school-based sports medicine centers, the taping and bandaging section is often one of the busiest, especially just before practices and games. For this reason, athletic trainers designing school sports medicine centers should carefully consider the location and space devoted to this function. Private and hospital-based sports medicine clinics generally perform much less taping and bandaging in their facilities, so the area they devote to it is usually minimal.

Several design elements are important for a functional taping and bandaging area. First, it must include an adequate number of taping stations. Taping stations can be individual tables or large platforms designed to accommodate several athletes at one time (Cady, 1979). Whichever style is chosen, the taping table should be a minimum 36 in. high, although some athletic trainers will be better served by taping tables that are taller.

Another important design element of the taping and bandaging area is adequate counter space. The counter should have an easily cleaned surface like formica, be large enough to allow easy access for all athletic trainers working in the area, and offer electrical outlets every 4 ft. Although the traditional placement of the counter is along a wall, an attractive alternative is an island counter in the middle of the taping and bandaging area—the island provides taping stations on both sides, allowing easy access for twice as many athletic trainers. The taping and bandaging area should include cupboards and drawers with locks for secure short-term storage of supplies needed routinely. One way to save space in the taping and bandaging section is to combine taping stations with cupboards (Ribaric, 1980).

Finally, the type of floor covering to use in the taping and bandaging area can be a difficult problem. Both adhesive sprays and petroleum-based ointments can permanently stain carpeting and vinyl tile. For this reason, it may be wise to contract with a company that provides carpet runners for doorways and entrances. When the runners become soiled, the company will replace them with clean ones.

Hydrotherapy

The hydrotherapy section of the sports medicine center is the one specialized function area that should be physically separated because of water spills and the noisy turbines used to power whirlpool baths. The ideal design would include a glass enclosure around the area, containing the noise, heat, humidity, and accidental spilling or flooding while allowing the athletic trainer to monitor activities there from another section of the facility.

Besides the sloped floor and expandable plumbing mentioned earlier, athletic trainers should consider other important features when planning the hydrotherapy area. Adequate space should be allotted for all the center's equipment that uses water, including hydrotherapy tanks, steam pack units, ice machines, freezers, and paraffin baths. In school sports medicine centers, water coolers and portable ice chests are usually stored here as well. Although very expensive to construct, operate, and maintain, multistation submersed whirlpools and two-lane training pools can be included in hydrotherapy areas. If so, plans must also include filtration units and water heaters. The floor of the hydrotherapy area should be covered with ceramic tile similar to what would be found in a shower room or toilet area. The walls can be constructed from cinder block if they are painted with a high-gloss epoxy paint that can be easily cleaned.

General Treatment

The general treatment area usually contains a number of treatment tables and any electro-therapeutic equipment, requiring one of the largest space commitments. After determining how many treatment tables will be required (figuring 20 athletes per table per day), you can determine a square footage estimate for this area (see the formula provided previously).

Allow approximately 30 in. between tables for placing three-shelved carts with therapeutic modalities. Place an electrical outlet between each treatment table. Provide a fluorescent light immediately above each table, each with its own light switch. Make sure at least some of the treatment tables have sliding drapes for privacy during treatment. Some treatment tables should also be adjustable to elevate swollen extremities. Treatment tables can double as storage cabinets if you fit them with cupboards, drawers, or shelves.

Materials for walls and floor coverings for this area should be light colored and easy to clean. Vinyl tile works well for this purpose, but it is slippery when wet. Carpet is difficult to clean, but it provides a warmer, more quiet atmosphere.

Rehabilitation

In most athletic training settings, the rehabilitation area is another section that requires a great deal of space—it may take up the majority of the space in private and hospital sports medicine clinics. A few commonly used pieces of equipment to rehabilitate injured athletes—isokinetic equipment, treatment and exercise tables, treadmills, upper and lower extremity ergometers, stair climbers, and isotonic weight machines—can easily fill a large area. In addition to the equipment, adequate "dead space" must be provided between exercise stations for safety purposes.

The location of the rehabilitation section is somewhat controversial. Most athletic trainers agree that it should not occupy the same space as the treatment or taping functions. Many athletic trainers have moved the rehabilitation function to a general-purpose weight-training facility. Although this has some advantages, exposing unsupervised athletes to expensive and potentially harmful devices, such as a Cybex or Biodex, is probably unwise. The best arrangement gives the rehabilitation area its own room within the confines of the sports medicine center, especially if the institution's weight-training facility is nearby in the same building. This scheme allows for careful, supervised rehabilitation of injured athletes while still maintaining a quiet atmosphere in the general treatment area. When rehabilitating athletes are ready to advance to heavier weights and general-purpose strengthening devices, they can go to the weight room.

As in the athletic trainer's office, the best alternative for floor coverings in the rehabilitation center may be carpeting. If dumbbells or other free weights are used, a carpeted floor will absorb the shock and noise of dropped equipment more effectively. If the rehabilitation room is located anywhere other than the ground floor, the architect may need to reinforce the floor to support heavy equipment.

Walls should be constructed of a material that allows insertion of hooks and screws because many of the rehabilitation tools may be stored by hanging them on the wall. A full-length mirror is also useful to give athletes visual feedback when performing rehabilitation exercises.

Storage

The storage section of the sports medicine center is commonly overlooked, perhaps because, calculated on a service delivery per square foot basis, storage rooms are expensive to construct. Given the cost, storage rooms should have several important features. First, the storage room should be located within the sports medicine center itself if at all possible. In addition, the closer the storage room is to the taping and bandaging section, the more convenient it will be for the athletic trainer to restock depleted expendable supplies. The storage room must be cool and dry at all times. Many expendable supplies commonly used in sports medicine, especially adhesive tape, deteriorate in warm, humid environments. Obviously, the storage room should be outfitted with plenty of shelves and cupboards. Finally, access to the storage room should be strictly controlled in order to prevent unauthorized removal of supplies.

Private Examination

Many occasions in sports medicine call for private examination of an injured client to preserve modesty or provide a calmer environment for the exam. Although the private examination area of the sports medicine center does not need to be large, it should provide a comfortable environment for the client and the athletic trainer or physician. Private examination rooms should include an examination table, a mobile lamp, a sink for washing hands, and a counter and cupboards to hold commonly needed supplies. Any supplies or equipment frequently used by the team physician should be readily available in the private examination room, as should appropriate gowns and drapes for clients. As already mentioned, the private examination room can be combined with the office if necessary.

■ Applications to Athletic Training: Theory Into Practice

Use the following two case studies to help apply the concepts in this chapter to real-life situations. The questions at the end of the studies have many possible correct solutions. The case studies can be used in class discussion or for homework or test questions.

CASE STUDY 1

Deanna Walsh is the athletic trainer for a large Wisconsin high school that offers 20 sports for 750 student-athletes. The voters of the school district have recently approved a bond issue to build a new, $30 million high school. Deanna was asked by the planning committee to meet with the architect to discuss her ideas for the new training room. Prior to the meeting, Deanna carefully considered the features she wanted to see incorporated into the new facility. She drew a sketch of the layout she desired, and she made a list of all the design features she wanted, including

- *total size of 2,500 square feet;*
- *separate but connected rooms for taping, treatment, rehabilitation, office, storage, and private examination;*
- *a "hanging" ceiling with acoustical tiles to reduce noise;*
- *one treatment and taping table for every 10 athletes she would have to service during peak service hours;*

- *floor coverings of vinyl tile for the taping, treatment, and storage areas; ceramic tile for the hydrotherapy area; and carpeting for the office and private examination room;*

- *air conditioning with separate thermostats for each of the six rooms.*

After considering Deanna's suggestions and attempting to incorporate them into the overall design of the athletic and physical education portion of the building, the architect informed her that the new sports medicine center was too expensive as proposed and its cost would have to be reduced by one third.

QUESTIONS FOR ANALYSIS

1. Did Deanna employ the proper planning process when developing her ideas for the new training room? What should she have done differently? How could she build a stronger case for her ideas?

2. What additional features should be included in Deanna's list? How can these features be justified?

3. Which features should Deanna modify or eliminate in order to meet the architect's requirement?

4. Place yourself in Deanna's position and produce your own schematic drawing of the training room you would propose for the new high school. Justify each of the features you would include.

CASE STUDY 2

Russ Emmons, A.T.,C./P.T. operates a successful 7-year-old physical therapy and sports medicine practice. His caseload had nearly doubled when three new orthopedic surgeons moved into town a couple years ago. When the local high school proposed a contractual relationship in which Russ would provide athletic training services for a fee plus referrals, he decided the time had come to expand out of his rented, cramped facility into his own building.

Russ consulted a friend who had recently built an auto parts store for advice about hiring an architect. "I know just the architect you want," his friend told him. "He did a great job for me and I'm sure you'll like him."

Russ decided to take his friend's advice, and he made an appointment to see the architect. When they finally met a couple of weeks later, Russ was pleased with his friend's advice. The architect listened carefully to Russ' ideas and offered many helpful suggestions Russ had not considered. Toward the end of the meeting Russ asked the architect about how he should go about locating a contractor to build the new clinic. "You wouldn't necessarily have to find anyone," the architect replied. "My firm could coordinate the construction internally. You'd only have to deal with one person and we could probably speed the whole construction process up quite a bit." Russ decided he liked the idea and several weeks later, after reviewing the project with his attorney and a loan officer from the bank, he signed a design/build contract with the architect's firm.

1. What advantages will Russ have in owning his building? What disadvantages?

2. Did Russ make any mistakes in hiring an architect? What could he have done to avoid those mistakes?

3. Russ chose to use the design/build model for developing his new building. Was this a wise decision? What kinds of problems is he likely to encounter? What advantages will he realize?

4. What factors should Russ consider in the location of his new practice?

∎ Summary

The design and construction of new sports medicine facilities is an infrequent but expensive and important role of the athletic trainer. The design stage of such projects is when trainers can exert the greatest influence over the final product. Mistakes during the design phase will increase the facility's cost or decrease its function. Most athletic trainers will work with planning committees consisting of program specialists and high-level administrators to design the sports medicine center. The design process involves ten steps: assessing needs, approving the project, selecting a construction model, selecting an architect, developing schematic drawings, securing funding, bidding the construction, analyzing bids and reacting to them, commencing construction, and monitoring construction.

Seven factors must be considered in the design of the sports medicine center: size, location, electrical systems, plumbing systems, ventilation systems, lighting, and specialized function areas. The specialized function areas of most sports medicine facilities will include separate space for an office, taping and bandaging, rehabilitation, general treatment, hydrotherapy, storage, and private examination of patients.

∎ Annotated Bibliography

Arnheim, D.D., & Prentice, W.E. (1993). *Modern principles of athletic training* (8th ed.). St. Louis: Mosby Year Book.

This is the classic text of introductory athletic training. Arnheim and Prentice cover several important sports medicine facility design issues in chapter 26 ("Organizational and Administrative Considerations").

Biehle, J.T. (1982). Construction costs and the "oh my gosh!" syndrome. *American School and University*, **54**, C10-C14.

This article discusses the advantages of the construction management model and provides a case study to demonstrate its effectiveness as a method for controlling construction costs.

Cady, C. (1979). A space saving taping table. *Athletic Training*, **14**(4), 224.

Cady has designed a taping station that accommodates four athletes, but uses only as much room as two conventional taping tables.

Cohen, A., & Cohen, E. (1979). *Designing and space planning for libraries.* New York: Bowker.

Although written for librarians, this book contains some excellent basic design concepts that can easily be transferred to the sports medicine setting. Chapters 4 and 5 are especially useful. Chapter 4 describes the relationships between owners, users, designers, and contractors. Chapter 5 contains excellent information on how to utilize space most effectively.

Dibner, D.R. (1982). *You and your architect.* Washington, DC: The American Institute of Architects.

This 16-page pamphlet is an excellent source of information for anyone who has not been involved with a construction project. Dibner describes in simple terms the processes involved with planning and constructing a new building and provides guidelines to help users understand the role the architect plays. He also includes a list of standard forms commonly used to confirm agreements between clients, architects, and contractors. This is a very important reference for any athletic trainer who will be involved in designing or constructing a new sports medicine facility.

Directory of architects. (1992). *Athletic Business,* **16**(6), 108-109.

The architects listed in this directory designed recreational and athletic facilities that have been listed among the top 45 in the nation by *Athletic Business.* Some of the facilities contain outstanding examples of sports medicine center design.

Dougherty, N.J., & Bonanno, D. (1985). *Management service in sport and leisure services.* Minneapolis, MN: Burgess International.

Chapter 7 ("Facility Development and Management") should be of particular interest to the athletic trainer. The chapter outlines a basic needs assessment procedure and takes the reader through the more important elements of the design and construction process.

Fahey, T.D. (1986). *Athletic training: Principles and practice.* Palo Alto, CA: Mayfield.

Fahey's text is a general introduction for the athletic training student. Chapter 2 ("The Athletic Training Room") offers useful suggestions for the design of school sports medicine facilities.

Fletcher, M.E., & Ranck, S.L. (1991). Building a committee. *Athletic Business,* **15**(8), 49-50.

Fletcher and Ranck suggest useful ways for tapping into the most important groups for planning committee members when designing a campus athletic or recreation facility.

Forseth, E.A. (1986). Consideration in planning small college athletic training facilities. *Athletic Training,* **21**(1), 22-25.

This article is one of the very few references that deal specifically with designing sports medicine facilities. Forseth offers a useful starting point for athletic trainers who will be involved in the construction of a new facility.

Muther, R., & Wheeler, J.D. (1973). *Simplified systematic layout planning*. Kansas City, MO: Management & Industrial Research Publications.

This book is written for both layout engineers and nonprofessionals who will be involved with design of new facilities. Although the information is old, Muther's method is simple to use and appeals to common sense.

Penman, K.A. (1977). *Planning physical education and athletic facilities in schools*. New York: Wiley & Sons.

Chapter 18 of this book presents design considerations for the school training room. Although much of the information will appear to be outdated, the book provides some good suggestions for athletic trainers considering the design of the sports medicine center.

Penman, K.A., & Penman, T.M. (1982). Training rooms aren't just for colleges. *Athletic Purchasing and Facilities*, **6**(9), 34-37.

This article highlights the major features to be considered in planning a high school athletic training facility.

Planning facilities for athletics, physical education, and recreation. (1979). North Palm Beach, FL: The Athletic Institute.

This text provides general advice to those contemplating the construction of a school athletic or physical education facility. Chapter 6 ("Service Areas") is devoted to design concerns about locker rooms, equipment rooms, and the school sports medicine center.

Porter, M.M., & Porter, J.W. (1981). Electrical safety in the training room. *Athletic Training*, **16**(4), 263-264.

This article outlines the basic functions of the ground fault interrupter and the role it plays in safeguarding against accidental electrocution in sports medicine settings.

Ribaric, R.F. (1980). Taping/storage table. *Athletic Training*, **15**(1), 50.

Ribaric has designed a combination taping table/storage cabinet that saves both money and space.

Secor, M.R. (1984). Designing athletic training facilities or "Where do you want the outlets?" *Athletic Training*, **19**(1), 19-21.

Although most of the suggestions in this useful article are self-evident, they are good reminders when developing the initial drawings for a new sports medicine center.

Snider, S.W. (1982, January). Planning a new building? Consider design/build. *Athletic Purchasing and Facilities*, pp. 50-51.

The author delineates the advantages and disadvantages of using the design/build method of construction and uses a case study from a YMCA to illustrate.

Theunissen, W. (1978). Planning facilities: The role of the program specialist. *Journal of Physical Education and Recreation*, **49**(6), 27-29.

Theunissen does a good job of explaining the broad concepts of physical education and recreation facility design. He emphasizes using the program specialist to assist the architect and other design and construction consultants in designing the facility.

CHAPTER 6

"The newest computer can only compound, at speed, the oldest problem in the relations between human beings, and in the end the communicator will be confronted with the old problem of what to say and how to say it."

Edward R. Murrow

Helping Athletic Trainers Remember: Information Management

STUDENT OBJECTIVES

▌ Understand the importance of documentation as part of a complete information management system in sports medicine.

▌ Understand and be able to describe the different methods of athletic injury and treatment documentation.

▌ Understand and describe the different types of information to be managed in a typical sports medicine program.

▌ Implement a system for organizing information in a sports medicine program.

▌ Understand how a computer could be used in the sports medicine information management process.

OPENING CASE

Karen Thompson is the certified athletic trainer at Central City High School in addition to having a three-fifths appointment as a physical education and biology teacher. Two months ago she had requested a computer for the school's training room as part of a large grant proposal by the school district entitled "Computers Across the Curriculum." She hoped a computer would help her with record keeping. Because she was the only athletic trainer at the school and had to spend most of her time taking care of injured student-athletes, she usually had to take paperwork home with her in the evening to keep up.

One day in September, after teaching her classes, Karen discovered several large boxes on a treatment table in the training room. Her computer had arrived! Since student-athletes were already starting to line up for taping and treatment, Karen moved the boxes to the corner of the room that doubled as her office. "Now that I finally have the equipment," she told herself, "I can start to think about how I can use it to improve our record-keeping system."

A week later the boxes were still there. When Karen called the school district's business manager to inquire about setup and training he informed her that only the equipment was covered by the grant. He suggested she consult with some of her colleagues if she had questions or problems. Karen had never worked with a computer before, so she was sure she was going to have more than a few of each.

Like many athletic trainers, Karen Thompson perceives her primary mission as providing high-quality health care to injured student-athletes. Her frustration is not due to having to meticulously document the care she administers, but rather to what she believes to be an excessive shift away from patient care to documentation for its own sake. Her view of the computer as a solution to her information management problems, whether valid or not, is common.

This chapter will provide athletic trainers with the basics about information management in the athletic health care setting. We are working in an information society. Over the last century our culture has moved from its agricultural base, through a period of industrial revolution, into the information age. In the United States, approximately half of all workers are employed in jobs that involve accumulating and transferring information (Synnott & Gruber, 1981). Athletic trainers will increasingly be expected to be effective managers of information.

As health care professionals, we do not have the luxury of deciding whether or not we will manage information. The question is not "Will I choose to manage information and communicate effectively?" but rather, "What skills and tools do I need to manage information and communicate effectively?" For many reasons, athletic trainers are expected to document every patient care activity and the response to it. Trainers must gather and disseminate the information necessary to accomplish a number of goals, including improvement of patient care, professional development, and improvement in education and counseling. Finally, athletic trainers are increasingly expected to be competent leaders for the sports medicine programs in their institutions. Athletic trainers who lack the information management skills to assume these leadership positions will quickly become frustrated. Their jobs, like Karen Thompson's, are likely to be characterized more by problems than by creative solutions.

■ Why Document?

Although documentation is only one of the information management tasks that athletic trainers must accomplish, it is common to all employment settings. Why is this skill so important? Why should busy athletic trainers concern themselves as much as they do with this task? There are many reasons.

Legal Protection

Medical documentation helps protect the legal rights of both the athlete and the athletic trainer by providing a written record of the care provided by the athletic trainer. Medical records are often the only defense athletic trainers have in legal actions taken by aggrieved athletes. The old adage ''If it isn't written down, it didn't happen'' is an increasingly appropriate guiding principle for all athletic trainers (Hawkins, 1989).

Memory Aid

Medical documentation acts as a memory aid for athletic trainers and other professionals involved in the care of the injured athlete. Human memory is a poor substitute for accurately recording medical facts, especially because an athlete's medical record may not need to be referred to for months or even years.

Legal Requirement

Medical documentation is, in many cases, required by law. For example, athletic trainers in professional sports are required to document player injuries for the Occupational Safety and Health Administration (OSHA). Athletic trainers in several different practice settings may be required to provide medical documentation for legally mandated workers' compensation insurance.

Professional Standards

Medical documentation is required to meet professional *standards of practice*. The National Athletic Trainers Association (1987) requires documentation of physician referral, initial evaluation and assessment, treatments, and dates of follow-up care for all athletes cared for in a ''service program'' typical of most educational settings. The requirements for athletic trainers

standards of practice
Widely accepted principles intended to guide the professional activities of a health care practitioner.

working in "direct service" programs, typically in sports medicine clinics, are more rigorous. In addition to meeting the service program standards, the athletic trainer in this setting must provide a program plan with estimated length, methods, results, and revisions and a discontinuation or discharge assessment and summary. Other professional organizations have other documentation standards. For example, the Joint Commission on Accreditation of Healthcare Organizations publishes minimum standards for health care documentation that apply to athletic trainers who work in hospitals and similar health care institutions (Marrelli, 1992).

Improved Communications

Medical documentation improves the quality of communication between the various professionals involved with the athlete's case (Kettenbach, 1990). Often, the only communication the athletic trainer has with the team or family physician is in writing. If the quality of the documentation is poor, either in content or writing style, misunderstandings could result between athletic trainer and physician.

Insurance Requirements

Reimbursement decisions by third-party payers, such as insurance companies and health maintenance organizations, are based on medical documentation. This rationale is especially relevant for private or hospital-based sports medicine clinics, but it can also be important in professional, high school, and college sports medicine programs.

Discharge Decisions

Medical documentation should be part of the basis for deciding when to discharge an athlete from the athletic trainer's care (Kettenbach, 1990). The medical record should act as a map to guide a reader unfamiliar with the case through the entire injury, treatment, and rehabilitation process. The reader, whether a physician, athletic trainer, or physical therapist, should be able to determine whether the athlete is ready to be discharged from reading the record.

Improved Care

When properly organized, medical documentation should help direct the athletic trainer to deliver better care. Well-written and well-organized medical documentation should be used as a tool for problem solving in difficult cases.

Medical documentation forms the raw material for program quality assessment. Setting both short-term and long-term goals should be part of every injured athlete's care. If the medical record shows care inconsistent with these goals, athletic trainers should be concerned that injured athletes are being discharged without receiving all the care they need to function competitively.

■ Two Kinds of Information in Sports Medicine

Information in sports medicine can be divided into two broad categories: medical records and program administration records. The two types of records are separate entities, and with a few exceptions there should be little overlap between them.

Medical Records

An athlete's medical record is a written outline of the athlete's health history during the time the athlete was under the athletic trainer's care. ***Medical records*** are patient-specific, and the only data that should be included is directly related to a specific athlete's health. Information not related to health, such as news clippings and academic information, has no place in the medical record and should be stored elsewhere. Marrelli (1992) recommends the following guidelines:

- *Write legibly or print neatly. The record must be readable.*
- *Use permanent ink (appropriate ink color may depend on hospital policy).*
- *For every entry, identify the time and date, sign it, and provide your title.*
- *Describe the care provided and the patient's response.*
- *Describe findings objectively (e.g., in terms of behaviors).*
- *Write entries in consecutive and chronological order with no skipped lines or gaps.*
- *Write entries as soon as possible after care is provided.*
- *Be factual and specific.*
- *Use patient (or family or caregiver) quotes.*
- *Document patient complaints or needs and their resolution.*
- *Write out what you are saying, avoiding potentially confusing abbreviations.*
- *Chart only the care you provided.*
- *Promptly document a change in the patient's condition and the actions taken based on that change.*
- *Write the patient's, family's, or caregiver's response to teaching. (pp. 11-12)*

Finally, Schneller and Godwin (1983) recommend that you not erase errors. Instead, draw a line through the error, enter the proper information next to the error, and date and initial the correction.

Examples of the different types of information contained in the medical record follow.

Physical Examination Forms

The athlete's physical examination results should come first in the medical record. Not only does the physical exam normally occur first chronologically,

medical record *Cumulative documentation of a person's medical history and health care interventions.*

the results can be a quick reference for athletic trainers or physicians. Some states mandate the use of specific physical examination forms for high school student-athletes. In other states and settings trainers can choose from a wide variety of forms. The form chosen should ask for the following information (see Figure 6.1):

- Personal data (name, address, date of birth, etc.)
- Health history questionnaire
- Vital signs
- Physician's review of systems
- Special procedures (blood and urine analysis, x-rays, echocardiograms, etc.)
- Functional tests (joint strength, aerobic capacity, etc.)

▌ Results of physical examination special tests become an important part of the medical record.

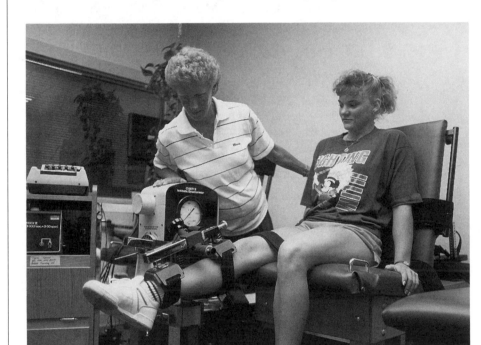

Injury Evaluation and Treatment Forms

Injury evaluation and treatment records should provide a concise record of the athlete's progress from time of injury until time of discharge. These forms often constitute the bulk of the athlete's medical record. Although many athletic trainers maintain separate records of injury evaluations and treatments, each treatment should be easily linked to a documented injury.

Athletic trainers can choose from five different methods for documenting injury evaluation and treatment data: problem-oriented medical records, focus charting, charting by exception, computerized documentation, and narrative charting.

problem-oriented medical record (POMR) *A system of medical record keeping that organizes information around a patient's specific complaints.*

Problem-Oriented Medical Record (POMR): The ***problem-oriented medical record*** (POMR) is a system of medical record keeping that organizes

HOPE COLLEGE HEALTH CLINIC
ATHLETIC PHYSICAL EXAMINATION SUMMARY

1. Name _____ (M or F) _____ Age _____ Date _____

2. S.S. # _____   Year in school   Fr   So   Jr   Sr

Sport _____

MEDICAL HISTORY SURVEY

3. Do you have now or have you had in the past, problems with:	YES	NO
a - Headaches - needing treatment		
b - Heart		
c - Breathing, e. g. - asthma		
d - Abdominal pain		
e - Dizzy spells		
f - Black outs		
g - Eyes (except glasses)		
h - Hearing or ears		
i - Arthritis		
j - Joint pain or swelling		
k - Knees - injury, giving out, swelling		
l - Spine - back or neck		
m - Broken bones		
n - Kidneys		
o - Bladder		
p - Diabetes		
q - High blood pressure		
r - Cancer		
s - Operations or surgery		
t - Varicose veins		
u - Skin disorders		
v - Other major injuries		
w - Drug allergies		
x - Eating disorder		

4. If you answered yes to any of #3 - give details below — Identify by letter.

5. Have you ever been knocked unconscious?   Yes ___ No ___
If yes, explain:

6. Have you ever had a cervical spine injury?   Yes ___ No ___
If yes, explain:

7. Do you have any permanent handicap or disability?   Yes ___ No ___
If yes, explain:

8. Are you under a physicians care at the present time?   Yes ___ No ___
If yes, explain:

9. Are you taking any medications or drugs at the present time?
Yes ___ No ___   Give details:

10. Year of last Tetanus. _____

11. Women — Do you have a monthly menstrual period?   Yes ___ No ___
Date of last period. _____   If no, explain

12. Do you have an intense fear of gaining weight?   Yes ___ No ___

(FOR EXAMINING PHYSICIAN ONLY)

13. Eyes:

Rt. Eye _____   Lt. Eye _____

14. General Information:

Ht. _____ Wt. _____ B/P _____ Pulse _____

Examination	Normal	Abnormal
15. Head		
16. Eyes		
17. Nose & Throat		
18. Ears		
19. Neck		
20. Lungs		
21. Heart		
22. Abdomen		
23. Hernia		
24. G - U		
25. Extremity		
26. Shoulders		
27. Knees		
28. Other:		
29. Nervous		
30. Knee Laxity		

31. Rt. _____ MCL _____ LCL _____ ACL _____ PCL _____

Lt. _____ MCL _____ LCL _____ ACL _____ PCL _____

PHYSICIAN'S STATEMENT

32. Approved for sports   Yes ___ No ___

33. Approved pending further study
Explain:

34. Approved with limitations
Explain:

35. Disapproved comments:

36. Date _____

Signature _____

White copy to Health Center, yellow copy to P.E. Dept.

Figure 6.1   Sample of a physical examination form. Reprinted by permission of the Hope College Health Clinic.

information around the athlete's specific complaint (Berni & Readey, 1978). Its greatest contribution for sports medicine settings is the **SOAP note** (see Figure 6.2). SOAP is an acronym for the following documentation parameters:

S   *Subjective evaluation of the athlete's problem. The subjective portion relates how the athlete conveys symptoms. It would include recording the athlete's statement that ". . . my right knee popped and gave out."*

O   *Objective evaluation of the athlete's problem. The objective portion of the evaluation includes physical data actually observed by the athletic trainer during evaluation. It would relate information such as the presence of intraarticular effusion, 2+ Lachmann sign, and AROM $\downarrow$ 15 degrees in extension.*

A   *Assessment of the athlete's problem. Assessment is the athletic trainer's judgment of the nature of the problem based on the subjective and objective evidence. Using the same knee injury case, a reasonable assessment of the problem would be internal derangement of the right knee with probable anterior cruciate ligament disruption.*

P   *Plan refers to the course of action the athletic trainer will implement to resolve the problem. Statements of both short-term and long-term goals for the athlete should be included for quality assurance.*

Focus Charting: *Focus charting* is a less cumbersome alternative to the POMR medical record keeping method (Iyer, 1991). Typical focus charting forms list pertinent *data* about the athlete's injury in the first column, describe the *action* the athletic trainer will take in response in the second column, and present the *response* to the athletic trainer's action plan in the third column (see Figure 6.3). As in all other forms of medical charting, each entry should be signed and dated, and time notations should be entered if appropriate.

Charting by Exception: *Charting by exception*, as its name implies, is a method in which only athlete responses that vary from predefined norms are noted on the record (Murphy & Burke, 1990). This method makes record keeping more efficient and less time consuming. Although charting by exception is obviously inappropriate for recording initial injury evaluation, it has many potential uses for recording treatments and rehabilitation. The use of this method, however, requires maintaining tightly controlled and frequently monitored treatment protocols.

Computerized Documentation: The use of computers for keeping sports medicine records was described as early as 1982 (Abdenour, 1982), and the products available to athletic trainers have been increasing in number and utility ever since. As the quality of microcomputers has increased and their price decreased, athletic trainers have gradually shifted from using large, centralized mainframe computers toward using stand-alone and networked microcomputers.

Individual Injury Evaluation and Treatment Record

Name _____ Sport _____ Body part _____

Date injury occurred _____ Date injury reported _____ New _____ Old _____

Primary complaint _____ Secondary complaint _____

Subjective evaluation:

Objective evaluation:

Assessment:

Plan:

Evaluator's initials _____

Date	Treatments and progress

▮ **Figure 6.2** Sample evaluation and treatment form using SOAP note format.

Athletic trainers see computerized record keeping as a way to decrease time spent documenting athletic injuries and treatments and thereby increasing time available for hands-on care of injured athletes. But the switch to a computerized system of medical record keeping will probably result in an initial *increase* in time spent on record keeping. It will take time to train athletic trainers to use the computer. In addition, record keeping and procedural changes will probably have to be made in order to adapt to the new technology.

Another potential problem is maintaining the confidentiality of computerized records. It is more difficult to safeguard digitally stored data than data on paper in locked file cabinets. The use of passwords can sometimes slow unauthorized retrieval of medical records but it is very difficult to effectively thwart a motivated computer hacker.

Sports Medicine Focus Chart			
Name:		Sport:	
Date	Data	Action	Response

Figure 6.3 Sample focus chart for use in recording injuries (data), treatments (action), and progress (response).

Finally, depending on the limitations of the computer software, computerized record keeping can limit the athletic trainer's flexibility in describing the case as fully as desired.

Nevertheless, athletic trainers should welcome the computer as a tool for effective and efficient medical record keeping in sports medicine. Computers allow athletic trainers to retrieve only those parts of the medical record desired for a specific purpose—trainers no longer need to physically search through a hundred-page medical record for a single entry. Nonprofessionals or students can perform some of the data entry, freeing the athletic trainer to spend more time with injured athletes. Athletic trainers can pull information from many individual medical records for writing reports. This feature allows them to prepare year-end injury and treatment summaries that used to take weeks in much less time. Later in this chapter I'll discuss different computerized medical record-keeping applications for sports medicine.

Narrative Charting: *Narrative charting* involves a more lengthy prose entry into the athlete's medical record. This is the most traditional method of medical record keeping. Athletic trainers make entries in paragraph form preceded by the date and time of the entry, relying very little on abbreviations or medical shorthand (see Figure 6.4). *Dictation* is useful in narrative record keeping. Although clerical transcription can be expensive, dictation can significantly reduce the amount of time required to document injuries, treatments, and progress notes. Dictation, like writing, is a skill that takes practice to perfect. The following suggestions will help improve the effectiveness of dictation:

- Organize the data to be dictated by taking notes in medical shorthand while interviewing the injured athlete. Use these notes to dictate a more comprehensive entry into the medical record.
- Speak clearly and slowly into the dictation machine. If possible, avoid dictating in a noisy room.
- Spell all proper names and medical terms that are used infrequently. This is especially important if the transcriber is inexperienced in medical transcription. Consider providing a medical dictionary to your transcriber.
- Review and initial all dictated narrations prior to filing them in the medical record.

Reports of Special Procedures

Include reports of all special procedures in the athlete's medical record. Although you should enter special procedure reports into the medical record

narrative charting A method of recording the details of a patient's assessments and treatments using a detailed prose format.

dictation The act of verbally recording, usually on a cassette tape, the details of a health care assessment or treatment for later transcription and filing.

Smith, Jon

April 7, 1992

Jon is a sprinter on the school's track team. He came in today to be evaluated for pain that he has been experiencing in his anterior shins for the past three weeks. He has been icing his shins prior to and after every track practice in order to relieve the pain, but the problem has progressed to the point where it is very uncomfortable to run. He also experiences some pain when he walks. He has some pain while laying in bed at night. The pain is a dull ache unless the anterior shin is touched when it becomes a sharp pain.

Visual examination is unspectacular. No swelling, discoloration, or deformity is noted. Palpation reveals point specific tenderness over the anterior surface of the distal one-third of both tibias. A mild elevation in local temperature is palpable. No crepitus is noted. The gastroc and soleus are both tight bilaterally, allowing only six degrees of passive dorsiflexion.

It is my impression that Jon may be suffering from bilateral tibial stress fractures. Jon is a member of an HMO and his physician while he is in college is Dr. Van Notten. I called Dr. Van Notten this morning to discuss Jon's case and was instructed to obtain a bone scan of Jon's tibias bilaterally. Jon is scheduled for the bone scan at Holland Community Hospital tomorrow morning at 9:30. He will be kept out of practice until Dr. Van Notten reviews the bone scan. He was placed on crutches and instructed to apply ice to his shins for 20 minutes every 2 hours while awake. He was told to return to the training room tomorrow after his bone scan.

Signed: Lydia Sanchez, A.T., C.

Figure 6.4 Example of the narrative charting method of injury documentation.

chronologically, annotate each to refer the reader back to an initial injury or illness assessment report. Special procedures include, but are not limited to the following:

- Isokinetic strength tests
- Blood tests
- Urinalysis
- X rays or other imaging procedures
- Surgical reports
- Cardiac assessments (echocardiogram, graded exercise tests, thallium uptake scans, etc.)

Communication From Other Professionals

You will commonly receive written documentation of an athlete's medical status from physicians, physical therapists, and other health care professionals involved with the injured athlete's case. One type of documentation is the referral form (Gabriel, 1981) sent with an injured athlete when he or she is sent to the physician's office or the emergency room (see Figure 6.5). The injured athlete referral form provides legally defensible proof that the athletic trainer consulted with a physician as required by the standards of professional practice and, in many states, by law. In addition, it improves communication between the athletic trainer and the physician by taking the burden of having to relay information off the injured athlete.

The referral form should include the athlete's name, sport, injury date, and appointment date and time. It should allow space for the athletic trainer to document the initial evaluation findings. Finally, it should provide space for the physician to write a diagnosis and orders for treatment or rehabilitation. The athletic trainer's and the physician's notes should be dated and signed.

Trainers can ensure that referral forms are returned in three ways. The most obvious is to ask the injured athlete to bring the form back at the next appointment. Trainers can ask the physician to mail the form back, but this method delays direct feedback from the physician. Finally, the athletic trainer could ask the physician to fax a response, which provides the information quickly and avoids the possibility of the athlete losing or forgetting the form.

A second method for communicating with other health care professionals is via the common professional courtesy of sending letters or copies of office notes to referring health care colleagues. Athletic trainers should enter these notes, often a useful source of information and documentation of the injured athlete's status, into the athlete's medical record. Athletic trainers should request a letter from all physicians and other health care professionals to whom they frequently refer injured athletes.

Emergency Information

Athletic trainers in high schools and colleges are frequently required to contact an injured student-athlete's parents or guardians, an urgent responsibility if the athlete has a serious accident or illness. To do so, the athletic trainer usually uses the emergency information form in the medical record

---

Sports Medicine Medical Referral

Name _____ Sport _____

Date _____ Time _____ Physician _____

Athletic trainer's impression _____

_____

_____

_____

Physician diagnosis & recommendation _____

_____

_____

_____

Recommended activity level (check all that apply):

      bedrest _____

      attend classes only _____

      no practice or competition _____

      limited physical activity as noted above _____

      practice as able _____

      no restrictions _____

Follow up appointment: _____ _____
                        Date   Time

_____
           Physician signature

Please instruct the athlete to return this form to the training room.

▌ Figure 6.5   Sample medical referral form.

(see Figure 6.6). This form should include athlete information, such as name, address, phone numbers, date of birth, and social security or student identification numbers. It should also include parents' names, addresses, and telephone numbers (home and business). Some athletic trainers have suggested that the form should contain the athlete's insurance information as well (Miles, 1987). This form should be readily accessible in the medical record, perhaps affixed to the inside cover of the athlete's folder. Emergency information forms could also be organized according to sport and placed in three-ring binders that teams can take with them wherever they go.

Permission to Provide Medical Treatment Forms

A widely recognized legal principle is that persons (or their parents in the case of minors) must consent to medical treatment. Any consent forms should

---

Emergency Information

Name _____   Sport _____

Date of birth _____   Address: _____

Phone: _____   _____

Parents' names: _____

Person to contact in an emergency: _____

   Relationship: _____   Phone: _____

Name of insurance company: _____

Policy numbers: _____

Is this insurance company a health maintenance organization (HMO)?   Yes _____   No _____

If so, list the HMO telephone number: _____

▌ **Figure 6.6**   Sample emergency information form. *Note.* From "Injuries on the Road: Good Information Reduces Problems" by B.J. Miles, 1987, *Journal of Athletic Training*, **22**, p. 127. Copyright 1987 by National Athletic Trainers Association. Adapted by permission.

be maintained in the athlete's medical record (see Figure 6.7). Although the use of such forms has been standard operating procedure in most hospital sports medicine programs, their use in school-based settings has been limited. Consent forms are especially important in the high school setting because most of these injured student-athletes are still minors.

Permission to Provide Medical Treatment Agreement

I HEREBY give my permission for my son/daughter, _____,
to undergo medical treatment for any injury or illness he/she may sustain or acquire while engaged in inter-scholastic athletics at Eagletown High School. I understand that the medical personnel of Eagletown High School, including athletic trainers, nurses, and team physicians will perform only those procedures which are within their training, credentialing, and scope of professional practice to prevent, care for, and rehabilitate athletic injuries. In the event that more serious medical procedures are required, such as surgery or other invasive procedures, I understand that attempts will be made to contact me for my consent. I understand that if my child suffers a potentially life threatening injury or illness, and in the event I am unable to be contacted within a reasonable period of time, that I authorize any duly licensed medical practitioner to perform such procedures as may be medically necessary to alleviate the problem.

I have had the opportunity to ask questions regarding this release and all of my questions have been answered to my satisfaction. Having understood the above agreement, I freely sign this Permission to Provide Medical Treatment Agreement.

_____   _____
            Date   Signature of Parent or Legal Guardian

▌ **Figure 6.7**   Sample agreement form for the parents or guardians of minors to grant permission to provide medical treatment.

Along with permission forms, signed releases from athletes or their parents that waive all future legal claims against the athletic trainer or the employing institution are commonly used. These *exculpatory clauses*, with very few exceptions, are legally unsupportable (Herbert, 1987). The primary legal argument against them is that such clauses are contrary to public policy and are therefore legally invalid. Because the public has a vested interest in quality health care, the courts have been hesitant to allow negligent practitioners to hide behind prospective waivers. In addition, in many states, parents cannot ''sign away'' the rights of their children. Any athletic trainer planning to use a prospective waiver with exculpatory language should first have it thoroughly evaluated by an attorney and liability insurance carrier.

exculpatory clause Language in a formal agreement that releases one party from any liability associated with a particular activity, often before the activity takes place.

Release of Medical Information Forms

Another commonly understood legal principle is that the health care provider may not release an athlete's medical records without consent. Many parties will want access to the athlete's medical records, including coaches, the press, insurance companies, and professional sports organizations. Before providing information the athletic trainer should make certain the athlete has formally agreed to the release by signing a waiver. Then the trainer must be certain to release only the information authorized by the athlete. Each time an athlete's medical information is released, the medical release form should show the content, purpose, and receiver of the information (see Figure 6.8).

Insurance Information

Financial documents, such as patient invoices and insurance claim forms, are not medical records. They have different purposes and uses and are protected by the laws governing confidentiality in different ways. Insurance information contained in the medical record should be limited to the following (Glondys, 1988):

- Expected payer(s)
- Insured's name
- Patient's relationship to insured
- Employment data and insurance numbers

Correspondence with insurance companies and other third-party payers should be maintained separately from the medical record. Letters and copies of insurance forms often contain information directly related to the description of the injury circumstances. Copies of medical records used to document claims should not be maintained in the insurance folder—to protect confidentiality a note referring to the supporting portion of the medical record should be used. This method protects the confidentiality of the medical record by ensuring that unauthorized individuals do not gain access through the insurance claims process.

Program Administration Records

Much of the information athletic trainers are required to manage is administrative. Whereas medical records are specific to only one athlete, *program*

program administration records Documentation of the activities of a program.

Release of Medical Information Authorization

I, _____, DO / DO NOT give consent for the team physician, athletic trainer, or other medical personnel employed by _____ College to release such information regarding my medical history, record of injury or surgery, record of serious illness, and rehabilitation results as may be requested by either the representatives of any professional or amateur athletic organization seeking such information.

I understand that the representatives of a professional or amateur athletic organization have made representations to the team physician, athletic trainer, or other medical personnel employed by _____ College that the purpose of this request for my medical information is to assist the organization being represented in making a determination as to offering me employment.

I understand that a record will be kept of all individuals requesting information and the date of the request. This information is normally confidential and except as provided in this Release will not be otherwise released by the custodian of the information. This Release remains valid until revoked by me in writing.

I have had an opportunity to ask questions regarding this Release and the process by which my medical information may be released. All of my questions have been answered to my satisfaction. Having read and understood the above, I freely sign this Release of Medical Information Authorization.

_____   _____
Date   Signature of Student-Athlete

Medical Information Release Log for: _____

_____
Purpose of Release

_____   Information Released:
Person to Whom Information Was Released
                                                              _____

_____   _____
Organization   _____

_____   _____
Date   _____

_____   _____
Method of Delivery (phone, interview, etc.)

_____   _____
Released By   Signature of Student-Athlete

Medical Information Release Log for: _____

_____
Purpose of Release

_____   Information Released:
Person to Whom Information Was Released
                                                              _____

_____   _____
Organization   _____

_____   _____
Date   _____

_____   _____
Method of Delivery (phone, interview, etc.)

_____   _____
Released By   Signature of Student-Athlete

❚ **Figure 6.8**   Sample authorization form and log for release of medical information.

administration records are more general in nature and usually organized around subfunctions of the sports medicine program. The absolute standards for confidentiality that apply to medical records are usually, but not always, significantly relaxed for many types of program administration records. Whenever program administration records deal with specific individuals, however, confidentiality should be maintained. Examples of various types of program administration records follow.

Reports to Coaches

A common practice of most athletic trainers who work in professional, high school, and college settings is to provide coaches with daily written reports of the health status of their athletes (see Figure 6.9). Daily reports can help improve communication between the athletic trainer and the coach. Coaches appreciate timely information about the health status of their athletes because it allows them to plan more effectively. Another important benefit of the daily report to coaches is that athletic trainers can easily document recommendations for participation status. For example, assume that the athletic trainer recommends in the daily report that an athlete be limited to noncontact football drills because of a resolving neck injury. If the coach allows the athlete to participate in a full-contact scrimmage and the athlete is reinjured, the athletic trainer can at least document that he recommended a reduced activity level for the injured athlete.

Budget Information

Athletic trainers with financial authority must maintain accurate records of all financial transactions. In school, college, and professional settings, financial

---

Daily Coaches Report

Sport: Football   Date: October 14, 1993

Name	Injury	Date Injured	Date Reported	Comments
Smith, Tim	L-wrist/old fx. pain	10-12-93	10-12-93	seen by Dr. West
Funk, Roger	L-shldr. sublx	10-12-93	10-12-93	seen by Dr. West, rest
DeHaan, Dirk	R-AC contusion	10-12-93	10-13-93	treatment, seen by Dr. West
Russell, Bob	R-ankle sprain	10-12-93	10-13-93	treatment, rest
Fernandez, Scott	neck strain	10-12-93	10-13-93	seen by Dr. West, treatment, play as able
Jones, Rick	L-arm contusion	10-10-93	10-11-93	seen by Dr. West, rest

No participation	Play as able	Removed from list
Funk, Roger	Smith, Tim	Nick, Art
DeHaan, Dirk	Fernandez, Scott	Rios, Manny
Russell, Bob		
Jones, Rick		

▌ **Figure 6.9**   Example of a computer-generated daily coaches report.

reports usually include monthly budget statements (produced in-house or sent from the institutional business office), purchase orders, and invoices. Documents that support budgetary decisions, such as bids and ***requests for proposals*** (RFP) should also be maintained in the program administration record system.

Nonmedical Correspondence

Nonmedical correspondence is comprised of letters and memoranda not associated with a specific athlete's health status. Unlike medical correspondence, which must be meticulously recorded and preserved, much of the routine nonmedical correspondence can be discarded after action is taken. Nonmedical correspondence that must be retained should be filed under the appropriate subject heading and not in a separate folder labeled "correspondence."

Equipment and Supply Information

Equipment and supply inventories and catalogs from medical supply vendors are another kind of program administration record. Institutions often require administrative units to keep an inventory of nonexpendable capital equipment on file. This inventory usually includes the type of equipment, the amount or number of units, and the serial numbers. Some institutions assign their own identification numbers for nonexpendable equipment, which should also be included as part of this record. Athletic trainers in all settings are frequently called upon to purchase or recommend the purchase of sports medicine products. A well-organized file of appropriate catalogs can be useful.

Personnel Information

Information on sports medicine staff members' employment constitutes an important part of the program administration record-keeping system. Like an individual athlete's medical record, the personnel record is confidential and should only be accessed by those with a documented need for the information. Personnel information should be kept in a secure place, preferably a locked filing cabinet. Records on student athletic trainer performance should be treated similarly. Examples of the kinds of records normally associated with the personnel function include

- performance evaluation records;
- salary and promotion records;
- employment application information, including application forms, resumes, and letters of recommendation; and
- employment contracts.

Reporting Information

Athletic trainers are often held responsible for documenting the activities of the sports medicine program either for institutional or for outside accreditation purposes. The information required to compile such reports constitutes another aspect of the program administration record-keeping system. Documentation of patient caseloads and summaries of any special program accomplishments are often compiled in an annual report. Accreditation agencies will require access to different kinds of information, depending on their purpose. Hospital accreditation agencies generally will request summary statistics on patient outcomes and evidence of compliance with professional standards of practice. Agencies that accredit educational programs, such as the American Medical Association's Joint Review Committee for Educational Programs in Athletic Training, will require data related to student outcomes such as graduation, certification, and employment rates.

Another kind of reporting information is required by law to show compliance with the **OSHA Bloodborne Pathogen Standard**. Part 1910 of Title 29 of the Code of Federal Regulations requires that employers develop programs that protect employees, including athletic trainers, from occupational exposure to bloodborne pathogens (Occupational Safety and Health Administration, 1991). These rules have significant record-keeping requirements. Records kept to comply with the OSHA rules must be retained for three years. Documents that must be entered into the employee's medical record, however, must be maintained for the duration of the employee's employment *plus* 30 years.[1]

OSHA Bloodborne Pathogen Standard   Federal government rules that require employers to protect employees against the accidental transmission of bloodborne pathogens, especially HIV and hepatitis-B.

Patient and Student Education Information

All athletic trainers should maintain an up-to-date data base of article reprints, handouts, and other educational materials that they can provide to both patients and student athletic trainers. The maintenance of such a data base as another type of program administration information is important because the body of knowledge in athletic training and sports medicine is changing so rapidly.

∎ Filing Sports Medicine Records

Although it may seem rather basic, an appropriate and effective system for filing sports medicine records is important. Like Karen Thompson in the opening case, most athletic trainers are too busy to spend time searching for important documents in poorly organized files. Although different sports medicine settings will require different filing systems, the following recommendations should prove useful in most cases (Needy, 1974):

- Develop a **master outline** of files contained in the system organized under major subject headings (see Figure 6.10).

- Maintain confidential files, such as medical records and personnel folders, in their own locked cabinets.

- Organize files according to major, primary, secondary, and if needed, tertiary classifications. A budget file classified in this manner would look like this:

master outline   A guide to the major sections of a filing system.

---

[1]A complete package of forms related to compliance with the OSHA Bloodborne Pathogens Standard is available from St. Clair Associates, University Research Park, 8701 Mallard Creek Rd., Charlotte, NC 28262.

```
Major classification ................................................. Budget
Primary ....................................................................1992
Secondary .......................................... Expendable supplies
Tertiary ................................................................. Invoices
```

- Use file labels of different shapes or colors to differentiate between the various filing classifications.

- Do not overfill file folders. Once a folder has reached its capacity, usually 3/4 in., begin a second folder.

- Organize material within a folder chronologically or alphabetically.

- Develop separate filing systems for temporary and permanent files.

- File records promptly.

- Go through all files yearly. Discard unneeded records and update the master outline.

■ The Computer as an Information Management Tool

As already mentioned, the computer has developed into a powerful tool for information management in sports medicine. Ribaric (1982) predicted over 10 years ago that the use of computers would become commonplace in sports medicine and he was correct. Although computers can, in most circumstances, help improve athletic trainer productivity, athletic trainers sometimes resist the change to a computerized information management system. Resistance can be overcome if the technology and specific computer applications are gradually introduced (Ray & Shire, 1986).

One of the most important questions that athletic trainers considering a change to a computerized system must answer is what specific problems the computer can provide a solution for (Priest, 1989). Mere attraction to the technology is a poor but common reason for computerizing. One of Karen Thompson's problems in the opening scenario is that she had not clearly identified her record-keeping problems and their possible solutions. Like many other athletic trainers, she simply assumed that the computer would resolve her problems. Only after receiving the equipment did she begin to think about its use in a more rational and organized way. A *computer resources needs assessment analysis* is the first step the athletic trainer should take to decide whether to automate the record-keeping system (see Figure 6.11).

Unless the athletic trainer has extensive training in computer systems and applications, she should seek the advice of professionals prior to attempting to choose a system. Most colleges and universities employ computer specialists for this purpose. Many hospitals contract with computer consultants who can assist the hospital-based athletic trainer. Many high school athletic trainers can receive the computer advice they need by contacting the instructors who teach computer science in the school district. The computer consultant should be able to advise the athletic trainer on performing a *cost-benefit analysis*, in addition to recommending specific hardware and software.

computer resources needs assessment analysis   A type of needs assessment focused on information management and its automation.

cost-benefit analysis   A type of program evaluation that estimates both the amount of resources and the potential advantages associated with a program.

Master Outline—Personnel

Personnel
  Applications for employment
    Current job openings and applications
  Absence from work
    Absence reports
    Absenteeism and lateness
  Bonding of employees
  Employee benefits
    Group life insurance
    Group medical and hospitalization
    Incentive awards
    Retirement program
    Severance pay
    Social security
    Unemployment compensation
    Workers' compensation
  Employee conduct rules
    Disciplinary measures for violation of rules
  Employee relations
    Collective bargaining
    Communications
    Employee parking
    Grievance procedures
  Hiring procedures and policies
    Qualifications
    Residence requirements
    Selection procedures and recruitment
      Advertising
      College contacts
      Employment agencies
      Job interviews
      Job announcements
      References required
  Health and medical program
    OSHA bloodborne pathogen standard
    Compliance
    Working conditions
  Individual personnel folders (*confidential*)
  Leave
    Compensatory
    Death in family
    Holiday
    Jury duty
    Leave of absence
    Maternity
    Military
    Paternal
    Sick
    Sabbatical
    Vacation
    Voting

  Payroll records
  Personnel record-keeping policies
    Personnel forms
  Publications
    Bulletins
    Newsletters
    Training manuals
    Requests
    Staff publications
  Safety and accident program
    Accident analysis
    Accident reports
    Elimination of hazards
      Safety inspection records
    First aid policies and procedures
    Legal liability
    Safety equipment
    Safety—in-service training
    Rules
  Termination of employment
    Death
    Discharge
    Layoff
    Retirement
      Early retirement program
    Resignation
    Termination interview
    Turnover analysis
  Training
    Employee induction program
    Employee training records
    Time off for study program
    Tuition refund program
    Workshops and conferences
  Wage and salary program
    Job analysis
    Job descriptions
    Job specifications
    Job evaluations
    Job classifications
    Organizational charts
    Pay policies
    Promotions
    Wage and salary structure
      Wage criteria
      Wage surveys
      Rate range structure

Figure 6.10 Example of a master outline for the personnel section of a sports medicine filing system. *Note.* From *Filing Systems* (pp. 26-29) by J.R. Needy, 1974, Arlington, VA: National Recreation and Park Association. Copyright 1974 by National Recreation and Park Association. Adapted by permission.

Computer Resources Needs Assessment Questionnaire

Instructions:

All members of the sports medicine staff should complete this questionnaire in order to obtain the perspectives of as many potential users as possible. Responses from all questionnaires should be transferred to a master list. The master list will help guide the discussion between the athletic trainer and the computer resources consultant.

List the primary information needs of the sports medicine program. Some of this information may be incoming and some will be outgoing. Include both types. For each of these information needs, answer the following question:

1) From what source does the information come? (Examples include injury logs, treatment logs, telephone conversations, etc.)

Answer the following questions for each type of information that pertains to the sports medicine program:

1) Who uses the information? Who has access? How is the information used?
2) Is there anyone else who could use the information if it were provided to them? How would they use it?
3) How is the information generated? Who prepares it? Where is it sent after preparation?
4) How is information presently organized? Is an alphabetical or numerical filing system used?
5) How often is the information accessed, changed, or used?
6) Is all the information generated used in some way, or is some of it simply stored?
7) How is the accuracy of the information verified? How critical is the accuracy of the information?
8) Is the information used in reports? If so, how? How often are the reports generated?
9) How could the information be managed more effectively? If you think a computer would help, why do you think so? Are you aware of any hardware or software applications that would address this need?

▌Figure 6.11   Computer resources needs assessment questionnaire.

The athletic trainer faces several important considerations in developing a computerized information management system, including hardware, software, and communication options. Priest (1989) recommends addressing the following issues:

- How will the hardware be protected, both from theft and unauthorized use?

- How will the software be protected, both from theft and unauthorized duplication?

- Who will be responsible for performing regular backups in order to insure data retention? How often will backups be performed?

- How will access to computer files be regulated, especially if there will be multiple users?

- Who will update the data base and how will the accuracy of the entries be verified?

- Who will maintain computer file organization?

- How will disk capacity be monitored? Who will be responsible for making sure that fixed disk space is not exhausted?

- Will the computer be networked to other computers? Is the software compatible with the network?

- Who will provide technical support and training?

Hardware Considerations

Computer hardware refers to the equipment required to input, process, and output data. The following items are commonly included in the array of computer hardware options (Christensen & Rupp, 1986):

- Central processing unit (CPU): the circuits and controls that actually process the digital data.
- Monitor: the cathode ray tube used for video display.
- Printer: the device that produces a paper copy of the computer output. Like all hardware, a wide variety of printer types are available in a wide range of costs.
- Disk drives: devices that store digital data on a magnetic platter. Hard disks are contained in the same housing as the CPU and store more data than floppy disks, which are removable.
- Mouse: a hand-held device that allows the user to move the cursor around the monitor. This has been a standard input device on Apple and Macintosh computers for many years and is now being used more frequently on IBM and compatible microcomputers as well.
- Keyboard: the typewriter-like device used to enter data into the computer.
- Modem: a communications device that when coupled with a telephone line can be used to transfer data from one computer to another.

Mainframe or Micro?

For athletic trainers employed by institutions that have a mainframe computer, the decision to use the mainframe or a microcomputer is important. In sports medicine settings without access to a mainframe, a microcomputer will certainly be the most cost-efficient computing alternative.

computer hardware   *The equipment required to input, process, and output data.*

❚ Using laptop computers allows athletic trainers great flexibility in managing information in a variety of settings.

mainframe *A type of large, powerful computer designed for multiple users in a centralized institutional setting.*

terminal *A combination cathode ray tube and keyboard that allows users to access a mainframe computer.*

microcomputer *Also known as a* personal computer. *A type of computer designed to sit on a desk and serve the needs of one, or at most, a few users.*

local area network (LAN) *A system that allows two or more microcomputers in different places to be linked so users can communicate and share software and data.*

clone *Lower cost microcomputers designed to be compatible with those produced by IBM.*

laptop computer *Microcomputers that have been reduced in size to be portable. The smallest of these machines are known as notebooks.*

A **mainframe** computer is a large, multiuser CPU capable of substantial and rapid data transformations. A mainframe is typically housed in the university's computer center or the data management department of a hospital. Mainframe computers are usually accessed via remote **terminals** that are either directly connected (hard wired) or connected by modem and telephone line.

A **microcomputer**, also known as a *personal computer*, is a much smaller CPU designed to sit on a user's desk. It has less memory, data transformation, and storage capacity than a mainframe. Microcomputers are usually intended to be used by one, or at most, a few users. Several microcomputers can be linked together to share software and communicate through a **local area network** (LAN) (Cheong & Hirschheim, 1983). In many settings, microcomputers connected by LANs are making the mainframe obsolete because LANs allow users the connectivity and shared software applications without the expense of a mainframe. Microcomputers can also act as terminals for mainframe computers if they are equipped with the appropriate communications hardware and software.

Two different kinds of microcomputers comprise the vast majority of the personal computer market. The first is the Apple and its more advanced counterpart, the Macintosh. The other is manufactured by International Business Machines (IBM). In addition, many companies manufacture personal computers compatible with IBM's, commonly known as **clones**.

Microcomputers come in many shapes and sizes. One increasingly popular micro is the **laptop computer**, sometimes called a *notebook*. Although designed to use the same software and perform all the functions of the normal micro, laptops are portable and are often small enough to fit into a briefcase. Although more expensive than traditional microcomputers, the laptop offers a great deal of computing flexibility in sports medicine settings because it can be transported easily to remote sites like playing fields and arenas.

Although microcomputers are attractive hardware options for many sports medicine settings, they do have their limitations. Likewise, the mainframe computer has strengths and weaknesses. The relative advantages and disadvantages of these two hardware options include the following:

- Micros can be used by only one person at a time. A mainframe can accommodate many users simultaneously.

- Microcomputer users must know how to use peripheral devices, such as disk drives and printers. The terminal is usually the only device mainframe users must manipulate.

- Mainframes have much greater data storage and computational abilities. Microcomputers continue to be improved, however, and their data transformation and storage resources are becoming adequate for most sports medicine needs.

- Several operations can be performed simultaneously on most mainframes whereas some microcomputers are limited to single tasks, which prevents use of the computer during long print jobs or computational processes. New software is becoming available that will allow more micros to overcome this limitation, however.

- Micros offer greater control over the computer resource because problems can be handled locally.

- There is a much greater amount and variety of software available for the microcomputer, including software developed specifically for athletic trainers. Most of the software is also much less expensive.

- Microcomputers are much less expensive than mainframes. Most athletic trainers could purchase the necessary microcomputer hardware, including peripheral devices, for under $2,000. Mainframes are many orders of magnitude more expensive.

- In many universities and hospitals, the library card catalogs are maintained on a mainframe computer. If athletic trainers have access to the mainframe, they can often search for books and journals without leaving the sports medicine center.

Important Hardware Questions

The following questions should be asked and answered prior to purchasing computer hardware:

- Will the desired software applications run on the hardware?

- What level and quality of technical support and service will accompany the hardware?

- Is the computer manufacturer well established? Will service be available in 5 years?

- Will the manufacturer or dealer provide training? What will it cost?

- Will the computer communicate with other machines?

- Does the cost quotation include all the necessary equipment including CPU, hard disk drive, monitor, keyboard, printer, cables, mouse, and modem?

Software Considerations

Computer software, also known as a *program*, is a set of instructions that tells the computer hardware what tasks to perform and how to perform them. A kind of software that must be installed on every computer is known as the *operating system*. Most operating systems are designed to be used with particular types of computers. For example, most IBM and compatible micros use a system known as DOS (disk operating system). Apple and Macintosh computers use a completely different operating system. Another kind of computer software that athletic trainers will have to purchase is *application software*. These programs are designed to carry out specific functions, such as word processing; data storage, manipulation, and retrieval; statistical analysis; graphics production; and communications. Many of the programs needed to carry out the information management function of the sports medicine program can be relatively expensive. There are thousands of very useful programs, however, known as *shareware* programs, that can be obtained at a reasonable cost. They are available from a variety of software distributors, usually for the cost of a floppy disk plus postage. If users like

computer software Also known as a computer program. *A set of instructions that controls the operations of the computer hardware.*

operating system The computer software necessary to operate the machine that integrates and controls the functions of the hardware and application software.

application software Computer programs designed to perform specific functions, such as word processing, statistical analysis, and graphics production.

shareware Application software available at greatly reduced cost, usually on a trial basis.

the programs, they are often asked to "register" by sending a modest fee to the software developer (Nehmer, 1992).

Before purchasing application software, athletic trainers should consider the following questions:

- Will the software help you accomplish the tasks that are required? Which tasks can't be accomplished? How important are they?

- Has the software functioned well in other settings similar to yours? Talk to other athletic trainers about their experiences with specific programs.

- How user friendly is the software? How much training will be required? Who will provide the training?

- Do the requirements of the software match the hardware you have?

- How expensive is the software? Are less expensive alternatives available?

- Does the software come with written documentation? What is the quality of the written documentation?

- Does your institution provide technical support for this software?

- Is the software available on a trial basis?

Word Processing Software

Word processing is one of the most basic information management functions. Athletic trainers have a wide choice of computer programs for this function. Word processing software is used for a variety of purposes, including:

- writing letters and memoranda,
- compiling reports,
- integrating text with graphics,
- merging lists for large mailings,
- manipulating text without having to retype,
- producing forms,
- checking spelling,
- searching text,
- managing computer files,
- performing simple calculations, and
- maintaining simple data bases.

macro An internal program available with some application software that allows a user to reduce a complex series of keystrokes to one command.

Many word processing programs can run *macros*, internal programs that make it possible to program a complex series of keystrokes with the touch of a key or two. For example, at Hope College macros are designed to generate a daily report to coaches in one of the most popular word processing programs, WordPerfect, by touching just two keys.

Data Base Software

Data base software allows the athletic trainer to input, store, manipulate, and retrieve a specific information set (Christensen & Rupp, 1986). In athletic training, data base software has been used primarily to store and retrieve information about athletic injuries and treatments. This segment of the software industry has been the most responsive to the needs of athletic trainers. Four data base software programs developed specifically for athletic trainers include Athletic Injury Management, Integrated Injury Tracking System, Sports Injury Monitoring System, and SportsWare Injury Tracking System.[2] In addition, athletic trainers may wish to consider the advantages and disadvantages of using a generic data base program.

Athletic Injury Management: Athletic Injury Management Software (AIM) is produced by Cramer, Inc. This data base management system (DBMS) is a refinement of the ALFIE system, an older Cramer data base product. AIM allows the athletic trainer to

- record injury type and circumstances,
- record treatments,
- record progress notes,
- create a student roster with important information about every athlete,
- record data from physical examinations,
- record insurance information and claims processing activities,
- record an athlete's medication history, and
- generate injury, treatment, and coaches reports.

AIM will operate on either Macintosh or IBM-compatible hardware running Microsoft Windows (Windows is a software program that allows IBM and compatible computers to operate with a graphical interface that allows the user to use a mouse rather than having to enter commands from the keyboard). Athletic trainers operating the old ALFIE system will have to purchase the entire AIM system if they wish to upgrade because the two programs' files are not compatible. AIM is available as a complete package for $395, or the injury reporting, daily treatment logs, and physical examination modules can be purchased separately for $295.

Integrated Injury Tracking System: The Integrated Injury Tracking System (IITS) is produced by Micro Integration Services, Inc. This injury and treatment data base program allows athletic trainers and physical therapists to record information on an athlete's past medical history, basic medical information, injury circumstances and supporting notes, surgery information, Cybex scores for quadriceps and hamstring strength, and medication histories. Some information is recorded as a code number, but all codes and their

data base software *Application software that allows a user to input, store, manipulate, and retrieve a specific information set. Sometimes referred to as a* data base management system (DBMS).

---

[2]All information on these athletic injury data base programs was current as of July 1, 1992. Since software is constantly being changed and upgraded, however, athletic trainers are strongly urged to contact individual software companies to inquire about up-to-date product capabilities and pricing.

corresponding injury factors can be found in pop-up windows on the screen. The predefined reports available from the IITS include

- a list of athletes sorted by grade (the system ranks athletes on a 1-6 scale according to their present state of health),
- injury examination findings,
- summary leg strength results,
- injury summaries sorted by body area,
- treatment reports, and
- an injury breakdown report.

IITS stores data in a format compatible with dBase III Plus (a powerful generic data base management program). By purchasing an optional report generation program along with dBase III Plus, the athletic trainer can produce reports from any of the fields entered in the IITS screens. When entering rehabilitation notes, IITS will access the athletic trainer's word processing software to simplify editing progress notes. IITS will run on IBM or compatible computers with 640K of *random access memory* (RAM). The price is $995.

Sports Injury Monitoring System: The Sports Injury Monitoring System (SIMS), produced by Med Sport Systems, Ltd., is the most sophisticated DBMS program available for athletic trainers. It is designed not only to document injury and treatment parameters, but also to improve communication between various members of the sports medicine team. This program allows the athletic trainer to record the specific circumstances of an athlete's injury and to document the injured athlete's follow-up care. Daily progress notes on range of motion, swelling, pain, and compliance with the treatment plan can be recorded. The software will produce several different reports, including

- daily coaches report,
- initial injury report,
- daily status report,
- daily progress notes,
- injury summaries by sport or position,
- year-end athlete injury reports,
- injury and illness summary statistic tables, and
- graphs of various functions, including percentage of injury resolution and percentage of normal function.

SIMS also allows development of an athlete roster and has a daily calendar feature. SIMS will only operate on an IBM or compatible computer with 640K of RAM. Macintosh and mouse-compatible Windows upgrades are being planned. Like the AIM program, SIMS can be purchased in two modules. Athletic trainers can purchase the entire SIMS package ($1,295) or the Sports Injury Reporting System (SIRS), which includes most of the basic features of SIMS but without graphics, player demographics, progress summaries, or player summary reports for $495. For additional fees, Med Sports Systems also offers report generators for SIRS and SIMS and various support packages. The SIMS program is also unique in that it can be installed on a LAN.

random access memory (RAM)   A type of computer memory in which specific information can be accessed in any order. Generally, the more powerful application software programs require greater amounts of RAM.

SportsWare Injury Tracking System: SportsWare, a product of Computer Sports Medicine, Inc., shares many characteristics with the other athletic injury data base programs, including the ability to generate player rosters and emergency information lists, chart injury evaluations and the circumstances under which an injury occurred, record treatments, and enter evaluation and treatment notes. SportsWare also has the capability to track medical insurance claims and maintain equipment and supply inventories. SportsWare's predefined reports include

- travel reports (emergency information for all members of a particular sport),
- injury evaluation reports,
- player status reports,
- injury statistic reports,
- athlete medical history reports,
- injury summary reports,
- treatment statistic reports, and
- treatment summary reports.

A useful feature of this program is that data can be entered with a mouse using pull-down menus and pop-up windows. Date-related information can be accessed via a pop-up calendar. The program comes with a text editor and telephone log. SportsWare is available for an IBM or compatible machine with 640K of RAM for $495. A Macintosh version is available for $545.

Generic Data Base Management Programs: In addition to the specialized athletic injury data base management programs mentioned above, generic DBMS programs are available for every type of computer (Leroy, 1990). Some programs are quite expensive and powerful and require a knowledge of DBMS programming. Other programs, such as PC-File, are available through shareware catalogs and are much easier to use. These programs offer athletic trainers the ability to define the kind of data they want to store and to sort the data and generate reports based only on the information desired. Many low-cost DBMS programs allow importing and exporting data to and from word processing and spreadsheet programs. This useful feature allows the athletic trainer to generate reports with graphic representations of various kinds of data. Although the commercially available sports medicine DBMS applications are the best option for most athletic trainers, athletic trainers with very limited funds may wish to experiment with a low-cost generic DBMS first.

Spreadsheet Software

A *spreadsheet program* manipulates the data stored in cells comprised of columns and rows in a table on the computer screen (Illingworth, 1990). Cells can contain numbers, text, or formulas. Spreadsheets are most commonly used when mathematical calculations are required. When the numerical values in a cell are changed, formulas automatically recalculate the values contained in other affected cells. The program's text capabilities describe the numerical data by providing titles and headings. Most of the best spreadsheets also

spreadsheet program   A type of application software that manipulates numerical data contained in cells formed by the intersection of rows and columns.

have graphics capabilities that allow the athletic trainer to depict numerical data as pie charts, bar charts, and other kinds of diagrams. Applied to sports medicine, spreadsheets are most useful for budget, inventory, purchasing, statistical analysis, and payroll functions.

Other Software

Athletic trainers often find it useful to employ computer software to perform complex statistical analyses, create graphic images for slides and overhead projections, organize their personal calendars, and send data to other computers. The Allen and Hanburys company, for example, distributes a free computerized athletic drug reference that is very useful for finding out whether a particular drug is banned by the NCAA or United States Olympic Committee (USOC).[3]

Electronic Mail

electronic mail *A system that allows users to communicate via computer.*

Athletic trainers are increasingly using ***electronic mail***, also known as *e-mail*, to share information with people or other computers. To do so they need a microcomputer (or a terminal if using a mainframe computer), modem, telephone line, and the appropriate terminal emulation and communications software (which is sometimes included in the purchase price of the modem).

Athletic trainers may use bulletin boards, networking, and list servers. In this context, a ***bulletin board*** is an on-line, interactive electronic data base system (Dewey, 1987). It allows a computer to call up another computer to access information. Bulletin boards are usually devoted to specific topics. For example, the NATA operates an employment bulletin board at its national headquarters. Users can leave messages, read messages, and transfer files to and from the bulletin board. Some bulletin boards are free (except for the long-distance telephone charge) whereas others require a membership fee or "connect time" fees. Dewey (1991) estimates that there are over 20,000 bulletin boards operating in the United States. Athletic trainers who work with large staffs in several different locations should consider the advantages of using a bulletin board to improve communication among staff members.

bulletin board *An electronic, on-line, interactive electronic data base system, usually organized by topic or interest group.*

network *A group of computers connected by either direct hardwire coupling or dedicated telephone lines for the purpose of communicating with each other.*

A ***network*** is a group of computers, usually three or more, connected either by direct hardwire coupling or dedicated telephone line that can communicate with each other. Computer networks can be relatively simple, such as a local area network connecting computers in a single sports medicine center, or very large and complex. For example, there are over 100 networks, including BITNET and INTERNET, that connect educational and research institutions. Athletic trainers employed in these institutions, typically colleges and universities, could send electronic mail to each other by using the networks (Frey & Adams, 1990).

---

[3]Contact Allen & Hanburys, Glaxo, Inc., Research Triangle Park, NC 27709.

Another way the athletic trainer can gather and disseminate information over a large area is by using a network to access a list server. A *list server* is a remote computer that compiles a list of user electronic mail addresses. When new items are added to the data base, the server will send the new item as an electronic mail message to all the users on the list. Like bulletin boards, discussion lists are usually topic specific (see Figure 6.12). Although

list server A remote computer that compiles a directory of users' computer addresses and distributes messages contributed by the members of a particular discussion list.

Figure 6.12 Examples of discussion lists available through computer networks.

List abbreviation	Network address	Discussion topic
AHL	AHL@GWUVM	American Health Line News Service
ALCOHOL	ALCOHOL@LMUACAD	Alcohol and drug studies
ATHTRN-L	ATHTRN-L@IUBVM	Athletic training
BIOMCH-L	BIOMCH-L@HEARN	Biomechanics and movement science
BIOMED-L	BIOMED-L@NDSUVM1	Biomedical ethics
COCAMED	COCAMED@UTORONTO	Computers in Canadian medical education
COMPMED	COMPMED@WUVMD	Comparative medicine list
DIET	DIET@UBVM	Weight loss
DISRES-L	DISRES-L@RYERSON	Disability research
DRUGABUS	DRUGABUS@UMAB	Drug abuse education information and research
EMERG-L	EMERG-L@MARIST	Emergency services
FAMILY-L	FAMILY-L@MIZZOU1	Family medicine
FIBROM-L	FIBROM-L@UIUCVMD	Fibromyalgia and fibrositis
FINAN-HC	FINAN-HC@WUVMD	Health care finance
FIT-L	FIT-L@ETSUADMN	Exercise, diet, and wellness
GRANOLA	GRANOLA@VTVM2	Vegetarianism
HEALTHCO	HEALTHCO@RPIECS	Communication in health/medicine
HEALTH-L	HEALTH-L@IRLEARN	Health research
H-PROMO	H-PROMO@RYERSON	Health promotion research
LASMED-L	LASMED-L@TAUNIVM	Laser medicine
MEDIMAGE	MEDIMAGE@POLYGRAF	Medical imaging
MOTORDEV	MOTORDEV@UMDD	Human motor skill development
PANET-L	PANET-L@YALEVM	Medical education and health information
PEDIATRIC-PAIN	PEDIATRIC-PAIN@AC.DAL.CA	Various topics related to pain in children
SAFETY	SAFETY@UVMVM	Safety
SMDM-L	SMDM-L@DARTCMS1	Medical decision making information
SPORTPSY	SPORTPSY@TEMPLEVM	Exercise and sport psychology
THPHYSIO	THPHYSIO@FRMOP11	Thermal physiology

there are hundreds of topics for discussion list users to choose from, be careful about choosing too many because you could generate an overwhelming amount of electronic mail. Discussion lists change constantly.[4]

▮ Applications to Athletic Training: Theory Into Practice

Apply the concepts discussed in this chapter to the following two case studies to help you prepare for such situations you might face in actual practice. The questions at the end of the studies have many possible solutions. The case studies can be used for homework, test questions, or in class discussion.

CASE STUDY 1

When Charles Olson, the athletic trainer at Eagletown High School, met with his student athletic trainer staff at the beginning of each school year, he always covered documentation procedures for injuries and treatments. The following procedures were to be used by all student athletic trainers:

- *Injury evaluation forms were to be completed only by the head athletic trainer. Student athletic trainers were expected to file the forms in individual medical files every Monday, Wednesday, and Friday.*

- *All treatments were to be recorded by student athletic trainers on the daily treatment log as soon as the treatment was administered. On Monday, Wednesday, and Friday afternoons, all treatments from the daily treatment log were to be copied onto the bottom half of the injury evaluation report by the student athletic trainers. Once a page of the log had been transferred, it was thrown away.*

One day Charles was surprised to find a subpoena in his mail for all medical records related to a former student-athlete who had graduated 5 years earlier. At first, Charles could not find the student's file. Finally, after several hours of digging through boxes in a storage closet in the gymnasium he found the file. When he looked up the injury evaluation form for the case in question, he was shocked to see that the treatment records were sloppy, often not dated, and usually illegible because they had been written with a fountain pen that had left blotches of smeared ink on the page. Although Charles complied with the subpoena and submitted all the requested records, he was left with an uneasy feeling about the quality of those records.

QUESTIONS FOR ANALYSIS

1. What are the advantages of the injury and treatment recording system used at Eagletown High School? What are the disadvantages?

---

[4]For a very helpful elementary discussion on using electronic mail on a network to access discussion lists, see *Zen and the Art of the Internet* by Brendan Kehoe (Widener University, Chester, PA 19013) or send an e-mail message to BRENDAN@CS.WIDENER.EDU to request an electronic copy.

2. What kinds of problems is the Eagletown High School system likely to foster? How could those problems be overcome? What kinds of resources would be required to implement these solutions? How much would it cost?

3. What are the legal implications for this record-keeping system? Which legal issues should be addressed when considering changes in the system?

CASE STUDY 2

Randy Waters is an athletic trainer for a double-A minor league professional baseball team. In addition to his duties as athletic trainer, Randy is also equipment manager and traveling secretary for the team. Because of his many duties, Randy is a very busy person without a lot of time for record keeping. He usually discusses the health of individual players with the team's manager over coffee and rolls each morning. Randy informs the manager of any new injuries and the manager can ask any questions he has.

One day in August as the playoffs were rapidly approaching, Randy was unable to have coffee with the manager and the other coaches because he had to make arrangements for an upcoming trip. During the game that night, the team's star pitcher's knee suddenly buckled after a pitch and he fell to the ground. He had to be removed from the game and was evaluated by the team physician in the locker room. After the game the physician told the manager the knee would be fine in a couple of days, but in the future it would be wise to rest players for a day or two following an accident like the one the pitcher had suffered. "What accident?" asked the manager with a puzzled look on his face. The physician related that during his exam the player told him he has twisted his knee in the parking lot the previous evening. He went to the athletic trainer and got some ice for it and in the morning it felt better. The manager immediately went to Randy and demanded to know why he hadn't been informed.

QUESTIONS FOR ANALYSIS

1. Why is the manager so upset with Randy? Is his anger justified?

2. What steps could Randy have taken to avoid this situation? How should Randy modify his information management system to avoid problems like this in the future?

3. What legal risks does Randy's system pose, both for the club and for himself?

4. If Randy decided to use a computer to help him with his information management needs, what kinds of hardware and software might serve him best?

▌ Summary

To succeed as professionals in an information society, athletic trainers must manage and communicate information effectively. Documentation is a central task in the athletic trainer's information management role. Medical documentation helps ensure legal rights, acts as a memory aid, satisfies laws and professional standards, and provides data on which to make informed decisions.

Information in sports medicine is usually made up of medical records and program administration records. Medical records are confidential and should contain injury and treatment reports, physical examination data, reports of special procedures, communications from other health care professionals, emergency information, permission to treat and medical waiver forms, release of medical information forms, and certain kinds of insurance records. Program administration records include reports to coaches, budget information, nonmedical correspondence, equipment and supply information, personnel information, patient and student education information, and information required for writing self-studies and other kinds of valuative reports.

Computers can be a useful tool in assisting the athletic trainer manage information if used thoughtfully and wisely. The athletic trainers should consider cost, types of problems to be solved, amount of available support, and the amount of human resources available to use the computer system when purchasing hardware and software. The decision to use a mainframe or a microcomputer is also important. Many kinds of software are available to help the athletic trainer manage information, including word processing, data base management systems, and spreadsheets. Several DBMS systems written specifically for athletic trainers are available, although a generic program may serve well. Athletic trainers can share information with other professionals by using the computer as a communication device. Bulletin boards, networks, electronic mail, and list servers are a few of the methods available to help athletic trainers use computers to expand their information base.

▮ Annotated Bibliography

Abdenour, T.E. (1982). Computerized training room records. *Athletic Training*, **17**(3), 191.

> Abdenour describes a system for using a university's mainframe computer for keeping a narrative log for each injured athlete.

Berni, R., & Readey, H. (1978). *Problem-oriented medical record implementation*. St. Louis: Mosby.

> This text describes the problem oriented medical record (POMR) approach to medical documentation. It includes sections on how to implement the system, how various medical and allied health practitioners can use it, and how to evaluate it.

Cheong, V.E., & Hirschheim, R.A. (1983). *Local area networks*. New York: Wiley & Sons.

> This highly technical discussion of the use of local area networks is beyond the scope of most athletic trainers.

Christensen, W.W., & Rupp, P.R. (1986). *The nurse manager's guide to computers*. Rockville, MD: Aspen.

> This useful book can help health care professionals make decisions regarding computers. Chapters 2, 4, and 5, which discuss the relative

advantages and disadvantages of mainframe and microcomputer systems, are the most useful.

Dewey, P.R. (1987). *Essential guide to bulletin board systems.* Westport, CN: Meckler.

This is a good manual for athletic trainers who are interested in developing their own bulletin board systems.

Dewey, P.R. (Ed.) (1991). *National directory of bulletin board systems—1992.* Westport, CN: Meckler.

This reference lists thousands of bulletin boards by topic and their telephone numbers. For athletic trainers interested in specific topics or in experimenting with bulletin boards, this book would be a useful source of information.

Frey, D., & Adams, R. (1990). *!%@:: A directory of electronic mail addressing and networks.* Sebastopol, CA: O'Reilly & Associates.

This reference provides information on over 100 computer networks and includes a useful section on electronic mail addressing standards.

Gabriel, A.J. (1981). Medical communications: Records for the professional athletic trainer. *Athletic Training,* **16**(1), 68-69.

Gabriel provides examples of forms used to document the medical status of high school student-athletes in a centralized, districtwide sports medicine program.

Glondys, B.A. (1988). *Today's challenge: Content of the health record.* Chicago: American Medical Records Association.

An excellent source of information for athletic trainers who must create and maintain a medical records system, this book discusses content of the medical record and legal aspects of medical record keeping. It also provides a bibliography on legal issues.

Hawkins, J.D. (1989). Sports medicine record keeping: The key to effective communication and documentation. *Sports Medicine Standards and Malpractice Reporter,* **1**(2), 31-35.

Hawkins suggests five rules for sports medicine records management: (1) Put it in writing, (2) cross-communicate written information, (3) cross-file records to provide duplication, (4) use multicopy forms, and (5) use interactive forms.

Herbert, D.L. (1987). The use of prospective releases containing exculpatory language in exercise and fitness programs. *The Exercise Standards and Malpractice Reporter,* **1**(6), 89-90.

Herbert provides useful information for anyone who uses waivers from liability for legal protection and explains why such waivers are often invalid.

Illingworth, V. (1990). *Dictionary of computing* (3rd ed.). New York: Oxford University Press.

A basic compendium of computing terminology that would be useful for those with no previous background in computing, but is unnecessary for those who are more experienced.

Iyer, P.W. (1991). New trends in charting. *Nursing91*, **21**(1), 48-50.

This article, intended primarily for health care practitioners in hospital settings, provides 15 forecasts of how medical documentation is likely to change. The sections on focus charting, charting by exception, and writing clear evaluation statements are especially good.

Kettenbach, G. (1990). *Writing S.O.A.P. notes*. Philadelphia: Davis.

This important text can acquaint students and other new athletic trainers with an important information management skill. In addition to a programmed learning approach on writing subjective-objective-assessment-plan (SOAP) notes, it offers a useful section on medical terminology and the use of abbreviations.

Leroy, L. (1990). A review of record keeping sports medicine computer software. *Athletic Training*, **25**(4), 321-328.

Leroy evaluates and reports on the relative merits of Cramer's ALFIE and Micro Integration Services' IITS computer software systems. In addition, he offers good advice to those interested in using generic DBMS software to create their own injury and treatment data bases.

Marrelli, T.M. (1992). *Nursing documentation handbook*. St. Louis: Mosby.

Part 1 of this book is especially useful for athletic trainers. The first four chapters provide an overview of the documentation process, content of the medical record, different systems of medical documentation, and a reprint of the Joint Commission on Accreditation of Healthcare Organizations' Standards Related to Documentation.

Miles, B.J. (1987). Injuries on the road: Good information reduces problems. *Athletic Training*, **22**(2), 127.

Miles provides an example of an emergency information form that he suggests the athletic trainer or coach should carry to games at other sites.

Murphy, J., & Burke, L.J. (1990). Charting by exception. *Nursing90*, **20**(5), 65-69.

This article describes the charting by exception method and provides an illustration from a nursing setting.

Needy, J.R. (1974). *Filing systems*. Arlington, VA: National Recreation and Park Association.

This short pamphlet describes a simple method to effectively organize files according to major subjects.

Nehmer, K.S. (Ed.) (1992). *Guide to free computer materials*. Randolph, WI: Educators Progress Service.

This reference contains thousands of computer programs for most of the popular brands of micros, including Apple, Amiga, Atari, Commodore, IBM, and Macintosh, that athletic trainers can obtain either free or for a small charge.

Occupational Safety and Health Administration. (1991). Occupational exposure to bloodborne pathogens. *Federal Register*, **56**(235), 64175-64182.

OSHA's Bloodborne Pathogen Standard took effect in 1992 and applies to all persons who are exposed to blood or potentially infectious materials in the workplace. Every athletic trainer must become familiar with the requirements of the rule because of its impact on the administration of sports medicine programs in all settings.

Priest, S.L. (1989). *Understanding computer resources: A healthcare perspective*. Owings Mills, MD: National Health Publishing.

This is an excellent primer on computer systems. Priest provides many examples of computer problems and solutions that apply directly to the health care professions.

Ray, R.R., & Shire, T.L. (1986). An athletic training program in the computer age. *Athletic Training*, **21**(3), 212-214.

This article provides guidelines for making hardware and software decisions in sports medicine and discusses examples of athletic training software applications for a mainframe computer.

Ribaric, R. (1982). The computer in sports medicine. *Athletic Training*, **17**(4), 309.

This is one of the earliest papers on the subject of computers in sports medicine. Much of its discussion of computer applications to the athletic training profession is still current and applicable today.

Schneller, T., & Godwin, C. (1983). *Writing skills for nurses*. Reston, VA: Reston.

This workbook is designed to improve the writing and medical record-keeping skills of nurses. It is general enough, however, that other allied health professionals such as athletic trainers would benefit from it. The first chapter, which is an introduction to writing skills for allied health professionals, is especially useful. Athletic training educators may find the many worksheets useful in teaching medical record keeping to preservice athletic trainers.

Standards of practice. (1987). Dallas: National Athletic Trainers Association.

An important foundation for the athletic training profession, the *Standards of Practice* defines a certified athletic trainer and sets minimal professional expectations for athletic trainers in service programs and direct service facilities.

Synnott, W.R., & Gruber, W.H. (1981). *Information resource management*. New York: Wiley & Sons.

This book is designed for information-management professionals in industry. Synnott and Gruber's opening chapter, however, offers an interesting and enlightening perspective that many athletic trainers may find useful as they begin to think of the information management function in broader terms.

Helping Athletic Trainers Pay the Bills: Athletic Injury Insurance

STUDENT OBJECTIVES

▌ Understand the difference between medical, health, and accident insurance.

▌ Understand and be able to define the terms used by the insurance industry to describe their products.

▌ Understand the advantages and disadvantages of self-insurance, primary coverage, and secondary coverage.

▌ Define the types of injuries covered by most athletic accident policies.

▌ Understand the basic legal responsibilities associated with third-party reimbursement.

▌ Understand the role of procedural coding in the third-party reimbursement system.

▌ Organize a claims processing system for a sports medicine program in an educational setting.

▌ Understand the steps required to file a claim for reimbursement from a third-party payer.

▌ Evaluate and purchase an athletic accident insurance policy for an educational institution.

OPENING CASE

Sven Olaf, a recent transfer student and star of the New Amsterdam High School soccer team, was racing down the sidelines during a game against the crosstown rivals when he collapsed in pain. The school's certified athletic trainer, Jennifer Smith, ran onto the field and discovered that Sven was suffering from severe spasm of the paraspinous musculature. The cause of the spasm was unknown, and the lower extremity neurological examination was normal. Because Sven was in such pain, Jennifer decided to have him transported to the local hospital by ambulance. While waiting for the ambulance to arrive, Sven's parents and the team's coach gathered around to provide support and reassurance. As Sven was being placed onto the spine board, the coach took Sven's father, who was unemployed, aside and told him, "Don't worry about the bills. The school has insurance for this kind of thing and I'm sure we'll be able to take care of it because it was an athletic injury." Two days later, Sven was discharged from the hospital after incurring a bill of over $2,000.

Because Sven had no personal medical insurance, Jennifer submitted the entire bill to the school's athletic accident insurance company. Three weeks later, Jennifer received a letter from the company denying the claim because the injury was substantially linked to a preexisting condition. Although Sven had never told Jennifer, he had suffered a similar injury 2 years earlier while a student at another school. The emergency room physician obtained this information during the examination and provided it to the insurance company in the medical records needed to process the claim. Because preexisting conditions were excluded in the athletic accident policy, the company denied the claim.

When Jennifer contacted Sven's parents and informed them the claim had been denied, Mr. Olaf angrily told her he had been assured the school would pay the bills. "The coach promised me!" he shouted over the phone. Jennifer told Mr. Olaf she would consult with the school administration and call him back. When Jennifer informed the athletic director of the problem, he immediately called a meeting of the coach, the school principal, and Jennifer to determine where they would find $2,000 to pay the bill that the coach, as an agent of the school, had promised they would pay.

Athletic trainers with any experience should be able to sympathize with Jennifer Smith's situation. Athletic administrators have long felt a moral responsibility to prevent the cost associated with athletic injury from barring access to school sports programs. The soccer coach's promise to Sven's father was simply an expression of that sense of responsibility. His promise probably would have been easy to keep in the 1970s when the majority of student-athletes' parents had their own comprehensive medical insurance. Unfortunately, this is no longer true. The Health Insurance Association of America (1991) reports that in 1979, 85% of the population was covered by some form of private health insurance. By 1991, however, this figure had dropped to approximately 72% (see Figure 7.1). The percentage of the population that has access to health insurance through the employer of a family member has dropped to 61% (Reynolds & Bischoff, 1990). Not only is access to private medical insurance declining, but also the terms of medical insurance policies are becoming increasingly restrictive. For example, between 1982 and 1984 alone, the number of companies that required deductibles for hospitalization doubled from 30% to 60% while the number of employers that required employees to make a contribution to the cost of their insurance premiums also increased (Fein, 1986).

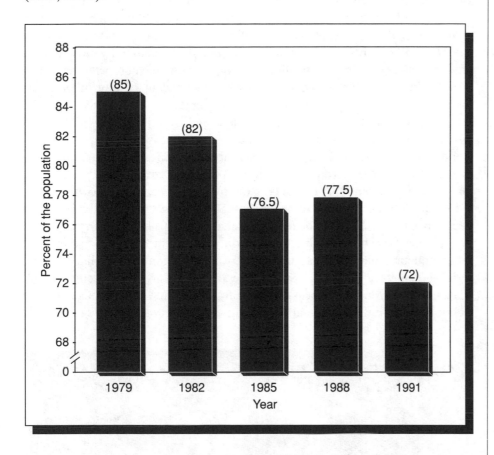

I Figure 7.1 Percentage of the U.S. population with access to private health insurance. *Note.* Data from *Source Book of Health Insurance Data* (p. 7) by the Health Insurance Association of America, 1991, Washington, DC: Health Insurance Association of America.

The cost of health care has become a political issue. Several proposals before Congress are intended to significantly modify the health care reimbursement system. These proposals range from minor reforms of the present private health insurance system to schemes that would create a national health care system similar to the Canadian model.

In the meantime schools and colleges face greater financial risks from medical costs than at any time in the past. This chapter, therefore, will provide athletic trainers with the information they need to manage insurance systems to more effectively safeguard the resources of the institutions they represent while living up to the moral responsibility to remove financial barriers to our nation's playing fields. In addition, this chapter will also examine the third-party reimbursement process to help athletic trainers working in hospitals and clinics get paid for what they do.

medical insurance *A contract between a policyholder and an insurance company to reimburse a percentage of the cost of the policyholder's medical bills.*

insurance policy *A contract between an insurance company and an individual or organization.*

health insurance *A type of policy designed to reimburse the cost of preventative as well as corrective medical care.*

athletic accident insurance *A type of insurance policy intended to reimburse medical vendors for the expenses associated with acute athletic accidents.*

exclusions *Situations or circumstances specifically not covered by an insurance policy.*

rider *A supplementary clause to an insurance contract that extends the terms of coverage beyond those associated with a standard policy.*

premium *The invoiced cost of an insurance policy.*

catastrophic insurance *A type of accident insurance designed to provide lifelong medical, rehabilitation, and disability benefits for the victims of devastating injury.*

▌ Athletic accident insurance is designed to provide coverage for only acute, traumatic injuries that occur in practices and games.

▌ Insurance Systems

Medical insurance is a contract between the holder of a *policy* and an insurance company to reimburse a percentage of the cost of the policyholder's medical bills, usually after a deductible has been paid by the policyholder (Rowell, 1989). *Health insurance*, on the other hand, is generally more comprehensive because it often includes provisions for maintaining good health rather than simply paying for illnesses and injuries. Both of these insurance classifications should be distinguished from the type of policy most educational institutions purchase for their student-athletes: *athletic accident insurance*, which is usually intended to supplement a student's family insurance plan and reimburses the cost of athletic accidents only (Chambers, Ross, & Kozubowski, 1986). The insurance industry defines *accident* differently from the concept of *injury* as understood by most athletic trainers, coaches, parents, and athletes. To the insurance company, accidents usually include acute, traumatic injuries, independent of any other cause or preexisting condition, that occur during practices and games. Specific *exclusions* in most accident insurance plans include injuries caused by overuse (tendinitis, bursitis, stress fractures, etc.), illnesses, and degenerative conditions. Some athletic accident insurance companies offer *riders* to cover the costs of these chronic conditions, but riders generally increase the *premium* significantly. A fourth type of coverage is *catastrophic insurance*, which usually takes effect after the first $25,000 in medical bills has been reached and provides lifetime medical, rehabilitation, and disability coverage for athletes who have suffered long-term, permanent handicaps as a result of an athletic injury. Member institutions of the National Collegiate Athletic Association have received catastrophic insurance at no cost since 1991. Catastrophic insurance is also available to non-NCAA institutions and high schools through their national governing organizations.

Experimental Therapy

Regardless of whether the athlete is covered by medical, health, accident, or catastrophic insurance, *experimental treatments* and procedures are usually excluded under the terms of most policies (Newcomer, 1990). A variety of medical and surgical techniques now common in sports medicine began as experimental therapies. Physicians, athletic trainers, and physical therapists frequently experiment with new methods to help athletes return to competition earlier and more safely. Unfortunately, the insurance industry often determines that a therapeutic method has made the transition from experimental to conventional several years after the medical profession. Different insurance companies define *experimental* in different ways, the best way being to simply list experimental procedures in the policy. Another method companies sometimes employ is to list the criteria by which they will determine if a procedure is experimental. This method is less exact and more difficult to defend in the courts. The final, and most common, method insurance companies use is to decide which methods are experimental on a case-by-case basis. The case-by-case decision method can be frustrating for patients and health care providers because they don't know what will be paid for and what will not.

experimental treatments *Therapies not proven to be effective.*

Usual, Customary, and Reasonable Fees

Another insurance concept athletic trainers should understand is *usual, customary, and reasonable (UCR)* reimbursement for medical services. The UCR concept is a flexible fee system originally developed by the federal government to reimburse health care providers through the Medicare system that is now used by most insurance companies. The amount of money that insurance companies will reimburse health care providers for a particular service under the UCR system is determined by a combination of the following factors:

usual, customary, and reasonable fee (UCR) *The charge consistent with what other medical vendors would assess.*

- The usual fee charged by each health care provider for the particular service
- The customary fee for the geographic area (either the average fee or the *90th percentile fee*, whichever is lowest)
- The reasonable fee (the lower of either the usual or customary fee)

90th percentile fee *The fee below which 90 percent of all other medical vendors in a particular geographic area charge for a specific service.*

To reduce the likelihood of having a claim denied, the athletic trainer should make sure that physicians and other health care providers the athlete will be referred to will perform only nonexperimental procedures and that they will accept the UCR fee as payment in full for services rendered. If the planned procedure could potentially be considered experimental, the athletic trainer should consult a representative of the insurance company before beginning it.

Even the most circumspect athletic trainer will have claims denied from time to time for reasons that may or may not seem fair. Lawsuits to recover the costs of denied claims should be the last possible option. The following suggestions may help resolve claims denied because of experimental treatment or UCR clauses:

- Find out the exact reasons the claim was denied. Insurance companies are required by law to provide this information.

- Obtain a statement from the physician or other health care provider explaining why the treatment was implemented and justifying the fee.

- If a student-athlete is covered through a parent's employer's self-insurance fund, correspond with the employer directly—the employer, not the insurance administrator, has final legal authority to reverse the denial.

- Provide evidence from clinical studies to support your claim that the treatment should not be considered experimental.

- Try to convince the physician or other health care provider to waive the portion of the fee above the UCR amount.

- Contact the state insurance commissioner and request assistance in challenging the denial.

Types of Athletic Insurance

Educational institutions can choose from three options when designing a medical insurance system for their student-athletes: self-insurance, primary coverage, and secondary coverage (Hart & Cole, 1992). As with any management option, each system has advantages and disadvantages, including cost.

Self-Insurance

Institutions that choose to self-insure are speculating that the amount of money they pay out for medical expenses will be less than the amount they would pay for insurance premiums. The institution purchases no medical or accident insurance except for catastrophic coverage and pays medical bills incurred by student-athletes. Many national governing organizations like the NCAA have rules that prevent educational institutions from paying for medical expenses not directly related to participation in intercollegiate or interscholastic athletics. Institutions that self-insure must be particularly careful to create and monitor procedures used to insure compliance with these rules.

Self-insuring offers several advantages (see Figure 7.2). Saving money is possible because the institution retains the potential profit earned by an

❚ Figure 7.2 Advantages and disadvantages of self-insurance.

Advantages	Disadvantages
• Potential savings	• High risk for large claims
• Simplified claims process	• Risk of bankrupting fund
• Greater flexibility	• Ties up institutional dollars

insurance company. Processing claims is also simplified because there are no insurance claim forms to complete. Institutions have the flexibility to pay for procedures that might be excluded under a normal insurance policy.

Although cost is an advantage with self-insurance, it can be a significant disadvantage as well. A large claim may deplete the institution's insurance fund, making it difficult or impossible to pay other, less costly claims. This possibility is one argument for setting aside leftover insurance funds in an endowment account that will eventually provide a cushion against large claims. The other disadvantage of this method is that it ties up a substantial amount of the institution's money that could be used for more productive purposes.

Primary Coverage

Primary coverage is medical or accident insurance that begins to pay for covered medical expenses as soon as the institution pays the deductible. The athlete's (or the athlete's parent's) personal medical insurance is not a source for payment of medical bills arising out of athletic participation. Institutions adopt primary insurance plans for a variety of reasons (see Figure 7.3). Some

- Sense of responsibility to pay all medical expenses
- Large percentage of uninsured student-athletes
- Simplified and accelerated claims processing

primary coverage A type of health, medical, or accident insurance that begins to pay for covered expenses immediately after a deductible has been paid.

I Figure 7.3 Reasons for purchasing primary insurance coverage.

feel a moral obligation to pay for all athletic medical expenses without involving families or their insurance companies. Others have a student population that is substantially uninsured anyway, so it is logical to choose primary coverage. Finally, primary coverage simplifies and accelerates claims processing because the family does not need to be involved.

The disadvantage of primary coverage is the expense. Because the insurance company takes on all the risk for an institution's student-athletes, as opposed to sharing the risk with personal medical insurance, it must charge a substantially higher premium for the coverage. Hart and Cole (1992) point out that the number of schools that purchased primary coverage for their athletic medicine program dropped from 30% in 1982 to about 5% in 1992.

Secondary Coverage

Secondary coverage, also known as *excess insurance*, is a policy that pays for covered medical expenses only after all other insurance policies, including the athlete's personal medical insurance, have reached their limit. This is the type of insurance plan selected by most institutions (Lehr, 1992). The most obvious benefit of this approach is that institutions can lower their costs by spreading the risk associated with athletic injuries to other potential payers (see Figure 7.4). Because the risk is shared with personal insurance

secondary coverage A type of health, medical, or accident insurance that begins to pay for covered expenses only after all other sources of insurance coverage have been exhausted. Also known as excess insurance.

I Figure 7.4 Advantages and disadvantages of secondary insurance coverage.

Advantages	Disadvantages
• Less costly	• Longer claims process
• Shared responsibility	• Requires more communication
• Promotes cost controls	• Labor-intensive claims process

companies, the costs associated with secondary coverage can be as much as 60% lower than those associated with primary coverage. Another less tangible benefit to this approach is that, if used properly, it can help develop a sense of shared responsibility for safety in the athletic program. Most parents want to provide a safe environment for their children. Presumably, their interest is heightened when they have a financial interest as well. Another advantage of the secondary approach is that it encourages athletic administrators to find ways to reduce and control medical costs. Premiums for secondary medical or accident insurance are closely linked to an institution's past claims history, enhancing the incentives for institutions to institute risk management programs and decrease medical costs.

The disadvantages of secondary coverage relate to claims processing. Because personal insurance is used as a primary layer of coverage, the institution must spend substantial time and energy communicating with parents and their insurance carriers to move claims along. This can delay settling insurance claims, which can frustrate medical vendors the institution wants to keep happy. Another potential problem is that the secondary system requires more communication and understanding about the shared responsibility for paying medical costs. In the opening case misunderstanding about how the school's policy worked was a major part of the problem. Errors in the chain of communication eventually placed the school in a position in which administrators felt pressured to pay for Sven's medical treatment, even though the injury occurred before Sven arrived at the school.

■ Third-Party Reimbursement

third-party reimbursement
The process by which medical vendors are reimbursed by insurance companies for services provided to policyholders.

third party *A medical vendor with no binding interest in a particular insurance contract.*

Third-party reimbursement is the process by which health care practitioners are reimbursed by a policyholder's insurance company for services they perform. A *third party* is defined as a person, in this case a medical vendor, who has no binding interest in a particular contract (the insurance policy). Third-party reimbursement is the primary mechanism to pay for medical services in the United States. Hospitals and private practice health professionals rely very heavily on third-party reimbursement to generate the income that keeps their practices in business.

Athletic trainers, unless they are also credentialed as physical therapists, have had a very difficult time obtaining third-party reimbursement for their services. In many cases, the lack of state credentialing for athletic trainers has created a barrier to third-party reimbursement. Even in those states that do credential athletic trainers, however, reimbursement for athletic training services has been difficult to obtain. Insurance companies, concerned about financial issues, have been slow to cover athletic trainers' services, even though the percentage of the population demanding them is increasing.

Even though athletic trainers have historically lacked direct access to third-party reimbursement, they are often responsible for generating significant amounts of reimbursable dollars for the clinics and hospitals that employ them and therefore they must understand this aspect of insurance. Many athletic trainers employed in sports medicine clinics perform tasks nearly identical to those performed by the physical therapists who countersign the athletic trainers' notes, thereby creating the basis for insurance reimbursement. Athletic trainers working in high school outreach programs are often responsible for bringing in referrals to the clinics that employ them. Many of these patients will pay for the services they receive by submitting a claim to their medical insurance carriers.

Some athletic trainers in university sports medicine programs have employed physical therapists, which allows their programs to seek third-party reimbursement from their student-athletes' personal insurance companies. This practice is controversial, however, and has been criticized by some leaders in the profession because it creates potential conflicts of interest about who will receive priority for the athletic trainer's services (Godek, 1992).

Types of Third-Party Payers

Among the different types of third-party payers are the following:

- Private medical insurance companies provide group and individual coverage for employees and their dependents.

- *Health Maintenance Organizations (HMOs)* provide participating health care practitioners with a fixed fee for services rendered to members. Fees are usually, but not always, determined using a *capitation* (per person) system. HMOs that do not use a capitation system usually reimburse providers based on a fixed fee schedule.

- *Preferred Provider Organizations (PPOs)* operate similarly to HMOs, but allow greater choice of health care providers and pay medical vendors on a fee-for-service, rather than a capitated, basis. PPOs allow policyholders to choose any health care provider they wish, but they provide financial incentives for policyholders who use providers identified by the PPO.

- Government-sponsored programs provide coverage for the elderly (Medicare), the needy (Medicaid), and members of the armed forces and their dependents (CHAMPUS).

Legal Requirements

Among the many legal considerations in third-party reimbursement, one of the most important is the requirement that health care practitioners obtain a signed authorization from the patient for release of medical records. Unless the patient authorizes such a release, the medical vendor is bound by the patient-practitioner relationship to keep information confidential. Third-party payers, however, will not process claims unless they have access to the information to substantiate them.

Another legal issue related to confidentiality of the medical record involves answering an insurance company's questions about the patient's case over the telephone. Athletic trainers should always verify the identity of the caller and be sure the patient has signed an authorization for release of medical records before answering questions over the phone. Rowell (1989) suggests the following steps:

- Once the patient's claim form is in hand, ask the caller to read a portion of the information to verify that the caller has the original.

health maintenance organization (HMO) A type of health insurance plan that requires policyholders to use only those medical vendors approved by the company.

capitation A system whereby medical vendors are paid a fixed amount per patient.

preferred provider organization (PPO) A type of health insurance plan that provides financial incentives to encourage policyholders to use those medical vendors approved by the company.

- If the caller is requesting a detailed explanation, ask that the questions be submitted in writing on company letterhead.

- Ask the caller for the insurance company's telephone number. Call the person back through the company switchboard to verify identity.

- Never answer questions from attorneys until the authorization for release of information is in hand, even if the attorney claims to have it. The best practice is to correspond by mail with attorneys regarding insurance reimbursement cases.

fraud　Criminal misrepresentation for the purpose of financial gain.

Fraud is another legal pitfall athletic trainers must avoid in the third-party reimbursement process. The athletic trainer must never change the date of an injury, treatment, or assessment or fail to record payments from an insurance company on a patient's bill. Other fraudulent acts committed by unscrupulous health care providers include claiming reimbursement for treatments that were not provided and increasing the charges for treatments for patients with insurance. The penalties for medical fraud are substantial and can include fines of $2,000 per occurrence plus twice the amount of the false claim.

CPT Coding

Current Procedural Terminology (CPT)　A coding system used to standardize the language associated with third-party reimbursement.

Reimbursement for sports medicine services is based on the coding system used when submitting claims to third-party payers. The **Current Procedural Terminology (CPT)** is a list of codes published by the American Medical Association that represents the vast majority of medical procedures. Initiated in 1966 to standardize language on insurance claims, CPT is in its fourth edition (CPT-4).[1] The person completing a claim form for sports medicine services would select the most appropriate code for each of the services rendered. The codes most likely to be used by athletic trainers are those listed under "physical medicine." These CPT codes range from #97010 (physical medicine treatment to one area: hot or cold packs) to #97752 (muscle testing with torque curves during isometric and isotonic exercise, mechanized or computerized evaluations with printout). Many CPT codes allow health care providers to bill for their time by listing additional specific codes, as the following choices describe:

Code	Service
97110	Physical medicine treatment to one area, initial 30 minutes, each visit; therapeutic exercises
97112	Neuromuscular reeducation
97114	Functional activities
97116	Gait training
97118	Electrical stimulation (manual)
97120	Iontophoresis
97122	Traction, manual

[1]Available by contacting Book and Pamphlet Fulfillment, OP-341/8, American Medical Association, P.O. Box 10946, Chicago, IL 60610-0946.

Code	Service
97124	Massage
97126	Contrast baths
97128	Ultrasound
97139	Unlisted procedure (specify)
97145	Physical medicine treatment to one area, each additional 15 minutes

The importance of carefully checking the accuracy of the CPT codes listed on the claim form cannot be overstated. Improper codes will significantly increase the time it takes the insurance company to process the claim or result in its denial.

A proposal by the American Physical Therapy Association (APTA) to create a new coding scheme by 1994 to address the present inequities of the physical therapy and sports medicine reimbursement system is being considered by the Health Care Financing Administration (HCFA) (Horn, 1992). If approved, this system would significantly affect the way sports medicine practitioners code their services for third-party reimbursement. The proposed system would combine the CPT and alphanumeric systems developed by the HCFA, specifically allowing practitioners to code for evaluations.

▌ Claims Processing

Filing claims quickly and properly is one of an athletic trainer's most important insurance functions. The claims process is distinctly different for athletic trainers in educational settings and athletic trainers in private or hospital-based sports medicine clinics. Athletic trainers in educational settings file all (or nearly all) claims with a single insurance company to pay other medical vendors for services rendered to the institution's student-athletes, whereas athletic trainers in sports medicine clinics will file claims with a wide range of insurance companies for reimbursement for services they provide. University athletic trainers who employ physical therapists so student-athletes' insurance companies can be billed also fall into the second category. The two settings will be discussed separately because the claims process is different in each.

Claims Processing in Educational Settings

The athletic trainer can take preliminary steps to make claims processing easier. One of the most important is to gather insurance information for every student-athlete in the program (Frankel, 1991). This task can often be accomplished well in advance of the season. For participants who are not identified until the beginning of the season, the preseason physical exam offers an excellent opportunity to collect the information. Personal insurance information forms should be updated annually. Another preparatory step that will save time and confusion after an injury occurs is to communicate by letter with the parents of all student-athletes, informing them of the limits of the school's accident insurance policy and the steps they will need to take to process an insurance claim in the event of an injury (see Figure 7.5).

Dear Student-Athlete and Parents:

At the beginning of every sports season, the athletic department sends the parents of each student-athlete information regarding our insurance coverage. We hope all participants will be injury free; however, if an athlete does become accidentally injured, the following information should be useful.

If a student-athlete is accidentally injured and generates medical expenses associated with the accident, all claims must be filed first with the student's or parents' personal insurance company. If a balance remains after the personal insurance company has paid its maximum, that balance will be submitted to the school's athletic accident insurance company. If covered, the school's insurance company will pay the balance of the eligible medical expenses not covered by the personal insurance company up to the maximum of the policy. This excess insurance program is being used at many of the nation's high schools and colleges.

The school's insurance policy covers only new accidents that are sustained during competition or supervised practice. Any bills related to injuries that fall into the category above should be mailed to the athletic department only after first being submitted to the personal insurance company. Preexisting injuries, off-season injuries, injuries incurred during the season that are not directly related to in-season competition or supervised practice (physical education injuries, intramural injuries, etc.), or routine medical care (eye care, dental care, care for illnesses) are NOT COVERED. Also not covered are injuries or "conditions" caused by overuse, such as tendinitis and stress fracture. *We strongly recommend that a personal health and accident insurance policy be maintained for all student-athletes.*

If you have any questions regarding the accident insurance program, please feel free to contact us at your convenience. We look forward to serving you again this year and hope that your experience will be enjoyable and accident-free.

Sincerely,

Athletic Director   Head Athletic Trainer

▌ Figure 7.5   Sample letter to parents and student-athletes explaining the athletic accident insurance plan.

insurance claim registry form   A worksheet that aids in tracking the progress of an insurance claim through the entire process.

explanation of benefits form (EOB)   A summary prepared by an insurance company and sent to the policyholder that documents how the insurance policy covered the charges associated with a particular claim.

If the school has a secondary policy, be sure to explain to parents that they must submit all medical bills to their insurance company before submitting the balance to the school.

When the athletic trainer receives a bill for processing, she should create an insurance file for the student-athlete. Because the status of the claim will change, it is useful to color code each file according to its status with adhesive labels—as the status of the claim changes, a different colored label can be applied over the old one. Consider the following system:

- Red label—Bills and other information being collected, claim not yet submitted.
- Yellow label—Full claim submitted but not yet paid.
- Green label—Claim paid in full and case closed.

In addition to creating an individual insurance folder, the athletic trainer should enter each claim on an *insurance claim registry form* (see Figure 7.6). This document provides the athletic trainer with a quick reference for determining which claims are paid and which are outstanding.

The athletic trainer should not submit any claim to the school's secondary insurance company before receiving an *explanation of benefits form (EOB)* from the athlete's personal insurance company. The EOB describes how benefits were paid for the claim. The EOB is proof of what bills the insurance company paid and to whom—medical vendors or the parents—the checks were written.

HMOs, part of a larger concept in the medical insurance industry known as **managed care**, are growing in popularity (see Figure 7.7). If a student's personal insurance carrier is an HMO, the student will be required to seek treatment from a physician designated as his or her **primary care provider** except in life-threatening emergencies. This requirement frequently poses problems for athletic trainers because it means student-athletes must seek medical treatment from physicians not associated with the school's sports medicine program. Most HMOs refuse to pay for treatment performed by a nonparticipating physician or other health care provider without prior approval. When the athlete is a high school student living in the same town as his or her HMO physician, the problem is merely an inconvenience. When the athlete is a college student living hundreds of miles from home, however, the problem can become more serious. Most secondary carriers will not pay the full cost of an athletic accident if the student's HMO denies the claim because the student sought treatment from a physician outside the plan.

The athletic trainer can take several steps with students who are insured through an HMO:

- Contact the HMO requesting information about the procedures to be followed in the event of an athletic accident (see Figure 7.8).
- Place an "HMO ALERT" label on the athlete's medical record as a reminder to contact the HMO in the event of an injury that will require outside medical care.
- If the student is in college and lives a great distance from the HMO service area, determine if the HMO will assign a physician in the local college community as the student's primary care provider during the time the student is in school.
- Be sure to remind the parents if the school's secondary insurance policy will not honor claims rejected by their HMO for noncompliance with the HMO plan. This will help prevent confusion and anger later.

Insurance claim forms must be complete and accurate to be processed as soon as possible. Athletic accident insurance claim forms have at least the following elements:

- Student's name and address (home and local when appropriate)
- Student's date of birth, sex, and year in school
- Sport in which the student was injured
- Date, time, and place of the accident
- Description of how the accident occurred
- Nature of the injuries suffered, including specific body parts
- Names and titles of witnesses to the accident
- Parents' medical insurance information

Finally, First Agency,[2] one of the oldest and largest athletic accident insurers, recommends that athletic trainers avoid the following claims processing pitfalls:

managed care A growing concept in the insurance industry emphasizing cost control through coordination of medical services, such as with an HMO or PPO.

primary care provider The physician selected by an HMO member who acts as the first source of medical service for the patient. Most HMOs require members to seek a referral from the primary care provider before seeking care from another medical vendor.

---

[2]First Agency, 5071 West H Avenue, Kalamazoo, MI 49009.

Sports medicine insurance registry form

Date filed	Athlete name	Insurance company	Amount due	Amount paid	Date paid

Figure 7.6   Sample insurance claim registry form. *Note.* From *Understanding Medical Insurance Reimbursement: A Step by Step Guide* (p. 63) by Jo Ann C. Rowell. Delmar Publishers Inc., Albany, NY; © 1989. ISBN: 0-8273-3352-8. Reproduced by permission.

- Do not wait until an injury occurs to collect the parent's insurance information from the student-athlete.

- Do not convey the impression that the institution will pay all expenses involving athletic injuries. This was one of the mistakes committed in the opening case study. One of the ways athletic departments can avoid this problem is to appoint a sole spokesperson who is responsible for managing the insurance program. All questions related to the insurance program should be directed to this person.

- Do not take primary responsibility for filing claims with the student's personal insurance company. This should be done either by the parents or the medical vendor.

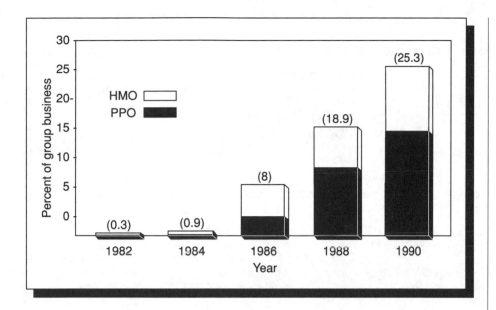

▌Figure 7.7 Growth of managed care in the commercial health insurance industry. *Note.* From *Source Book of Health Insurance Data* (p. 22) by the Health Insurance Association of America, 1991, Washington, DC: Health Insurance Association of America. Copyright 1991 by the Health Insurance Association of America. Reprinted courtesy of the publisher.

- Do not prepay medical vendors from the athletic budget—prepaying can result in duplicate payments and arouse animosity between physicians and parents.
- Do not delay filing claims with either the primary or secondary insurers. Many policies have time limits beyond which they will not pay.
- Do not assume that medical bills have been filed with the parent's insurance company. Athletic trainers should contact parents soon after an injury occurs to remind them of the process for settling claims. It is not uncommon for parents to receive a bill and assume that the institution is taking care of it, causing delays in claim processing that lead to past due accounts.
- Do not submit incomplete claims. Make sure bills are itemized and accompanied by the parent's insurance information.

Claims Processing in Sports Medicine Clinics

The claims process in sports medicine clinics is fundamentally different from the process in educational institutions for two reasons. First, the athletic trainer or clinic administrator must integrate claims processing within the context of a larger patient billing system. Because of this, the livelihood of the sports medicine clinic depends on the ability to obtain reimbursement from third-party payers for patient bills. The second fundamental difference is that the money generally does not pass through the hands of the athletic trainer in the educational setting but instead is sent directly to medical vendors. In contrast, sports medicine clinics receive direct payments from third-party payers. This is an important distinction because it places a greater accounting burden on the sports medicine clinic than athletic trainers in educational institutions face.

One of the most important steps athletic trainers in sports medicine clinics can take to ensure a smooth claims process is to seek prior authorization from a patient's insurance company before providing treatment. For some

HMO/PPO Authorization Form   Name of Student-Athlete _____

Name of Covered Person _____
(Parent or Guardian)

Name of Employer _____

HMO/PPO Certificate # _____

Dear __(HMO/PPO name here)__ :

_____ is a student-athlete at _____College and has indicated that he/she is covered under your plan for health and accident coverage while he/she is a student here.

_____ is participating in our intercollegiate sports program and there is a possibility that he/she may suffer an accidental injury while competing. The athletic accident coverage purchased by _____College is an excess policy that requires all medical bills be first submitted to the student's primary health plan for payment before it assumes any liability. It also requires that all student-athletes must follow any procedures required by their HMO/PPO, should they be covered by such a plan.

As the Head Athletic Trainer, it is my responsibility to process any insurance claims that are made by our student-athletes. I am requesting your assistance in properly administering your plan for _____
_____.

If you have any printed material that would assist in this matter, please send it to me as soon as possible. If there is a phone number that should be called prior to _____ receiving any medical treatment, I request that you send it to me as well. It is most important that I be informed of all medical vendors in the immediate area of _____College that qualify under your plan to treat _____.

At various times our athletic teams will be several hundred miles from our campus and I need to know the proper procedures for handling any emergency that might take place. I also need to know if your coverage has a particular definition of "emergency," and if there is a different procedure for treating a life-threatening emergency and a less serious problem, such as a fractured leg or dislocated shoulder that requires the immediate attention of a physician.

Thanks in advance for your help. I look forward to your early reply.

Sincerely,

Head Athletic Trainer

▌Figure 7.8   Sample HMO/PPO authorization form. *Note*. Adapted with permission from 1st Agency, Kalamazoo, MI.

third-party payers, such as HMOs and PPOs, this is a requirement—reimbursement usually will not be provided without preapproval by the primary care physician. Some Blue Cross plans will reimburse for physical therapy and other sports medicine services whereas other plans may not. The prudent clinic administrator should use the toll free number provided by Blue Cross to determine in advance the limitations of the patient's policy.

Rowell (1989) suggests the following nine steps for filing insurance claims with third-party payers:

- Complete the patient's charge slip listing the patient's name, date of service, type of service, and balance due.
- Convert all the procedures performed to CPT codes and list prices.

- List all procedures, charges, and payments in a daily office ledger and the patient's individual ledger.
- Complete the claim form. Most third-party payers will accept the ***HCFA 1500*** claim form from private practice clinics (see Figure 7.9). The ***UB-92***, also known as the ***HCFA 1450***, is the appropriate form for hospitals (see Figure 7.10).
- Obtain the authorized signature on the claim form. In most sports medicine clinics, the chief physical therapist must sign claims. In clinics owned by physicians, usually one of the physicians must sign.
- Place a copy of the insurance claim form in the patient's record.
- Enter the claim on the insurance claim registry form.
- Mail the claim form to the insurance company.
- Note that the claim has been submitted to the insurance company on the patient's ledger and mail an informational copy of the ledger to the patient.

Some insurance companies will allow medical vendors to submit their claims either in the traditional manner described above or in a scannable format. Preparing the scannable claim form (according to insurance company specifications) allows for quicker claims processing because a scanner automatically enters it into the insurance company's computer system. Claims that require any written explanation, however, will usually be held for review by a processing clerk. Another option available through some insurance companies allows medical vendors to submit claims electronically. A claim "form" is completed on the computer screen and then downloaded to the insurance company's computer with a modem and communications software. This is the quickest way to assure reimbursement for standard claims because the claim arrives at the insurance company, for all practical purposes, as soon as it is sent from the clinic.

■ Purchasing Insurance Services

The athletic trainer may have the responsibility for evaluating and purchasing an athletic accident policy for a school sports medicine program. A variety of persons, including athletic directors, business office personnel, and risk managers, often share this function. Even if athletic trainers are not directly involved in evaluating and selecting insurance, they should not hesitate to offer their input, especially if they will be responsible for implementing the system.

Insurance is usually purchased through an ***agent***. The U.S. Small Business Administration (1981) suggests that well-qualified insurance agents should be able to

- provide advice on the type and amount of insurance required,
- provide suggestions on the specific details of insurance policies, and
- provide timely service in the event of a claim.

Like sports medicine supplies and equipment, athletic accident insurance can be purchased in a variety of ways. One method is to simply contact a

HCFA 1500 *A claim form for private practice clinics developed by the Health Care Financing Administration for use in filing Medicare claims that has become accepted by most insurance companies.*

UB-92 (HCFA 1450) *A universally accepted insurance claim form for use by hospitals.*

insurance agent *A representative of an insurance company or an independent insurance agency who sells and services insurance policies.*

HEALTH INSURANCE CLAIM FORM
(CHECK APPLICABLE PROGRAM BLOCK BELOW)

FORM APPROVED
OMB NO. 0938-0008

MEDICARE (MEDICARE NO.)	MEDICAID (MEDICAID NO.)	CHAMPUS (SPONSOR'S SSN)	CHAMPVA (VA FILE NO)	FECA BLACK LUNG (SSN)	OTHER (CERTIFICATE SSN)

PATIENT AND INSURED (SUBSCRIBER) INFORMATION

1. PATIENT'S NAME (LAST NAME, FIRST NAME, MIDDLE INITIAL)

2. PATIENT'S DATE OF BIRTH

3. INSURED'S NAME (LAST NAME, FIRST NAME, MIDDLE INITIAL)

4. PATIENT'S ADDRESS (STREET, CITY, STATE, ZIP CODE)

5. PATIENT'S SEX

MALE ☐ FEMALE ☐

6. INSURED'S I.D. NO. (FOR PROGRAM CHECKED ABOVE, INCLUDE ALL LETTERS)

TELEPHONE NO.

7. PATIENT'S RELATIONSHIP TO INSURED

SELF ☐ SPOUSE ☐ CHILD ☐ OTHER ☐

8 INSURED'S GROUP NO (OR GROUP NAME OR FECA CLAIM NO.)

☐ INSURED IS EMPLOYED AND COVERED BY EMPLOYER HEALTH PLAN

9. OTHER HEALTH INSURANCE COVERAGE (ENTER NAME OF POLICYHOLDER AND PLAN NAME AND ADDRESS AND POLICY OR MEDICAL ASSISTANCE NUMBER)

10. WAS CONDITION RELATED TO:

A. PATIENT'S EMPLOYMENT

YES ☐ NO ☐

B. ACCIDENT

AUTO ☐ OTHER ☐

11. INSURED'S ADDRESS (STREET, CITY, STATE, ZIP CODE)

TELEPHONE NO.

11.a. CHAMPUS SPONSOR'S :

STATUS | ACTIVE DUTY ☐ DECEASED ☐ | BRANCH OF SERVICE
RETIRED ☐

12. PATIENT'S OR AUTHORIZED PERSON'S SIGNATURE (READ BACK BEFORE SIGNING) I AUTHORIZE THE RELEASE OF ANY MEDICAL INFORMATION NECESSARY TO PROCESS THIS CLAIM. I ALSO REQUEST PAYMENT OF GOVERNMENT BENEFITS EITHER TO MYSELF OR TO THE PARTY WHO ACCEPTS ASSIGNMENT BELOW.

SIGNED _____ DATE _____

13. I AUTHORIZE PAYMENT OF MEDICAL BENEFITS TO UNDERSIGNED PHYSICIAN OR SUPPLIER FOR SERVICE DESCRIBED BELOW.

SIGNED (INSURED OR AUTHORIZED PERSON) _____

PHYSICIAN OR SUPPLIER INFORMATION

14. DATE OF: | ILLNESS (FIRST SYMPTOM) OR INJURY (ACCIDENT) OR PREGNANCY (LMP)

15. DATE FIRST CONSULTED YOU FOR THIS CONDITION

16. IF PATIENT HAS HAD SAME OR SIMILAR ILLNESS OR INJURY, GIVE DATES

16.a. IF EMERGENCY CHECK HERE

17. DATE PATIENT ABLE TO RETURN TO WORK

18. DATES OF TOTAL DISABILITY

FROM ___ THROUGH ___

DATES OF PARTIAL DISABILITY

FROM ___ THROUGH ___

19. NAME OF REFERRING PHYSICIAN OR OTHER SOURCE (e.g. PUBLIC HEALTH AGENCY)

20. FOR SERVICES RELATED TO HOSPITALIZATION GIVE HOSPITALIZATION DATES

ADMITTED ___ DISCHARGED ___

21. NAME AND ADDRESS OF FACILITY WHERE SERVICES RENDERED (IF OTHER THAN HOME OR OFFICE)

22. WAS LABORATORY WORK PERFORMED OUTSIDE YOUR OFFICE?

YES ☐ NO CHARGES:

23. A. DIAGNOSIS OR NATURE OF ILLNESS OR INJURY. RELATE DIAGNOSIS TO PROCEDURE IN COLUMN D BY REFERENCE NUMBERS 1, 2, 3, ETC. OR DX CODE

1.
2.
3.
4.

B.

EPSDT YES ☐ NO ☐

FAMILY PLANNING YES ☐ NO ☐

PRIOR AUTHORIZATION NO.

24. DATE OF SERVICE		B. * PLACE OF SERVICE	C. FULLY DESCRIBE PROCEDURES, MEDICAL SERVICES OR SUPPLIES FURNISHED FOR EACH DATE GIVEN		D. DIAGNOSIS CODE	E. CHARGES	F. DAYS OR UNITS	G. * T.O.S.	H. LEAVE BLANK
FROM	TO		PROCEDURE CODE (IDENTIFY)	(EXPLAIN UNUSUAL SERVICES OR CIRCUMSTANCES)					

25. SIGNATURE OF PHYSICIAN OR SUPPLIER (INCLUDING DEGREE(S) OR CREDENTIALS) (I CERTIFY THAT THE STATEMENTS ON THE REVERSE APPLY TO THIS BILL AND ARE MADE A PART THEREOF)

26. ACCEPT ASSIGNMENT (GOVERNMENT CLAIMS ONLY) (SEE BACK)

YES ☐ NO ☐

30. YOUR SOCIAL SECURITY NO.

27. TOTAL CHARGE

28. AMOUNT PAID

29. BALANCE DUE

31. PHYSICIAN'S, SUPPLIER'S, AND/OR GROUP NAME, ADDRESS, ZIP CODE AND TELEPHONE NO.

DATE:

32. YOUR PATIENT'S ACCOUNT NO.

33. YOUR EMPLOYER I.D. NO.

I.D. NO.

*PLACE OF SERVICE AND TYPE OF SERVICE (T.O.S.) CODES ON THE BACK
REMARKS:

APPROVED BY AMA COUNCIL ON MEDICAL SERVICE 6/83

Form **HCFA-1500 (C-2) (1-84)** Form **OWCP-1500**
Form **CHAMPUS-501** Form **RRB-1500**

790-0072 (2-PLY C-2 W/C)

▌ **Figure 7.9** HCFA 1500 insurance claim form.

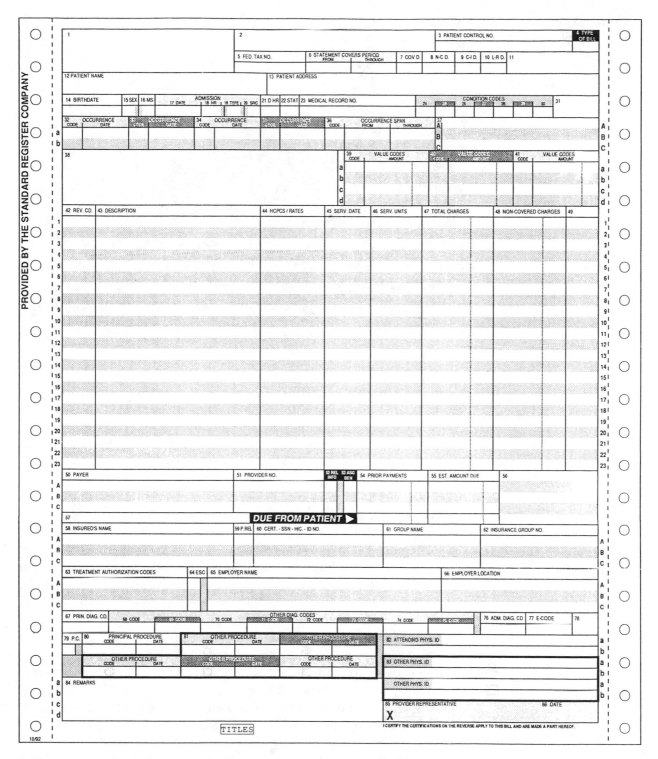

■ **Figure 7.10**   UB-92 (HCFA 1450) insurance claim form.

❚ Athletic accident policies should cover all athletic program participants, including cheerleaders, coaches, athletic trainers, and managers.

local insurance agency and ask that a policy be written covering the elements desired by the institution. This method requires the least time and effort from the athletic trainer but it is without question the least desirable. Without investigating the wide range of insurance products and their prices, the athletic trainer can never be sure of obtaining the best protection for the lowest cost.

Another method commonly employed by educational institutions is to use a formal bidding process to purchase insurance services. The advantage to the bidding method is that it allows institutions to obtain athletic accident insurance at the lowest possible cost. There are disadvantages to this system, however. First, every insurance plan has hidden costs, the most significant of which is usually the time it takes the institution's employees to learn the system and file the claims. If an institution awards athletic accident contracts to the lowest bidder annually, the employees will spend a great deal of time that could be spent on more productive work learning new insurance systems. Another disadvantage of the bidding system, especially for institutions that bid for multiyear contracts, is that the initial price of the premium may seem low, but as the institution establishes a claims history with the company, the premiums will undoubtedly rise to assure the company of a profit.

An alternative to both the bidding and direct purchasing systems described above is for the athletic trainer and other institutional representatives to interview several insurance companies and carefully evaluate their products and prices. This process allows for easy clarification of questions and provides an opportunity to determine what processing claims would require.

No matter what purchasing method is used, each proposal should be evaluated with the following points in mind:

layered coverage *A method of using different insurance companies to underwrite different levels of coverage in a common policy.*

- What are the monetary limits of the coverage? What are the time limits of the coverage? Does the policy offer *layered coverage*? If so, what are the limits for each layer of coverage? Is there a layer of cata-strophic coverage?

- What specific exclusions to the coverage are listed? What riders are available to cover these exclusions?

- Does the policy provide primary coverage or secondary (excess) cover-age? If secondary, how does it interface with personal insurance? How does it handle student-athletes whose parents are covered by HMOs or PPOs?

- What deductibles, if any, apply to the policy? Who will be responsible for paying the deductible?

- What *copayments*, if any, are required by the policy? Who will be responsible for the copayments?

- Who is covered by the policy? Are ancillary and support personnel, such as athletic trainers, coaches, student managers, and cheerleaders covered?

- Under what circumstances are covered individuals protected? How does the policy handle out-of-season injury?

- What is the annual premium? If a multiyear contract, how and under what circumstances will the annual premium change?

- What specific steps must the institution take to file claims? How much staff time and effort will be required to do so?

copayments The percent-age of a medical bill not paid for by the insurance company.

▮ Applications to Athletic Training: Theory Into Practice

Apply the concepts discussed in this chapter to the following two case studies to prepare for situations you may face in actual practice. The questions at the end of the studies are open-ended—there are many possible correct solutions. Use the case studies for homework, exam questions, or class discussion.

CASE STUDY 1

Barbara Cummings, A.T.,C./P.T., was beginning to have second thoughts about her decision 4 months ago to sell her private sports medicine and physical therapy practice to Universal Health Care Services. She had thought that by selling the practice to Universal, a huge medical practice conglomer-ate operating in 47 states, she would be able to improve her bottom line while the parent company assumed the risk of adding the new, expensive equipment she so desperately needed in order to remain competitive with the local hospital's sports medicine clinic. Unfortunately, she soon discov-ered that Universal put so much pressure on her to increase revenue that patient care was beginning to suffer. Still, she felt she had to do something to meet Universal's expectations or she would be forced to leave the practice she had worked so long to establish.

When Bob Thaxton, Universal's manager of clinic operations for 10 northern states, visited Barbara's clinic a week ago, he told Barbara she would have to institute the following billing and insurance practices immediately:

- *All new patients were to be discharged immediately when their insurance limits were met.*

- *No patients were to be discharged until their insurance expired.*

- *Every patient was to be billed for a minimum of 1 hour of therapy to cover expenses associated with overhead at the home office.*

- *Patients without insurance would not be accepted.*

Although Barbara was upset with the new regulations, she felt she had no choice but to conform to the standards established by the company. The day after Bob Thaxton's visit, the new regulations were implemented.

QUESTIONS FOR ANALYSIS

1. What potential legal pitfalls do the new billing and insurance regulations pose for Barbara and her staff? What ethical dilemmas, if any, are posed by these regulations?

2. How could Barbara implement the regulations without violating the law? Would her patients be well served by these actions? Why or why not?

3. What other revenue-enhancing procedures, besides those mandated by Universal, could Barbara implement? How would they serve her patients more efficiently and effectively than the procedures required by Universal?

CASE STUDY 2

Libby Wilson, Northwest State University's head athletic trainer, was called into the athletic director's office and told that a new university policy required all service contracts to be awarded to the lowest bidder. The new rule was to take effect beginning with the next fiscal year, which was only 2 months away. Libby would have to put together a bidding package for the university's athletic accident insurance, the ambulance service, and the team physician's contract. The athletic director gave her 1 month to secure the bids. This would give him enough time, he felt, to evaluate the bids, award the contracts, and have the services in place by the time the new fiscal year began.

Although Libby was not happy about having to put these services out for bid, she went to work right away. She knew that the insurance bid would be the most complicated, so she decided to tackle this part of the project first. She put together a bidding document that requested cost quotations based on the following requirements:

- *Excess coverage for 500 student-athletes in 18 sports, including football and gymnastics*

- *Excess coverage for all ancillary and support personnel*

- *Coverage limits up to $25,000 with lifetime catastrophic coverage for amounts above $25,000*

Libby included a copy of the university's claims history for the past 5 years (an average of 75 claims per year) and sent the bidding package to three insurance companies that specialized in athletic accident insurance.

Two weeks later she received the bids. She developed Table 7.1 to help the athletic director understand the bids:

Table 7.1   NSU Medical Insurance Bid Summary

Company	Coverage	Premium Deductable per claim		
		0	100	250
Professional Underwriters	$25,000	$20,000	$17,500	$15,000
Best Insurance Company	$25,000	$18,000	$16,000	$14,000
Good Insurance Company	$15,000	$12,000	$10,000	$ 8,000

QUESTIONS FOR ANALYSIS

1. What advantages and disadvantages are likely to accompany the university's new policy with reference to the athletic accident insurance program?
2. If you were in Libby's position, would you have followed the same process in securing bids for insurance? Why or why not? What would you have done differently?
3. Based on the information contained in the table above, which company's insurance policy represents the best value? Do you need any other information to reach this conclusion?
4. The Good Insurance Company will only write a policy with a maximum of $15,000 per claim. The university's catastrophic insurance coverage does not take effect until $25,000 in medical bills have been paid. If the university decided to purchase the Good Insurance Company's policy, what options should they investigate to decrease their risk between $15,000 and $25,000?

▪ Summary

As the cost of medical care continues to rise and the quality of medical insurance continues to deteriorate, it is becoming increasingly important for athletic trainers to thoroughly understand insurance systems. Insurance not only protects the assets of educational institutions that sponsor athletic programs, but also safeguards the income and livelihood of athletic trainers employed by sports medicine clinics. Athletic trainers should be able to distinguish medical, health, and accident insurance from each other. Most athletic accident policies cover only acute injuries with no connection to preexisting conditions and do not pay for illnesses or overuse conditions.

Most insurance companies refuse to pay for experimental therapy or to reimburse medical vendors beyond usual, customary, and reasonable fees. The three choices available to most educational institutions when purchasing insurance services include self-insurance, primary coverage, and secondary or excess coverage. Secondary coverage is by far the most common type of insurance plan.

Sports medicine clinics generate the vast majority of their income through third-party reimbursement. Although athletic trainers have historically lacked direct access to third-party reimbursement, they provide a wealth of billable services for the clinics that employ them. Different kinds of third-party payers include typical medical insurance companies, HMOs, PPOs, and government-sponsored programs. CPT coding lists procedures on insurance claim forms in the form of a code. Claims can be submitted on the standard HCFA 1500 form, on a scannable form, or electronically using a computer modem. Claims processing in educational settings is different in purpose and process than in a sports medicine clinic. In each case, patients enrolled in HMO or PPO insurance plans must receive authorization from their primary care provider before services are rendered.

Athletic trainers are frequently responsible for purchasing or recommending the purchase of athletic accident insurance. Price, policy exclusions, limits of coverage, deductibles, and claims processing workload should all be considered when evaluating the policies offered by different insurance companies.

■ Annotated Bibliography

Chambers, R.L., Ross, N.V., & Kozubowski, J. (1986). Insurance types and coverages: Knowledge to plan for the future (With a focus on motor skill activities and athletics). *Physical Educator*, **44**(1), 233-240.

This article discusses the various types of insurance available for athletic programs, including liability, health, catastrophic, and accident insurance. It contains a good bibliography.

Fein, R. (1986). *Medical care, medical costs*. Cambridge, MA: Harvard University Press.

This text is an academic discussion of the problems in financing modern medical care. The first two chapters will be of most interest to athletic trainers because they focus on the most important issues and on the history of private medical insurance in the United States.

Frankel, E. (1991). Handle with care. *College Athletic Management*, **3**(3), 11-13.

This is a good article for school athletic trainers. Frankel offers several practical suggestions that should help streamline the sports medicine program's insurance system.

Godek, J.J. (1992). Sports rehabilitation in the '90s: Who's who? *Journal of Sport Rehabilitation*, **1**, 87-94.

Joe Godek, a leader in the profession of athletic training, discusses the relationships between physicians, physical therapists, and athletic trainers and offers a model for a limited scope of practice for athletic trainers and physical therapists. Godek also argues that athletic trainers should approach the concept of third-party reimbursement cautiously because it could undercut the traditional role played by athletic trainers in schools and colleges and with professional and amateur athletic organizations.

Hart, P.M., & Cole, S.L. (1992). Subtracting insult from injury. *Athletic Business*, **16**(5), 39-42.

In this well-written article on athletic accident insurance for schools and colleges, the authors offer several practical suggestions about reducing medical insurance costs through more efficient management. This article is highly recommended for athletic trainers who have responsibility over their athletic department insurance program.

Horn, J. (1992). HCFA considers revisions of coding system. *P.T. Bulletin*, **7**(28), 3, 40.

Horn describes the system of coding reform proposed to take effect in 1994. The new system is intended to better reflect what physical therapists actually do in their practices.

Lehr, C. (1992). Status of medical insurance provided to student-athletes at NCAA schools. *Journal of Legal Aspects of Sport*, **2**(1), 12-22.

This study describes the common elements of collegiate athletic accident plans. The introduction and discussion sections provide good information for the athletic trainer planning to implement an athletic accident insurance system in a school setting.

Newcomer, L.N. (1990). Defining experimental therapy: A third-party payer's dilemma. *The New England Journal of Medicine*, **323**(24), 1702-1704.

Newcomer discusses the experimental therapy clauses found in most insurance policies, listing the advantages and disadvantages of the various methods for defining what treatments are to be considered experimental.

Reynolds, J.D., & Bischoff, R.N. (1990). *Health insurance answer book*. Greenvale, NY: Panel.

This useful book's question-and-answer format covers the most common questions of insurance plan administrators. Chapters of special importance for athletic trainers include 1 through 4 and 6 through 8.

Rowell, J.C. (1989). *Understanding medical insurance reimbursement: A step by step guide*. Oradell, NJ: Medical Economics.

This book is required reading for athletic trainers in clinics and hospitals. It not only defines the many insurance industry terms, but it also helps health care practitioners understand how to file insurance claims and cut through the red tape of third-party reimbursement.

Source book of health insurance data. (1991). Washington, DC: Health Insurance Association of America.

Published in annual editions since 1960, the *Source Book of Health Insurance Data* is loaded with facts, figures, and analysis about health care insurance in the United States. It is an excellent resource to help athletic trainers evaluate the cost-effectiveness of their insurance programs.

U.S. Small Business Administration. (1981). *Risk management and insurance*. Washington, DC: U.S. Government Printing Office.

This 40-page pamphlet describes the basic elements of small business insurance. It is particularly useful for athletic trainers who own sports medicine clinics, but it also offers useful exercises that will help any athletic trainer determine if the premium charged by an insurance company represents a good value.

CHAPTER
8

Protecting Athletic Trainers: Legal Considerations in Sports Medicine

STUDENT OBJECTIVES

▌ Define and discuss the legal principles most applicable to athletic training settings.

▌ Identify the types of situations most likely to hold liability concerns for athletic trainers.

▌ Understand the different types of credentialing laws that affect the practice of athletic training.

▌ Understand the elements required to prove negligence on the part of an athletic trainer.

▌ Be aware of the various legal defenses available to athletic trainers against charges of malpractice.

▌ Identify the most important elements of providing effective legal testimony.

▌ Identify and put into practice methods that avoid legal liability while improving the quality of athletic training care.

OPENING CASE

As the only certified athletic trainer for a large metropolitan high school, Todd Russell has over 500 student-athletes to care for. One Thursday, as Todd was in the training room packing for a Friday night football game on the other side of the state, the assistant soccer coach and one of his players carried in Enrique Vasquez, the team's back-up goalkeeper, and laid him on a treatment table. Todd examined Enrique's injured left ankle. Enrique explained that he had been involved in a collision in front of the goal, but he wasn't sure how he had injured the ankle. Most of his pain was located over the medial malleolus. Mild swelling was present. Active range of motion was painful in inversion and eversion, but not too bad in plantar and dorsiflexion. Todd told Enrique that he had probably sprained the deltoid ligament on the medial aspect of his ankle. He applied ice with an elastic bandage and elevated the injured foot. Because the team physician usually stopped in on Thursdays, Todd decided to keep Enrique in the training room and have the ankle examined. Todd returned to his packing while Enrique iced the ankle.

Todd removed the ice after 30 minutes, and the team physician arrived 10 minutes later. After evaluating the problem, the physician told Enrique that Todd's assessment was probably correct, but that he wanted Enrique to be seen by his family doctor the next day to get an X ray. Todd, who was present when these instructions were given, made sure that Enrique understood what he needed to do. He gave Enrique a pair of crutches and returned to his preparation for the football game.

Because the game was to be played nearly 300 miles away, Todd was not in school on Friday. Enrique, whose parents had no medical insurance, decided not to see his family physician or get an X ray. He used the crutches only sparingly, thinking that walking on the injured ankle would decrease the stiffness he felt. When he woke up on Saturday, however, his ankle was so swollen and painful that his mother took him to the emergency room, where a displaced fracture of the tibial malleolus was diagnosed.

Enrique underwent surgery later that day to stabilize the fracture. Unfortunately, he developed an infection and was hospitalized for the next 2 weeks. The infection caused scarring of the articular surfaces of the joint, leaving Enrique with a permanently stiff, sore ankle.

Several months later, both Todd and the team physician were surprised to learn that they, along with the school board, were being sued by Enrique's family.

Todd Russell faces the same pressures as many athletic trainers: too many athletes to care for and only student assistants to help provide that care. Yet the expectations he faces from coaches, physicians, parents, and administrators are substantial. He is expected to be caring, thorough, tireless, and wise every day (and night and weekend) he comes to work. If he makes a mistake, it is typically overlooked. But if he were to make the wrong mistake with the wrong person, his professional standing, his personal assets, and his self-respect could be seriously jeopardized.

Athletic trainers have been aware for some time that they need a general understanding of certain legal principles to protect themselves and the institutions that employ them from the risk of lawsuit (Gieck, Lowe, & Kenna, 1984). Wise athletic trainers, however, also realize that basic knowledge of legal principles, when applied thoughtfully and consistently, helps inform and improve their professional practice. These legal standards often provide extra incentive for athletic trainers to do what they ought to be doing routinely in their professional practice, whether they will be sued or not (Danzon, 1985).

This chapter cannot, of course, provide definitive, comprehensive coverage of all the law related to the practice of athletic training. But it will present to student athletic trainers the legal issues they are likely to encounter in their professional practice. If an athletic trainer is confronted with a specific legal issue or problem, the best source of information is an attorney who is experienced in handling similar cases (Horsley & Carlova, 1983). Effective policies and procedures, informed by consultation with both attorneys and insurance companies, also will help guide athletic trainers through the minefield of legal perils they face daily.

▮ Credentialing

Athletic trainers in every state are impacted in some way by the laws governing medical practice (Herbert, 1990). Such laws, emanating from public interest in self-protection, help to ensure that health care providers are competent. Athletic trainers have established a legal basis for their practice in 30 states.[1] In states without state-sponsored credentialing, athletic trainers may be able to carry out their duties by having them legally delegated by a supervising physician. But this possibility varies between states, and even in states where delegation is allowed, the circumstances under which athletic training tasks may be delegated are often unclear and open to legal interpretation (Hawkins, 1988).

Athletic trainers must become familiar with the practice acts that regulate the profession, which vary a great deal between states (see Appendix B). The acts define *athlete* and *athletic trainer* differently. Some limit the scope and setting in which the athletic trainer may practice. Some allow athletic trainers to charge a fee for service (Delaware and Massachusetts), whereas others prohibit fee-for-service billing (New Jersey and North Dakota). Many limit the athletic trainer to the use of certain types of therapeutic modalities. Most have very specific educational requirements that may or may not correspond to those required for certification by the NATA Board of Certification. A majority of state laws require physician supervision. Some states also allow other health professionals, such as physical therapists, chiropractors, and dentists to supervise the athletic trainer under certain circumstances. In those states without specific athletic training credentialing, the athletic

---

[1]As of October 1, 1993. For the most current list, contact Governmental Affairs, National Athletic Trainers Association, 2952 Stemmons, Dallas, TX 75247.

trainer should obtain a copy of the state's **medical practice act** to determine the scope and setting of practice the law permits athletic trainers and other health care providers.

Four types of credentialing laws regulate the practice of athletic training: licensure, certification, registration, and exemption.[2] Athletic trainers practicing in states with athletic training practice acts should review the state law to determine what type of credentialing is required—each type has different implications. In addition, the definitions and level of restrictiveness of each type of credentialing vary from state to state.

Licensure

Licensure is the most restrictive form of governmental credentialing. Licensure is intended to protect the public by limiting the practice of athletic training to those who have met the requirements of a licensing board established under the law. Licensure laws generally prohibit unlicensed individuals from calling themselves athletic trainers. More importantly, they prohibit unlicensed persons from performing the tasks reserved for athletic trainers under the law. States that license athletic trainers (see Figure 8.1) usually

▌Figure 8.1 States that license athletic trainers. *Note.* From "Governmental Affairs" by the National Athletic Trainers Association, 1992, *NATA NEWS*, **4**(2), p. 21. Copyright 1992 by the National Athletic Trainers Association. Adapted by permission.

• Alabama	• New Mexico	• Texas
• Delaware	• North Dakota	
• Georgia	• Ohio	
• Massachusetts	• Oklahoma	
• Mississippi	• Rhode Island	
• Nebraska	• South Dakota	

require a specific educational background comprised of both course work and experience in addition to passing a licensing examination administered by the board. Some states that license athletic trainers will accept the equivalent of the NATA Board of Certification standards, but many have different requirements as well. Licensing boards are powerful legal entities because they are usually empowered to set the rules, in accordance with the law, that govern who may practice and who may not. They also set the fee required for license applications and renewals.

Certification

Certification is a less stringent form of professional regulation than licensure. A person who is certified is generally recognized to possess the basic knowledge and skills required of practitioners in the profession. Both states and professional associations can certify health care practitioners. The NATA Board of Certification (NATABOC), for example, is the recognized certifying agency for ensuring that athletic trainers have the basic knowledge and skills

---

[2]For an excellent discussion of the various types of credentialing laws that govern the practice of athletic training, see the governmental affairs section of the *NATA News*, **4**(2-6).

to carry out the duties of an athletic trainer as defined by the *Competencies in Athletic Training*. Athletic trainers who meet the requirements for NATABOC certification and maintain their certification are entitled to use the board's credential. Some states also certify athletic trainers (see Figure 8.2). States get the authority to certify athletic trainers from a credentialing

• Indiana	• New York	• Tennessee
• Kentucky	• Pennsylvania	
• Louisiana	• South Carolina	

Figure 8.2 States that certify athletic trainers. *Note.* From "Governmental Affairs" by the National Athletic Trainers Association, 1992, *NATA NEWS*, **4**(2), p. 21. Copyright 1992 by the National Athletic Trainers Association. Adapted by permission.

law passed by the state legislature and signed by the governor, the same process that gives them the authority for licensure. Unlike licensure, however, state certification usually protects only the athletic trainer's title, not the specific tasks performed by the athletic trainer. Noncertified persons could not call themselves athletic trainers, but they could perform the duties of an athletic trainer.

Registration

Registration is another form of professional regulation that is less restrictive than licensure. In states that have athletic trainer registration laws, athletic trainers are required to register with the state before practicing (see Figure 8.3). Some states allow a grace period in which athletic trainers may practice

registration *A type of state credentialing that requires qualified members of a profession to register with the state in order to practice.*

• Idaho	• Minnesota	• New Jersey
• Illinois	• Missouri	

Figure 8.3 States that register athletic trainers. *Note.* From "Governmental Affairs" by the National Athletic Trainers Association, 1992, *NATA NEWS*, **4**(2), p. 21. Copyright 1992 by the National Athletic Trainers Association. Adapted by permission.

without being registered, as long as they begin their application for registration within the time frame established by the state's board governing athletic trainers. Because unregistered persons are prohibited from practicing, the registration law becomes a form of title protection for the athletic trainer. States that require registration may or may not require screening devices such as examinations, although most prescribe the educational requirements necessary to register as an athletic trainer.

Exemption

Some states have provided the legal basis for athletic trainers to practice by exempting them from complying with the practice acts of other professions, typically physical therapy, physician assistant, medical, and masseuse practice acts (see Figure 8.4). Although *exemption* is often viewed as the least restrictive form of professional regulation, athletic trainers may still be required to meet a variety of standards, usually related to educational background or certification by the NATABOC, to qualify. In addition, athletic

exemption *A legislative mechanism used to release members of one profession from the liability of violating another profession's practice act.*

trainers are required to act according to the standards of the profession and the boundaries of their training.

Figure 8.4 States that exempt athletic trainers from other health professions' practice acts. *Note.* From "Governmental Affairs" by the National Athletic Trainers Association, 1992, *NATA NEWS*, **4**(2), p. 21. Copyright 1992 by the National Athletic Trainers Association. Adapted by permission.

• Arizona	• Hawaii
• Colorado	• New Hampshire
• Connecticut	

Legal Principles

Athletic trainers can be subject to judicial claims based on a wide variety of legal theories, and trainers in different settings must be aware of the legal concepts specific to their setting. Athletic trainers also employed as high school teachers, for example, must understand the law that applies to their teaching role as well as to their allied health care role. Athletic trainers employed in professional sports must at least be aware of the basic principles of employer-employee law, especially as it applies to health care.

The common threat faced by all athletic trainers who provide sports medicine services to patients is athletic trainer ***malpractice***. Scott (1990) defines health care malpractice as "liability-generating conduct associated with the adverse outcome of patient treatment. Liability may be based on:

malpractice *Liability-generating conduct associated with the adverse outcome of patient treatment (Scott, 1990).*

- Negligent patient care
- Failure to obtain informed consent
- Intentional conduct
- Breach of a contract
- Use/transfer of a defective product
- Abnormally dangerous treatment" (p. 6)

Torts

breach of contract *An unexcused failure to perform the obligations created by a negotiated agreement, either formal or informal.*

tort *A legal wrong, other than breach of contract, for which the court system provides a remedy, typically in the form of monetary damages.*

Although athletic trainers may enter patient-practitioner relationships that are implied contracts, unhappy patients are less likely to bring a legal action based on ***breach of contract*** than on an accusation that the athletic trainer committed a ***tort*** (Wadlington, Waltz, & Dworkin, 1980). A tort is a legal wrong other than breach of contract for which a remedy will be provided, usually in the form of monetary damages. Actions based upon tort are pressed by plaintiffs in civil legal proceedings, as opposed to criminal cases, which are initiated by the government. All the legal bases for malpractice, other than breach of contract, are based on tort law. Of the three types of tort, intentional tort, negligent tort, and strict liability tort, most malpractice actions are based upon negligence, which focuses on the conduct of the practitioner.

Negligence

negligence *A type of tort in which a professional fails to act as a reasonably prudent practitioner would act under the circumstances.*

Athletic trainers are usually sued under a negligent tort theory (Leverenz & Helms, 1990a). ***Negligence*** is a type of tort in which the athletic trainer fails to act as a reasonably prudent athletic trainer would act under the circumstances (Drowatzky, 1985). Athletic trainers can be negligent either by *omission* or *commission*. Omission is the failure to do something that should have been done under the circumstances. Commission occurs when the athletic trainer performs an act that should not have been committed. To prove an athletic trainer was negligent, the aggrieved patient must be able to substantiate the following five components (Ciccolella, 1991):

- Conduct by the athletic trainer
- Existence of duty
- Breach of duty
- Causation
- Damage

omission *A failure to act in accordance with the standard of care required of an individual when there was a legal duty to do so.*

commission *An action that violates the legal standard of care when a legal duty exists.*

Conduct

To substantiate a charge of negligence, the plaintiff must be able to prove that the athletic trainer, either by commission or omission, actually did something that links him to the case. Nonactions, such as thoughts, attitudes, or intentions, cannot render the athletic trainer negligent. Only when athletic trainers take an action (or fail to take an action) can they be successfully accused of negligence. In the opening case, Todd Russell's failure to contact Enrique's parents may constitute proof of the conduct portion of a negligence claim.

Duty

When does an athletic trainer owe a duty to an injured athlete? Generally speaking, athletic trainers employed by educational institutions have a duty to provide athletic training services to athletes actively engaged in the institution's athletic program. Athletic trainers employed by professional sports teams have the same duty toward team members. This duty has its legal origin in the athletic trainer's contract, in which the athletic trainer agrees to provide these services in return for payment. Whether the high school or university athletic trainer owes a duty to the student who becomes injured in an intramural basketball game or a physical education class is less clear—it depends on the responsibilities defined by the employment contract. This is a good reason that athletic trainers should have an employment contract with a clearly written position description delineating their specific responsibilities.

Athletic trainers employed by sports medicine clinics have greater leeway in deciding who they will accept as patients. Consequently, the injured athletes they owe a duty to should, in theory, be only those patients they choose to treat in their clinics. There are enough exceptions to this general rule, however, that sports medicine clinic owners should consult with their attorneys to find out who they may owe a duty to and under what circumstances. For example, sports medicine clinics that have a contract to provide services to an HMO may have a duty to provide services to the HMO's subscribers.

abandonment   *The desertion of a patient-practitioner relationship by the health care provider without the consent of the patient.*

Abandonment is another issue related to duty that affects athletic trainers. Once an athletic trainer chooses to provide services to an injured athlete, whether a duty originally existed or not, the athletic trainer does not have the legal freedom to simply walk away from the case except under certain circumstances. The trainer cannot forsake even athletes who do not cooperate or who fail to pay their bills—unless they provide adequate warning and enough time to find alternative care.

If the injured athlete recovers and the athletic trainer and the patient agree that further treatment is no longer necessary, they can jointly terminate the relationship. If the athlete has been referred, the athletic trainer has a duty to inform the referring agent, usually a physician, that treatment is being discontinued.

The athletic trainer can also discontinue services without fear of being charged with abandonment if the patient voluntarily terminates the relationship. The athletic trainer should make sure (and should be able to prove), however, that the patient understands the consequences of discontinuing the therapy.

If the athletic trainer is away from the sports medicine center and leaves the athlete's care in the hands of another practitioner, abandonment may also be charged. If the practitioner substituting for the athletic trainer commits a negligent act, the trainer may be found negligent as well. Athletic trainers should avoid this problem by informing patients when they plan to be gone and making sure that the patient agrees to be treated by the substitute practitioner. The athletic trainer owes a duty to the patient to make sure that the substitute is competent and is capable of providing the same standard of care as the athletic trainer.

In general, the duties owed by the athletic trainer to the athlete are those described in the NATA's *Competencies in Athletic Training*. Specific duties identified by the courts include the duty to

- provide or obtain reasonable medical assistance for injured athletes as soon as possible under the circumstances in such a way as to avoid aggravation of the injury (a probable breach of this duty occurred in the opening case). This implies having an effective emergency action plan, complete with necessary first aid supplies and communications with ambulance services;

- maintain the confidentiality of the patient's medical records;

- provide adequate and proper supervision and instruction;

- provide safe facilities and equipment; and

- fully disclose information about the athlete's medical condition to the athlete in question.

Breach of Duty

The next step in proving negligence against an athletic trainer requires the aggrieved athlete to establish by a preponderance of the evidence that the athletic trainer actually breached a duty owed the athlete. The issue here is whether the athletic trainer exercised the ***standard of care*** that other reasonably prudent athletic trainers would have exercised under the circumstances. The athletic trainer can consult the standards of practice of various medical and athletic professional organizations to determine a standard of care if questions arise.[3] It is important to recognize that the standard of care does not require the athletic trainer to be the *most* knowledgeable or competent athletic trainer in the profession. If this were the case, nobody could meet the standard. Instead, the standard requires athletic trainers to perform their duties as other competent athletic trainers would under similar circumstances. In determining whether athletic trainers have met the standard of care, the laws of various states require that their actions be compared to those of other athletic trainers in one of the following three settings (Scott, 1990):

- The same locality
- Similar communities
- The same or similar circumstances

The standard of care expected of athletic trainers in fulfilling their duties to injured athletes can depend on whether the state has credentialed the profession. Herbert (1990) posits that in those states without statutory credentialing, the athletic trainer may be held to the standard of care of other regulated health professionals, including physicians. Indeed, in Gillespie v. Southern Utah State College,[4] a student athletic trainer was held to the standard of care of a physician in the treatment of a sprained ankle that later developed serious complications (Leverenz & Helms, 1990b).

Causation

Once the aggrieved athlete has demonstrated that the athletic trainer breached a duty to exercise reasonable care, the athlete must prove that the breach was in fact the legal cause of the injury (or made the original injury worse). The courts use two tests to determine causation. First, the plaintiff must prove ***actual cause***. Actual cause will be established if the athlete can demonstrate that the athletic trainer's actions were a considerable determining factor in the damage claimed. The athletic trainer may be found only partially responsible for causing or aggravating the injury. Team physicians, coaches, and institutions may be named as codefendants in negligence cases because all of them may have contributed to the injury. If more than one defendant was responsible for causing or aggravating the injury, they will be found jointly and severally liable for the negligence.

The second causation test is the requirement to demonstrate the existence of ***proximate (legal) cause***. Proximate cause exists when an athletic trainer takes an action that foreseeably leads to harm or injury to another or to an event that injures another. Inherent in the notion of proximate cause is the ***foreseeability*** of the harm allegedly precipitated by the athletic trainer. The requirement that harm must be foreseeable is positive for athletic trainers—it

standard of care *The legal duty to provide health care services consistent with what other health care practitioners of the same training, education, and credentialing would provide under the circumstances.*

actual cause *The degree to which a health care practitioner's actions are associated with the adverse outcomes of a patient's care.*

proximate (legal) cause *An act that naturally and foreseeably leads to harm or injury to another or to an event that injures another.*

foreseeability *The knowledge or notice that a result is likely to occur if a certain act occurs.*

---

[3]For a useful guide to standards in sports medicine, see Herbert, D.L. (1992). *The sports medicine standards book.* Canton, OH: Professional Reports Corporation.

[4]Gillespie v. Southern Utah State College, 669 P.2d. 861 (Ut. 1983).

doesn't penalize them for results that were improbable or unlikely. One of the problems in the opening case is that the team physician and athletic trainer did not ensure that an X ray of Enrique's injured ankle was obtained, even though they should have known that if a fracture was present it could have been aggravated by delayed or improper treatment. In short, they should have foreseen serious consequences.

Damage

The final element in establishing negligence is to determine if the aggrieved athlete actually suffered damages. If the athletic trainer breached a duty without causing any harm, no negligence has occurred. The athletic trainer who oversteps his level of training by suturing a wound, for example, cannot be found negligent unless the plaintiff can prove that she suffered harm as a result (a charge of practicing medicine without a license would probably have merit, however). Although physical damage is the most common and easily proved, the law recognizes other forms of damage as well. Emotional distress and loss of consortium (injury to the marital relationship) are just two examples (Herbert, 1990).

■ Legal Defenses

Athletic trainers accused of malpractice have several possible legal defenses. None of these should be viewed as ironclad protection against lawsuit, however—each defense has exceptions that could leave the athletic trainer liable, even though the general principle may be valid. The best defense, of course, is to provide high-quality athletic training services consistent with the standard of care expected in the profession and the statutory regulations of the state. The following legal defenses may apply to claims of athletic trainer malpractice:

- statute of limitations
- sovereign immunity
- assumption of risk
- Good Samaritan immunity
- comparative negligence

Statute of Limitations

statutes of limitations
Laws that fix a certain length of time beyond which legal actions cannot be initiated.

Statutes of limitations are state laws that fix a certain length of time in which an aggrieved patient may sue a health care provider. The statute of limitations applies in most states to health care providers who have been statutorily recognized by the state. States in which athletic training practice is regulated, therefore, probably extend the statutes of limitations to cover athletic trainers, but other states may not. Athletic trainers in states that don't provide credentials who are employed by physicians, hospitals, or physical therapists may also be protected because their employers are regulated. Although the time period established by the statute of limitations usually begins when the injury occurs and extends through a fixed period of time, many exceptions can lengthen the period of time in which the athlete can bring suit.

Sovereign Immunity

Sovereign or *governmental immunity* is a legal doctrine that holds that neither governments nor their agents can be held liable for negligent torts (Baley & Matthews, 1984). In theory, athletic trainers employed in public schools, colleges, and universities are immune from legal liability because they are agents of governmental entities. In fact, however, many governmental units, including the federal government, have substantially lowered this traditional shield against legal liability (Herbert & Herbert, 1989). Athletic trainers employed in public institutions should not proceed as if they are immune by virtue of their positions, even though Leverenz and Helms (1990b) have identified three cases in which athletic trainers avoided liability based on a claim of governmental immunity.[5]

sovereign (governmental) immunity A legal doctrine that holds that neither governments nor their agents can be held liable for negligent actions.

Assumption of Risk

One of the oldest and most common defenses that educational institutions and their employees have used against legal liability in athletic injury cases is *assumption of risk*. In this defense, the athletic trainer asserts that the injured athlete was aware of the risks involved and decided to proceed anyway, thereby absolving the institution and the athletic trainer from any liability for damages. Scott (1990) points out that this defense is only valid when two conditions are met. The athlete must "fully appreciate" the type and magnitude of the risk involved in participating in the activity. The athlete must also "knowingly, voluntarily, and unequivocally" choose to participate in the activity in the face of the inherent risks. Skillful attorneys usually have little trouble defeating this defense, especially when the injured party is a minor. To protect against legal liability and improve their chances of being able to use this defense should the need arise, many schools and colleges provide educational sessions, complete with videos and printed materials, that warn student-athletes and their parents of the specific dangers inherent in their sports. Following these sessions, participants are asked to sign a statement affirming that they have been warned of the dangers associated with their sport (including permanent disability and death), that they understand these risks, that they have been offered the opportunity to ask questions regarding the risks, and that they voluntarily choose to participate irrespective of the risks.

assumption of risk A legal defense to a tort action in which the plaintiff is said to have voluntarily chosen to face the risk or danger that occurred and therefore has no right to complain of its occurrence.

Good Samaritan Immunity

A defense that may be used by athletic trainers in a very limited number of settings is immunity by virtue of a *Good Samaritan law*. Good Samaritan laws enacted in some states protect health care providers who voluntarily come to the aid of an injured person. These statutes may or may not cover athletic trainers. Specific Good Samaritan laws in some states protect volunteer team physicians from legal liability (Benda, 1991). Because athletic

Good Samaritan laws Statutes intended to shield certain health care practitioners from certain types of legal liability when they voluntarily come to the aid of an injured or ill person under specific circumstances.

---

[5]Garza v. Edinburg Consolidated Independent School District, 576 S.W.2d. 916 (Tx. 1979), Lowe v. Texas Tech University, 540 S.W.2d. 297 (Tx. 1976), and Sorey v. Kellett, 849 F.2d. 429 (5th Cir. 1988).

trainers are increasingly volunteering to serve at state games and charitable athletic events, this defense may become more popular. Generally, the Good Samaritan defense applies only when no compensation of any kind has been provided or will be expected. The injured person, of course, must consent to be treated. The statutes do not protect the athletic trainer from willful or wanton misconduct or from gross or intentional negligence.

▌ Some states protect some medical professionals from the threat of legal liability when they volunteer their services.
Photo by Rob Anderson/Special Olympics International.

Comparative Negligence

comparative negligence
A means of measuring negligence whereby the negligence of the plaintiff is compared with that of the defendant and the award to the plaintiff is reduced by the amount of negligence attributed to the plaintiff.

As was true in the opening case, patients sometimes ignore the prescriptions of their health care providers, which leads to injury or aggravates an injury. The courts often use the doctrine of *comparative negligence* to determine if the liability for an athlete's injuries should be divided between the plaintiff and the defendant(s). Comparative negligence determines the degree of fault the athletic trainer and the injured athlete have for causing the injury. The athletic trainer's financial liability depends on the formula used in the state in which the case is tried. In most states, injured athletes can only collect damages if their comparative culpability is less than half the total. In some states, however, injured athletes can be awarded financial restitution equal to the athletic trainer's percentage of fault. For instance, if Enrique's negligence accounted for 25 percent of the total fault for the aggravation of his injury, Todd Russell and his team physician may have to pay 75 percent of the damage claim.

testimony   Statements offered under oath, subject to cross-examination, as evidence to the facts in a legal proceeding.

▌ Providing Testimony at Deposition or Trial

Even though athletic trainers are sued infrequently, they may be called to provide *testimony* in a court. The athletic trainer may give testimony at a deposition, which is an informal series of questions posed under oath prior to the trial during the course of case preparation. A second type of testimony is provided under oath at trial. The athletic trainer may be called either as a "fact" witness or as an "expert" witness. As a fact witness, the athletic trainer either had responsibility for treating an injured athlete or has knowledge of the facts of the case. The athletic trainer has few choices about appearing in court under these circumstances since the court may issue a *subpoena* ordering appearance.

subpoena   An order issued by a court compelling the testimony of a witness at deposition or trial.

An attorney may retain an athletic trainer as an expert to testify on behalf of a client. Expert witnesses are paid to provide testimony that will educate the judge and jury about the standard of care that should be applied in the particular case. As an expert witness, the athletic trainer should agree with the positions she will be asked to take at trial. She should also be sure the attorney who hired her has the facts to support the case. Otherwise she may appear ignorant and foolish on the witness stand.

Whether an athletic trainer is subpoenaed or appears as an expert witness, the following guidelines should be observed to be perceived as a credible witness (Horsley & Carlova, 1983):

- Avoid memorizing the testimony.

- Never guess. If you're unsure of the answer to a question, admit lack of knowledge on that point.

- Testify only about issues for which you are an expert. Do not testify beyond the boundaries of your experience.

- Prepare for your testimony by carefully studying the records of the case before entering the courtroom. If you need to refer to the medical records while on the stand, understand that the records will be considered evidence that the opposing attorney will be able to access.

- Discuss your testimony with your attorney or the attorney retaining you as a witness prior to actually giving it in the courtroom.

- Use common language. Whenever you use medical language, attempt to interpret it for the judge and jury.

- Be absolutely sure that your testimony in court is consistent with any depositions you may have made prior to the beginning of the trial. Always review the deposition prior to taking the stand.

- Ask the judge if you feel the need to expand on a yes/no question posed by an attorney.

- Ask the judge if you feel that answering a question would violate the athletic trainer–patient relationship.

- Use illustrations (charts, drawings, slides, photographs, etc.) to help make your point when appropriate.

- If charged with malpractice and your malpractice insurance company has provided a lawyer you feel uncomfortable with, hire your own attorney.

- Maintain a professional, dignified demeanor at all times. Dress neatly, answer in a normal tone of voice at an even rate, and be respectful of the judge, jury, and attorneys.

▌ Strategies for Avoiding Legal Liability

At the beginning of this chapter, I suggested that a knowledge of legal liability should help improve the quality of care offered by the athletic trainer. To place that rather sweeping statement into context, consider the following suggestions as part of a strategy to avoid the threat of legal liability (Graham, 1985).

Build Relationships

Develop and maintain good relations with athletes, parents, co-workers, subordinates, and other health care professionals with whom you work or to whom you commonly refer injured athletes. You should not only build trust relationships, but also promote a constant flow of two-way communication with these groups.

Insist on a Written Contract

Have a written contract supported by a detailed position description that clearly delineates the athletic trainer's job functions. This is one of the most important defenses the athletic trainer can offer against a charge of negligence because it helps establish those to whom the athletic trainer may owe a legal duty.

Obtain Informed Consent

Obtain informed consent for the services you perform. In the case of minors, obtain informed consent from their parents. Warn athletes and parents of the dangers, including permanent disability and death, inherent in their particular sport. Repeat such warnings annually.

▌ A comprehensive physical examination by a licensed physician is an essential first step in avoiding legal liability in sports medicine.

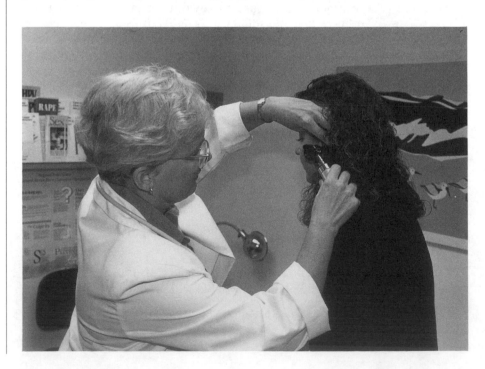

Provide Physical Examinations

Be certain that every athlete undergoes a physical examination by a medical practitioner licensed by the state to perform such examinations. Make certain that the content of the physical examination is consistent with nationally recognized standards.

Know the Profession

Develop and maintain a data base of information about injuries and illnesses that are most common to each sport you work with. This will enhance your qualifications as an expert in your field.

Document Hazards

Make a documented attempt to reduce injuries by recommending or personally taking action to remove or modify potential hazards. Consider establishing a safety committee that would be charged with conducting an ongoing program of risk assessment and reduction. Be aware, however, that a "paper trail" documenting safety hazards can also be used against the athletic trainer or the institution, especially if the hazards are not corrected or the corrections go undocumented.

Establish Policies

Adopt and scrupulously adhere to policies and procedures designed to reduce the incidence of injury and to guide the actions of sports medicine personnel when injuries do occur. Keep all emergency first aid equipment in working order and available to those who will need to use it.

Document Activities

Document the details of all injuries, treatments, and rehabilitative procedures so a chronology of events can easily be determined after the fact. Maintain medical records until well after the statute of limitations for malpractice liability has expired.

Maintain Confidentiality

Maintain the confidentiality of the athlete's medical record. When you wish to share the information with others, obtain the written permission of the athlete first.

Participate in Continuing Education

Take part in continuing athletic training education by attending seminars and symposia and reading sports medicine literature. Alter your techniques as technology and knowledge advance. Document your continuing education activities and the changes that result.

Recognize Your Qualifications

Practice only within the limitations of your state's law and the boundaries of your training. Be consistent with the standard of care expected of other reasonably prudent athletic trainers. Be quick to refer injured athletes to physicians.

Insurance

All athletic trainers, certified and student alike, should have malpractice and liability insurance to safeguard personal assets in the event of a legal action. Even if a malpractice suit is frivolous and eventually dismissed, the costs associated with defense are usually beyond the means of most athletic trainers. In some cases, the employer's general liability policy will adequately protect the athletic trainer. In many cases, however, health care activities are specifically excluded from institutional liability insurance policies. In addition, the maximum benefit of institutional policies may not cover the fantastic costs associated with medical litigation. Athletic trainers who are inadequately protected through their employer's liability insurance policy should seriously consider purchasing their own policy.[6]

▌ Applications to Athletic Training: Theory Into Practice

Apply the concepts discussed in this chapter to the following two case studies to help you prepare for similar situations in actual practice. The questions at the end of the studies have many possible correct solutions. Use the case studies for homework, exam questions, or to spur class discussion.

CASE STUDY 1

Larry Donelson was pleased when the management of the professional football team that employed him allowed him to hire an additional student athletic trainer for the preseason training camp. The preseason was always one of the most hectic times, and he was grateful for the help that students were able to provide. One of the students he had decided to hire this year, Rich Hayes, was only a sophomore. Larry usually only hired students who had completed their junior year, but Rich had come highly recommended from his supervising athletic trainer, an old friend of Larry's, so he had decided to take a chance on Rich.

James Star was a 10th-round draft choice trying to make the team that summer. James had played college football at the same university Rich was attending. Although he felt good about his performance in the first two weeks, a knee injury suffered in the first scrimmage had kept him out of practice since then. Fortunately, the knee was starting to feel better and James hoped he could return to limited practice within a couple of days.

---

[6]The National Athletic Trainers Association offers malpractice and liability insurance to its members through Maginnis & Associates. Contact Maginnis & Associates, 332 South Michigan Avenue, Chicago, IL 60604.

One day the head coach surprised everybody by announcing that the team would have the next morning off. The student trainers, knowing they wouldn't have to wake up at the usual 5:30 a.m., decided to visit a local pub that night. It was the only bar in the small college town where the team had its training camp, so most of the players went there as well.

Rich saw James at the pub and joined him. Three beers later, the topic of James's knee injury came up. When James told Rich he was feeling better and would probably be back in a couple of days, Rich confided that he had heard Larry Donelson, the team physician, and the head coach talking about James a couple of days ago while he was cleaning a whirlpool. When James asked what they had said, Rich told them they were simply discussing the details of James's knee injury and his prospects for full recovery. After two more beers, James had the whole story.

When James was released from the team the next week, he immediately contacted his agent, an attorney, who filed a lawsuit on his behalf alleging that the team had concealed the true nature of James's injury, which resulted in his termination and subsequent unemployment.

QUESTIONS FOR ANALYSIS

1. What legal principles are involved in this case? How do they apply? Does James have a strong case? Why or why not?

2. How could this situation have been avoided? What policies and procedures should Larry Donelson institute to prevent this kind of problem?

3. Who, if anyone, is at fault in this case? If more than one person, how is a judge or jury likely to determine the percentage of each person's liability?

4. What records could Larry use to defend himself and the team?

CASE STUDY 2

Christine Campbell, the assistant athletic trainer for Northwest State University, was off the bench like a shot when she saw the basketball team's star center fall to the floor holding her knee. After conducting an examination on the floor, Christine decided to take the player to the training room for a more complete examination by the team physician. She and the student manager, who were both at least 10 in. shorter than the player, helped her hobble off the court toward the training room. As they were passing the locker room, the student manager slipped on a wet spot, causing the player to put her full weight on the injured knee. She cried out in pain and told Christine that she felt a "pop."

After the team physician, a general practitioner employed by the student health service, completed his examination, he informed the player that she had torn the anterior cruciate and medial collateral ligaments in her knee and would need surgery to correct the problem. He instructed Christine to do the following things, all of which he recorded in his postevaluation dictation for the athlete's medical record:

- *Apply an elastic wrap from the toes to midthigh.*
- *Apply a knee immobilizer.*
- *Fit the athlete with crutches.*

- *Arrange an orthopedic consultation for the next day.*
- *Give enough 600 mg ibuprofen for 3 days.*

Later that night, a phone call from the athlete's roommate woke Christine, who found out that the athlete had become violently ill and had to be rushed to the hospital by ambulance after suffering a reaction to the medication Christine had given her.

QUESTIONS FOR ANALYSIS

1. What legal principles are involved in this case? What liability concerns should be addressed? What policies and procedures should be implemented to address these concerns?

2. What would you have done differently, if anything, if you were in Christine's position?

3. Who, if anyone, is at fault in this case? If more than one person, how should a judge or jury determine the degree to which each person is liable?

▌ Summary

Although the thought of legal action against an athletic trainer is unsettling, prudent athletic trainers will take advantage of their legal knowledge to improve the quality of the service they provide to their athletes. The best and most important source of legal advice, of course, is an attorney experienced in dealing with health care malpractice issues.

Credentialing laws, including licensure, certification, registration, and exemption, are designed to insure basic competencies to protect the public. All athletic trainers should become familiar with the laws in their states to determine their legal basis for practice. Athletic trainers who practice in states without credentialing laws, although they may be protected by the delegatory clause of the medical practice act, may be held to the standard of care of a physician in a malpractice case.

Torts are legal wrongs, other than breach of contract, for which a court will determine a remedy, usually in the form of monetary damages. Negligence is the kind of tort most commonly charged against athletic trainers. To prove negligence, the aggrieved athlete must demonstrate conduct by the athletic trainer, existence of duty, breach of duty, causation (including actual and proximate cause), and damage. Athletic trainers will be held to the same standard of care as other reasonably prudent athletic trainers in the same or similar circumstances.

Although several defenses against charges of malpractice exist, including statutes of limitations, sovereign immunity, assumption of risk, Good Samaritan immunity, and comparative negligence, the athletic trainer's best defense is to practice in a manner consistent with the standards of the profession.

Should an athletic trainer be called to provide testimony, either as a fact witness or as an expert witness, he should prepare by reviewing the records of the case, consulting with the attorney, and speaking to only the facts of the case within the limits of his experience and training.

■ Annotated Bibliography

Baley, J.A., & Matthews, D.L. (1984). *Law and liability in athletics, physical education, and recreation.* Boston: Allyn & Bacon.

> This book, intended primarily for athletic administrators and coaches, also has value for the school athletic trainer. It includes descriptions of legal duties in school settings, administrative procedures for avoiding lawsuits, and procedures for reducing injuries in school-sponsored athletic programs.

Benda, C. (1991). Sideline Samaritans. *The Physician and Sportsmedicine,* **19**(11), 132-142.

> This article applies the Good Samaritan law to team physicians. For athletic trainers who work with nonpaid team physicians, it is a useful source of information to help protect the sports medicine program's team physician from threat of legal liability.

Ciccolella, M. (1991). Caught in court. *College Athletic Management,* **3**(4), 10-13.

> The author discusses, in plain language, the concept of negligence as it applies to athletic injuries in higher education settings. Of particular merit are the sections that discuss in detail the five components of negligence.

Danzon, P.M. (1985). *Medical malpractice.* Cambridge, MA: Harvard University Press.

> This book discusses the medical malpractice crisis. Athletic trainers are especially encouraged to read the first chapter, "Tort Liability as a System of Quality Control," to appreciate how the legal system should help provide an incentive for quality care.

Drowatzky, J.N. (1985). Legal duties and liability in athletic training. *Athletic Training,* **20**(1), 10-13.

> This well-written article summarizes the major legal principles athletic trainers should be familiar with to improve their practice and avoid lawsuits. Drowatzky offers six suggestions to help athletic trainers avoid legal complications.

Gieck, J., Lowe, J., & Kenna, K. (1984). Trainer malpractice: A sleeping giant. *Athletic Training,* **19**(1), 41-46.

> This article covers a few of the basic principles of negligence, including proximate cause and foreseeability. The authors place special emphasis on the importance of using written policies and protocols to avoid legal problems.

Graham, L.S. (1985). Ten ways to dodge the malpractice bullet. *Athletic Training,* **20**(2), 117-119.

As the title implies, the author describes the four most common liability threats to athletic trainers and provides 10 suggestions for avoiding these threats.

Hawkins, J. (1988). The legal status of athletic trainers. *The Sports, Parks and Recreation Law Reporter*, **2**(1), 6-9.

Hawkins discusses the implications for athletic training practice in states without statutory credentialing. He also discusses the standard of care expected of athletic trainers.

Herbert, D.L. (1990). *Legal aspects of sports medicine*. Canton, OH: Professional Reports Corporation.

This is an excellent source of legal information for athletic trainers and other members of the sports medicine team. It is well referenced and includes information on the legal aspects of a wide variety of tasks in sports medicine, including policy development, record keeping, preparticipation physical exams, medications, and communications with athletes. This book is highly recommended for all athletic trainers.

Herbert, D.L., & Herbert, W.G. (1989). *Legal aspects of preventative and rehabilitative exercise programs*, (2nd ed.). Canton, OH: Professional Reports Corporation.

This book is an excellent source of legal information for athletic trainers. It includes sections defining basic legal terms and their application to sports medicine settings.

Horsley, J.E., & Carlova, J. (1983). *Testifying in court*. Oradell, NJ: Medical Economics.

Horsley, an experienced medical malpractice attorney, explains the process of providing medical testimony in court. Although most athletic trainers will never need the advice he offers, those involved in legal actions, either as a defendant or as an expert witness, will find his suggestions useful.

Leverenz, L.J., & Helms, L.B. (1990a). Suing athletic trainers: Part I. *Athletic Training*, **25**(3), 212-216.

Leverenz and Helms searched the legal literature for cases involving athletic trainers. They identified the most common legal theories used to sue athletic trainers and the types of situations most likely to give rise to legal actions against athletic trainers.

Leverenz, L.J., & Helms, L.B. (1990b). Suing athletic trainers: Part II. *Athletic Training*, **25**(3), 219-226.

This article continues the authors' survey of the case law pertaining to athletic trainers. They analyze the law in the context of the NATA's *Competencies in Athletic Training*. Although the authors found no contradictions between the law and the *Competencies*, they were able to identify several issues that have legal implications but are not addressed by the *Competencies*.

Scott, R.W. (1990). *Health care malpractice*. Thorofare, NJ: Slack.

This excellent primer on malpractice in allied health care settings, written by an attorney-physical therapist, addresses many of the major legal problems athletic trainers face daily. The book would be especially appropriate for athletic trainers employed in sports medicine clinics, but athletic trainers in any setting will find it very helpful.

Wadlington, W., Waltz, J.R., & Dworkin, R.B. (1980). *Law and medicine*. Mineola, NY: Foundation Press.

This is a very comprehensive text that uses a case study approach to explain the principles of medical malpractice. Most of the discussion is about physician liability, but most of the legal concepts can be applied to athletic training.

WOTS UP Analysis for a Sports Medicine Program

The following nine worksheets constitute a WOTS UP analysis for a sports medicine program. This worksheet package has been adapted by permission of Donald A. Campbell and Company.

WORKSHEET 1
Benefits and concerns relative to strategic planning

Instructions:

1. List the benefits you expect from our strategic planning as well as any concerns.

2. Note possible ways to overcome each of your concerns. Circle the best ideas.

Benefits expected

Concerns

Ways to overcome concerns

WORKSHEET 2
Organizing the planning process

Instructions:

Indicate how each of the following issues should be handled. Outline the steps, responsibilities, and time lines for developing the strategic plan.

1. We should develop a strategic plan for:

_____ The entire sports medicine program

_____ Only part of the sports medicine program (which part?)

_____ The entire sports medicine program and each of its subprograms

_____ Other _____

2. For what period of time should we plan?

_____ Next 2 years	_____ Next 5 years
_____ Next 3 years	_____ Next 6 years
_____ Next 4 years	_____ Other _____

3. What critical issues do you hope the planning will address?

4. How much time should we spend planning?

5. Should we use a consultant or other resource person in developing our plan?

    _____ Yes

    _____ No

    _____ Unsure

    If so, what kind of help do we need?

6. Who should be part of the planning team? Check all that apply.

_____ Athletic trainers		_____ Consultants	
_____ Team physicians		_____ Student athletic trainers	
_____ Athletic administrators		_____ Patients	
_____ Coaches		_____ Others _____	

7. How large should the planning team be?

_____ 5-8	_____ 17-20
_____ 9-12	_____ More than 20
_____ 13-16	

8. Are there any others we should involve in the development of the plan? In the review of the plan?

9. Who should manage the overall planning effort?

10. Who should lead or chair the planning meetings?

11. By what date should we have the plan completed for approval?

12. Outline the steps you envision us using as we develop our plan.

Steps	Person(s) responsible	Deadline

WORKSHEET 3
History and present situation

Instructions:

Review the history and present situation of the sports medicine program as they pertain to your area of responsibility. List any historical trends that will need attention as we plan for the future. Do not hesitate to comment on areas *outside* of your realm of responsibility if you so desire.

WORKSHEET 4
Questions about mission

Instructions:

1. Describe below what you understand the mission of the sports medicine program to be.

2. List any questions, ideas, or concerns you have about the present mission of the sports medicine program.

3. Do you envision any changes in the mission of the sports medicine program? If so, what do you want to accomplish? Who will be served by such a change?

WORKSHEET 5
Client, customer, and stakeholder needs

Instructions:

1. List the needs of present or potential "customers" that the sports medicine program might address. Note ideas for how the sports medicine program might meet those needs.

2. List the significant groups that have a stake in what the sports medicine program does. How can the program meet their needs?

Clients and Customers

Describe existing or possible target groups	Their needs	Ways to meet those needs

Other stakeholders	Their needs	Ways to meet those needs

WORKSHEET 6
Competitors and allies

Instructions:

1. List present and possible new competitors, what the sports medicine program competes for, and our program's relative advantages and disadvantages (price, services, etc.).

2. List possible allies and how the sports medicine program might team up with each organization, person, or group.

Competitors   What we compete for

Existing

New

Our advantages   Our disadvantages

Allies of the sports medicine program

How can we team up with our allies?

WORKSHEET 7
Opportunities and threats

Instructions:

1. List and rank the major opportunities and threats that you believe the sports medicine program will face in the next five years that will determine its success or failure.

2. Use the information from worksheets 5 and 6 to help provide a more detailed analysis of our clients and stakeholders.

3. Be sure to consider the social, cultural, economic, political, and technological forces that may impact the sports medicine program in the next five years.

Opportunities

Threats

WORKSHEET 8
Strengths and weaknesses

Instructions:

1. List the major strengths and weaknesses of the sports medicine program as it looks toward the future.

Strengths and assets

Weaknesses and liabilities

WORKSHEET 9
Critical issues for the future

Instructions:

1. Review worksheets 3-8 and list critical issues or choices that the sports medicine program faces over the next 5 years.

Critical issues or choices

State Credentialing Boards[1]

The following list includes the names, addresses, and phone numbers of the state boards regulating athletic training through licensure, certification, or registration laws in the United States. The boards can provide information on regulatory requirements, fees, and forms. Although 30 states regulate athletic training, only the listed 25 states have regulatory boards. The other five states regulate through exemption laws; therefore, they do not have regulatory boards.

ALABAMA
Address not available[2]

DELAWARE
Board of Athletic Trainers
O'Neal Building
P.O. Box 1401
Dover, DE 19903
302-739-4522

GEORGIA
Georgia Board of Athletic Trainers
166 Pryor Street, SW
Atlanta, GA 30303
404-656-6719

IDAHO
Idaho State Board of Medicine
208 North Eighth Street
#202 State House
Boise, ID 83720
208-334-2822

ILLINOIS
Department of Professional
  Regulation
302 W. Washington, 3rd Floor
Springfield, IL 62786
217-785-0800

INDIANA
Address not available

KENTUCKY
Kentucky Board of Medical
  Licensure
310 Whittington Parkway, Ste. 1B
Louisville, KY 40222
502-429-8046
Attn: Angela Baker

LOUISIANA
Louisiana State Board of Medical
  Examiners
830 Union Street, Ste. 100
New Orleans, LA 70112-1499
504-524-6763

MASSACHUSETTS
Board of Allied Health Professions
State Office Building, 15th Floor
100 Cambridge Street
Boston, MA 02202
617-727-3071

MINNESOTA
Jeanne Hoffman
State Board of Medical Examiners
2700 University Ave., West #106
St. Paul, MN 55114-1080
612-642-0533

MISSISSIPPI
Mississippi State Department of
  Health
Office of Special Licensure
P.O. Box 1700
2423 North State Street
Jackson, MS 39215-1700
601-987-4153

MISSOURI
Missouri State Board for the
  Healing Arts
P.O. Box 4
Jefferson City, MO 65102
314-751-2334

NEBRASKA
Department of Health
Bureau of Examining Boards
301 Centennial Mall South
P.O. Box 95007
Lincoln, NE 68509-5007
402-471-2115

NEW JERSEY
The Board of Medical Examiners
28 West State Street
Trenton, NJ 08608
609-292-4843

---

[1]Reprinted with permission from National Athletic Trainers Association. (1993). Governmental affairs. *NATA NEWS*, **5**(9), 16.

[2]This list is accurate as of October 1, 1993. For the most up-to-date list, please contact the National Athletic Trainers Association, 2952 Stemmons, Dallas, TX 75247, 800-879-6282.

NEW MEXICO
Department of Regulation/Athletic
Trainers
P.O. Box 25101
Santa Fe, NM 87540
505-827-7164

NEW YORK
New York Education Department
Professional Education Office
Room 2039 Cultural Education
Center
Albany, NY 12230
518-474-3842

NORTH DAKOTA
Joe Kroeber, ATC
Jamestown High School
1210 Seventh Avenue, SE
Jamestown, ND 58401
701-252-0559

OHIO
Kent B. Carson
Executive Secretary
OT, PT, AT Board
77 South High Street, 16th Floor
Columbus, OH 43266-0317
614-466-3774

OKLAHOMA
Board of Medical Licensure &
Supervisions, State of Oklahoma
P.O. Box 18256
Oklahoma City, OK 73154
405-848-6841

PENNSYLVANIA
Bureau of Professional &
Occupational Affairs
P.O. Box 2649
Harrisburg, PA 17105-2649
717-783-7134

RHODE ISLAND
Rhode Island Department of
Health
Professional Regulations
75 Davis Street, Room 104
Providence, RI 02908
401-277-2827

SOUTH CAROLINA
Department of Health and
Environmental Control
2600 Bull Street
Columbia, SC 29201
803-737-4120

SOUTH DAKOTA
South Dakota Board of Medical
Examiners
1323 South Minnesota Avenue
Sioux Falls, SD 57005
605-336-1965

TENNESSEE
Melissa Haggard
Board of Medical Examiners
State Department of Health
283 Plus Park Blvd.
Nashville, TN 37247-1010
615-367-6393

TEXAS
Becky Berryhill
Texas Department of Health
Professional Licensing &
Certification Division
Advisory Board of Athletic
Trainers
1100 W. 49th Street
Austin, TX 78756
512-834-6615

abandonment   The desertion of a patient-practitioner relationship by the health care provider without the consent of the patient.

accuracy standards   Performance evaluation standards intended to improve the validity and reliability of the employee appraisal process.

actual cause   The degree to which a health care practitioner's actions are associated with the adverse outcomes of a patient's care.

adversaries   Persons who are unsupportive of both a program and a particular plan related to the program.

agreement-trust matrix   A model that identifies and types the most important people in developing support for a plan.

allies   Persons who exhibit a high level of support for a plan.

allocator of resources role   A type of decisional role in which the leader exercises authority to determine how organizational assets will be deployed.

application software   Computer programs designed to perform specific functions, such as word processing, statistical analysis, and graphics production.

assumption of risk   A legal defense to a tort action in which the plaintiff is said to have voluntarily chosen to face the risk or danger that occurred and therefore has no right to complain of its occurrence.

athletic accident insurance   A type of insurance policy intended to reimburse medical vendors for the expenses associated with acute athletic accidents.

authority   That aspect of power, granted to either groups or individuals, that legitimizes the right of the group or individual to make decisions on behalf of others.

bedfellows   Persons who exhibit support for a particular plan but who have a history of untrustworthy behavior and vacillation.

bidding   A process whereby vendors provide cost quotations for goods and services they wish to sell.

bidding documents   The package of materials prepared by the architect and sent to contractors, including the invitation to bid, the bid form, and special bidding instructions.

breach of contract   An unexcused failure to perform the obligations created by a negotiated agreement, either formal or informal.

bubble diagram   An abstract, graphic representation of the relationship of one function of a building to another based on the "closeness" established by the relationship chart.

budget   A type of operational plan for the coordination of resources and expenditures.

bulletin board   An electronic, on-line, interactive electronic data base system, usually organized by topic or interest group.

business plan   A written description of a business' activities, market analysis, historical and projected financial statements, and other associated information. Used by commercial loan officers to assess the viability of a business.

capital campaign   A program, usually of fixed length, designed to raise funds for program creation, development, and improvement.

capitation   A system whereby medical vendors are paid a fixed amount per patient.

catastrophic insurance   A type of accident insurance designed to provide lifelong medical, rehabilitation, and disability benefits for the victims of devastating injury.

certification   A form of title protection, established by state law or sponsored by professional associations, designed to ensure that practitioners possess essential knowledge and skills sufficient to protect the public.

charting by exception   A type of medical record that notes only those patient responses that vary from predefined norms.

clinical supervision   The process of direct observation of an employee's work, with emphasis on measurement of specific behaviors, and the subsequent development of plans to remediate deficiencies in performance.

clone   Lower cost microcomputers designed to be compatible with those produced by IBM.

collegial culture   A type of organizational culture characterized by consensus, teamwork, and participatory decision making.

commercial loan   An amount of money borrowed from a lending institution for the purpose of establishing, improving, or maintaining a business.

commission   An action that violates the legal standard of care when a legal duty exists.

comparative negligence   A means of measuring negligence whereby the negligence of the plaintiff is compared with that of the defendant and the award to the plaintiff is reduced by the amount of negligence attributed to the plaintiff.

computer hardware   The equipment required to input, process, and output data.

computer resources needs assessment analysis   A type of needs assessment focused on information management and its automation.

computer software   Also known as a *computer program*. A set of instructions that controls the operations of the computer hardware.

construction documents   The highly detailed, technical drawings a contractor will use to determine building costs and guide construction.

construction management   A method that involves the general contractor as part of the design team from the beginning of the building process.

copayments   The percentage of a medical bill not paid for by the insurance company.

cost-benefit analysis   A type of program evaluation that estimates both the amount of resources and the potential advantages associated with a program.

counterpower   The potential to influence the behavior of a superior.

Current Procedural Terminology (CPT)   A coding system used to standardize the language associated with third-party reimbursement.

data base software   Application software that allows a user to input, store, manipulate, and retrieve a specific information set. Sometimes referred to as a *data base management system (DBMS)*.

data port   A dedicated phone line used to connect computers in different locations.

decisional role   That portion of a manager's work that requires her to use authority to make decisions.

definers   People who use or receive the services of a program.

design/build   A method that uses only one firm to both design and construct a new building.

developmental supervision   A supervisory model that emphasizes collaboration between supervisors and those supervised to help them solve problems and develop professionally.

dictation   The act of verbally recording, usually on a cassette tape, the details of a health care assessment or treatment for later transcription and filing.

disseminator role   A type of informational role that requires the leader to communicate with members of the group.

disturbance handler role   A type of decisional role in which the leader manages conflict.

electronic mail   A system that allows users to communicate via computer.

endowment   That portion of an institution's assets in cash and investments not normally used for operational purposes.

entrepreneur role   A type of decisional role in which the leader initiates and designs controlled change within an organization.

exclusions   Situations or circumstances specifically not covered by an insurance policy.

exculpatory clause   Language in a formal agreement that releases one party from any liability associated with a particular activity, often before the activity takes place.

exemption   A legislative mechanism used to release members of one profession from the liability of violating another profession's practice act.

experimental treatments   Therapies not proven to be effective.

explanation of benefits form (EOB)   A summary prepared by an insurance company and sent to the policyholder that documents how the insurance policy covered the charges associated with a particular claim.

express warranty   An explicit statement specifying the conditions, circumstances, and terms under which a vendor will replace or repair a product if found to be faulty.

external evaluators   Experts not affiliated with the organization who are retained to assess the various programs within the organization.

feasibility standards   Performance evaluation standards intended to help foster practicality in the employee appraisal process.

figurehead role   A type of interpersonal role that requires the authority holder to represent the group, usually in a visible public capacity.

fixed budgeting model   A budgeting method whereby expenditures and revenues are projected on a monthly basis, thereby providing an estimate of cash flow.

focus charting   A medical record that registers a patient's complaint *data*, the health care practitioner's *actions*, and the patient's *response*.

foot pedal activator   A water flow device controlled by a foot pedal and used with hand-washing stations.

forecast   A process of predicting future conditions on the basis of statistics and indicators that describe the past and present situation.

foreseeability   The knowledge or notice that a result is likely to occur if a certain act occurs.

formalistic culture   A type of organizational culture characterized by a clear chain of command and well-defined lines of formal authority.

formative evaluation   An assessment designed primarily to improve a program.

fraud   Criminal misrepresentation for the purpose of financial gain.

freight-on-board (f.o.b.) point   The point at which the title for shipped goods passes from vendor to purchaser.

Gannt chart   A graphic planning and control technique that maps discrete tasks on a calendar.

general contractor   The company responsible for coordinating the actual construction of a building.

Good Samaritan laws   Statutes intended to shield certain health care practitioners from certain types of legal liability when they voluntarily come to the aid of an injured or ill person under specific circumstances.

ground fault interrupter (gfi)   A highly sensitive device designed to discontinue the flow of electricity in an electrical circuit during a power surge.

HCFA 1500   A claim form for private practice clinics developed by the Health Care Financing Administration for use in filing Medicare claims that has become accepted by most insurance companies.

health insurance   A type of policy designed to reimburse the cost of preventative as well as corrective medical care.

health maintenance organization (HMO)   A type of health insurance plan that requires policyholders to use only those medical vendors approved by the company.

honeymoon effect   The period of time, usually immediately after arriving in a new position, in which persons are more likely to be granted extra authority to make decisions.

implied warranty   An unstated understanding that a vendor will ''make good'' if a product is faulty.

influencers   Organization decision makers.

informational role   Those functions that require the manager to collect, use, and disseminate information.

inspection-production   A supervisory model that emphasizes the use of formal authority and managerial prerogatives in order to improve employee efficiency and efficacy.

insurance agent A representative of an insurance company or an independent insurance agency who sells and services insurance policies.

insurance claim registry form A worksheet that aids in tracking the progress of an insurance claim through the entire process.

insurance policy A contract between an insurance company and an individual or organization.

interpersonal role A type of managerial role, emanating from the possession of formal authority, that requires the manager to interact and form relationships with others in the organization.

inventory management The process of controlling equipment and supply stocks so that services can be provided without interruption while the use of institutional resources is maximized.

job description A written description of the specific responsibilities a position holder will be accountable for in an organization.

job specification A written description of the requirements or qualifications a person should possess in order to fill a particular role in an organization.

laptop computer Microcomputers that have been reduced in size to be portable. The smallest of these machines are known as *notebooks*.

layered coverage A method of using different insurance companies to underwrite different levels of coverage in a common policy.

leadership A subset of power that involves influencing the behavior and attitudes of others to achieve intended outcomes.

legitimacy That aspect of power that gives the leader the right to make a request and provides the obligation of the subordinate to comply.

liaison role A type of interpersonal role that requires the leader to interface with others in the group, including superiors, subordinates, and peers.

licensure A form of state credentialing, established by statute and intended to protect the public, that regulates the practice of a trade or profession by specifying who may practice and what duties they may perform.

line item budgeting A method that allocates a fixed amount of money for each subfunction of a program.

list server A remote computer that compiles a directory of users' computer addresses and distributes messages contributed by the members of a particular discussion list.

local area network (LAN) A system that allows two or more microcomputers in different places to be linked so users can communicate and share software and data.

lump sum bidding A process whereby general contractors provide cost quotations for the right to construct or renovate a building.

lump sum budgeting A method that allocates a fixed amount of money for an entire program without specifying how the money will be spent.

macro An internal program available with some application software that allows a user to reduce a complex series of keystrokes to one command.

mainframe A type of large, powerful computer designed for multiple users in a centralized institutional setting.

malpractice   Liability-generating conduct associated with the adverse outcome of patient treatment (Scott, 1990; full reference in chapter 8).

managed care   A growing concept in the insurance industry emphasizing cost control through coordination of medical services, such as with an HMO or PPO.

management   The element of leadership that involves planning, decision making, and coordination of the activities of a group.

market analysis   A written description detailing a business' competitive advantages, analysis of competition, pricing structure, and marketing plan.

master outline   A guide to the major sections of a filing system.

matrix structure   A type of chart that describes an organizational structure in terms of both functions and services.

medical insurance   A contract between a policyholder and an insurance company to reimburse a percentage of the cost of the policyholder's medical bills.

medical practice act   A state law regulating the practice of medicine, usually by specifying who may practice and under what circumstances.

medical record   Cumulative documentation of a person's medical history and health care interventions.

microcomputer   Also known as a *personal computer*. A type of computer designed to sit on a desk and serve the needs of one, or at most, a few users.

mission statement   A written expression of an organization's philosophy, purposes, and characteristics.

mixing valve   A type of plumbing fixture designed to blend hot and cold water, eliminating the need for separate hot and cold water controls.

monitor role   A type of informational role that requires the leader to observe and keep abreast of changes that will affect the group and its activity.

narrative charting   A method of recording the details of a patient's assessments and treatments using a detailed prose format.

natural lighting   Outside light used to illuminate indoor spaces, usually through windows or skylights.

needs assessment   A process of evaluating the present status and future requirements of a program.

negligence   A type of tort in which a professional fails to act as a reasonably prudent practitioner would act under the circumstances.

negotiation   The process of bargaining.

negotiator role   A type of decisional role in which the leader uses authority to bargain with members of the internal or external audience.

network   A group of computers connected by either direct hardwire coupling or dedicated telephone lines for the purpose of communicating with each other.

90th percentile fee   The fee below which 90 percent of all other medical vendors in a particular geographic area charge for a specific service.

nonmedical correspondence   Letters and memoranda not associated with a specific patient's health status.

omission   A failure to act in accordance with the standard of care required of an individual when there was a legal duty to do so.

operating system   The computer software necessary to operate the machine that integrates and controls the functions of the hardware and application software.

operational plans   A type of plan that defines organizational activities in the short term, usually no longer than 2 years.

opponents   Persons who support a particular program but dispute the implementation of a plan related to that program.

organizational chart   A graphic representation of an organization's structure, usually arranged by function or service or in a matrix format.

organizational culture   The values, beliefs, assumptions, and norms that form the infrastructure of the organizational ethos.

organizational structure   A model that defines the relationships between the members of an organization.

OSHA Bloodborne Pathogen Standard   Federal government rules that require employers to protect employees against the accidental transmission of bloodborne pathogens, especially HIV and hepatitis-B.

performance budgeting   A method that allocates funds for discrete activities.

performance evaluation   The process of placing a value on the quality of an employee's work.

personal power   The potential to influence others by virtue of personal characteristics and personality attributes.

personalistic culture   A type of organizational culture characterized by autonomy in decision making and problem solving.

planning   A type of decision-making process in which a course of action is determined in order to bring about a future state of affairs.

planning committee   A group of institutional employees who work with an architect to develop the design of a building.

planning, programming, budgeting, and evaluation system (PPBES)   A long-term budgeting process based on strategic planning and program evaluation.

plumbing fixtures   The external hardware used to control the flow and temperature of water.

policy   A type of plan that expresses an organization's intended behavior relative to a specific program subfunction.

pooled buying consortium   A group of similar institutions that merge resources to purchase goods in large quantities to receive volume discounts.

position description   A formal document that describes the qualifications for and work content, accountability, and scope of a job.

position power   Power vested in people by virtue of the role they play in an organization.

power   The potential to influence others.

preferred provider organization (PPO)   A type of health insurance plan that provides financial incentives to encourage policyholders to use those medical vendors approved by the company.

premium   The invoiced cost of an insurance policy.

primary care provider   The physician selected by an HMO member who acts as the first source of medical service for the patient. Most HMOs require members to seek a referral from the primary care provider before seeking care from another medical vendor.

primary coverage   A type of health, medical, or accident insurance that begins to pay for covered expenses immediately after a deductible has been paid.

primary decision makers   Institutional members who have formal authority over large units or subunits of an organization.

problem-oriented medical record (POMR)   A system of medical record keeping that organizes information around a patient's specific complaints.

procedure   A type of operational plan that provides specific directions for members of an organization to follow.

process   A collection of incremental and mutually dependent steps designed to direct the most important tasks of an organization.

program administration records   Documentation of the activities of a program.

program evaluation   A systematic and comprehensive assessment of the worth of a particular program.

program evaluation and review technique (PERT)   A method of graphically depicting the time line and interrelationships for the different stages of a program.

program statement   A document, prepared by the users, the architect, or both, that specifies the anticipated space requirements based on known work patterns provided by the users.

propriety standards   Performance evaluation standards intended to help ensure that the process is legal and fair.

proximate (legal) cause   An act that naturally and foreseeably leads to harm or injury to another or to an event that injures another.

purchase order   A document that formalizes the terms of a purchase and transmits the intentions of the buyer to purchase goods or services from a vendor.

purchasing   The process of acquiring goods and services.

random access memory (RAM)   A type of computer memory in which specific information can be accessed in any order. Generally, the more powerful application software programs require greater amounts of RAM.

receiving   The process of accepting delivery on goods purchased from a vendor.

recruitment   The process of planning for human resources needs and identifying potential candidates to meet those needs.

registration   A type of state credentialing that requires qualified members of a profession to register with the state in order to practice.

relationship chart   A table used to justify the placement of various rooms within a building.

request for quotation (RFQ)   A document that provides vendors with the specifications for bidding for the sale of goods and services.

requests for proposals (RFP)   Notices from internal and external funding sources announcing the details of grant programs.

requisition   A type of formal or informal communication, usually written, used for requesting authorization for purchasing goods or services.

rider   A supplementary clause to an insurance contract that extends the terms of coverage beyond those associated with a standard policy.

schematic drawings   A graphic representation, derived from the program statement, that illustrates the relationships between the principal functions of a building.

secondary coverage   A type of health, medical, or accident insurance that begins to pay for covered expenses only after all other sources of insurance coverage have been exhausted. Also known as *excess insurance.*

secondary decision makers   Professional staff members primarily responsible for delivering a program within an organization.

shareware   Application software available at greatly reduced cost, usually on a trial basis.

SOAP note   Medical appraisal organized by subjective and objective evaluation, assessment of the patient's problem, and development of a plan for treatment.

sovereign (governmental) immunity   A legal doctrine that holds that neither governments nor their agents can be held liable for negligent actions.

span of control   The number of subordinates supervised by a particular individual in an organizational setting.

spending ceiling model   A type of expenditure budgeting that requires justification only for those expenses that exceed those of the previous budget cycle. Also known as the *incremental model.*

spending reduction model   A type of budgeting used during periods of financial retrenchment that requires reallocation of institutional funds, resulting in reduced spending levels for some programs.

spokesperson's role   A type of informational role that requires the leader to communicate with organizational influencers and members of the organization's public.

spreadsheet program   A type of application software that manipulates numerical data contained in cells formed by the intersection of rows and columns.

staff selection   Any procedure used as a basis for any employment decision, including recruitment, hiring, promotion, demotion, retention, and performance evaluation.

standard of care   The legal duty to provide health care services consistent with what other health care practitioners of the same training, education, and credentialing would provide under similar circumstances.

standards of practice   Widely accepted principles intended to guide the professional activities of a health care practitioner.

standpipe drain   A type of drain that is raised above floor level.

statutes of limitations   Laws that fix a certain length of time beyond which legal actions cannot be initiated.

strategic planning   A type of planning that involves critical self-examination in order to bring about organizational improvement.

subcontractor   A company hired by the general contractor to complete a portion of the building project. The subcontractor's work is usually devoted to a particular skilled trade, such as plumbing, electricity, and landscaping.

subpoena   An order issued by a court compelling the testimony of a witness at deposition or trial.

summative evaluation   An assessment designed primarily to describe the effectiveness or accomplishments of a program or employee to determine appropriate actions.

supervision   A process whereby authority holders observe the work activities of an employee to improve the outcomes of the employee's work or the employee's professional development.

tax exempt bonds   Bonds authorized and sold by governmental agencies to provide funding for construction projects.

terminal   A combination cathode ray tube and keyboard that allows users to access a mainframe computer.

testimony   Statements offered under oath, subject to cross-examination, as evidence to the facts in a legal proceeding.

thermostat   A device that controls heating and cooling equipment.

third party   A medical vendor with no binding interest in a particular insurance contract.

third-party reimbursement   The process by which medical vendors are reimbursed by insurance companies for services provided to policyholders.

tort   A legal wrong, other than breach of contract, for which the court system provides a remedy, typically in the form of monetary damages.

traffic patterns   The anticipated flow of people from one area of a building to another.

transactional leadership   The simple exchange between leaders and followers of one thing for another.

transformational leadership   That aspect of leadership that uses both change and conflict to elevate the standards of the social system.

UB-92 (HCFA 1450)   A universally accepted insurance claim form for use by hospitals.

usual, customary, and reasonable fee (UCR)   The charge consistent with what other medical vendors would assess.

utility standards   Performance evaluation standards intended to ensure that employee appraisal is useful to workers, employers, and others who need to use the information.

variable budgeting system A budgeting method that requires that monthly expenditures be adjusted so they do not exceed revenues.

vision statement A concise statement that describes the ideal state to which an organization aspires.

WOTS UP analysis A data collection and appraisal technique designed to determine an organization's strengths, weaknesses, opportunities, and threats in order to facilitate planning.

zero-based budgeting A budgeting model that requires justification for every budget line item without reference to previous spending patterns.

zone of indifference A hypothetical boundary of legitimacy, outside of which requests or orders will be met with mere compliance or refusal.

AUTHOR INDEX

A

Abdenour, T.E., 146, 172
Acheson, K.A., 67, 80
Ackoff, R.L., 25, 44
Adams, R., 168, 173
Adams, S.H., 69, 83
Aldrich, J.W., 57, 80
Ammer, C., 30, 44
Ammer, D.S., 30, 44
Arnheim, D.D., 129, 135
Athletic Business, 117, 136
Athletic Institute, the, 129, 137

B

Baird, L.S., 72, 83
Baley, J.A., 213, 221
Barlow, C.W., 98, 108
Barnard, C.I., 4, 17
Bass, B.M., 2, 17
Bateman, T., 4, 6, 20
Beatty, R.W., 72, 83
Beckham, J., 82
Benda, C., 213, 221
Bennis, W., 49, 80
Bernardin, H.J., 70, 80
Berni, R., 146, 172
Biehle, J.T., 123, 135
Bischoff, R.N., 179, 201
Blake, R.R., 11, 18
Block, P., 20, 36, 37, 45
Bonanno, D., 114, 136
Bruce, S.D., 57, 80
Burke, L.J., 146, 174
Burns, J.M., 4, 6, 11, 18
Bushardt, S.C., 56, 72, 81

C

Cady, C., 130, 135
Carlova, J., 205, 215, 222
Cartwright, D., 18
Cascio, W.F., 70, 80
Castetter, W.B., 25, 31, 45, 59
Chambers, R.L., 180, 200
Chang, R.S., 67, 81
Cheong, V.E., 162, 172
Christensen, W.W., 161, 165, 172
Ciccolella, M., 209, 221
Cochran, D.S., 23, 45
Cohen, A., 119, 136
Cohen, E., 119, 136
Cole, S.L., 182, 183, 201

D

Dale, E., 7, 18
Danzon, P.M., 205, 221
Dejnozka, E.L., 4, 18

Dewey, P.R., 168, 173
Dibner, D.R., 115, 117, 122, 124, 136
Dobbins, G.H., 69, 80
Dorfman, P.W., 74, 81
Dougherty, N.J., 114, 136
Dowling, J.B., 50, 82
Drake, J.D., 63, 81
Drowatzky, J.N., 209, 221
Dworkin, R.B., 208, 223

E

Equal Employment Opportunity
    Commission (EEOC), 54, 81

F

Fahey, T.D., 125, 136
Fayol, H., 7, 18
Fein, R., 179, 200
Fitz-Gibbon, C.T., 39, 40, 45
Fletcher, M.E., 113, 136
Forseth, E.A., 117, 136
Fowler, A.R., 56, 72, 81
Frankel, E., 187, 200
French, J.R.P., 4, 18
Frey, D., 168, 173
Friedrich, C.J., 4, 18

G

Gabriel, A.J., 150, 173
Gall, M.D., 67, 80
Garofalo, M.J., 31, 45
Gibson, C.K., 23, 45
Gieck, J., 205, 221
Glondys, B.A., 153, 173
Godek, J.J., 185, 200
Godwin, C., 143, 175
Good, C.V., 4, 18
Graham, L.S., 216, 221
Gruber, W.H., 140, 175
Gulick, L., 7, 18

H

Haddad, S.A., 56, 81
Hagerty, B.K., 67, 81
Hart, P.M., 182, 183, 201
Hawkins, J.D., 141, 173, 208, 222
Health Insurance Association of
    America (HIAA), 178, 179, 191,
    201
Helms, L.B., 208, 211, 213, 222
Herbert, D.L., 153, 173, 205, 211,
    212, 213, 222
Herbert, W.G., 213, 222
Hirschheim, R.A., 162, 172
Hollander, E.P., 4, 19
Horine, L., 87, 108
Horn, J., 187, 201

Horsley, J.E., 205, 215, 222
Huber, V.L., 69, 81

I

Illingworth, V., 167, 173
Iyer, P.W., 146, 174

J

Jacobs, T.O., 4, 19
Joint Committee on Standards for
    Educational Evaluation, 39, 45,
    73, 74, 75, 82
Jones, R.L., 88, 94, 108

K

Kahn, R.F., 4, 19
Kahn, R.L., 4, 19
Kaplan, A., 4, 19
Karelis, C.H., 4, 19
Katz, D., 4, 19
Keaveny, T.J., 73, 82
Kenna, K., 205, 221
Kess, S., 103, 108
Kettenbach, G., 142, 174
Kilmann, R.H., 12, 20
King, A.A., 4, 19
Kolodny, H.F., 53, 82
Kozubowski, J., 180, 200

L

Lasswell, H.D., 4, 19
Lehr, C., 183, 201
Leroy, L., 167, 174
Leverenz, L.J., 208, 211, 213, 222
Loveland, J., 74, 81
Lowe, J., 205, 221

M

Marrelli, T.M., 142, 143, 174
Matthews, D.L., 213, 221
Mayo, H.B., 87, 109
McCarthy, M.M., 60, 82
McGann, A.F., 73, 82
Miles, B.J., 151, 152, 174
Mintzberg, H., 7, 8, 9, 13, 20
Morris, L.L., 39, 40, 45
Mouton, J.S., 11, 18
Murphy, J., 146, 174
Muther, R., 119, 120, 137
Myers, O.J., 55, 82

N

Nanus, B., 49, 80
National Athletic Trainers Association
    (NATA), 141, 175, 206, 207,
    208
Needy, J.R., 157, 159, 174

251

Nehmer, K.S., 164, 174
Newcomer, L.N., 181, 201
Newton, D.J., 23, 45

O

Occupational Safety and Health
       Administration (OSHA), 157, 174
Organ, D.W., 4, 6, 20
Ouchi, W.G., 50, 82
Owens, R.G., 49, 82

P

Parks, J., 69, 82
Pearce, J.A., 23, 46
Penman, K.A., 69, 83, 118, 127, 128,
       137
Penman, T.M., 128, 137
Penton/IPC Education Division, 34, 46
Pettigrew, A.M., 3, 20
Podsakoff, P.M., 69, 81
Porter, J.W., 126, 137
Porter, M.M., 126, 137
Posner, B.Z., 34, 46
Prentice, W.E., 129, 135
Priest, S.L., 158, 160, 175

R

Ranck, S.L., 113, 136
Randolph, W.A., 34, 46
Rankin, J.M., 86, 109
Raven, B., 4, 18

Ray, R.R., 55, 70, 71, 83, 88, 95, 109,
       158
Readey, H., 146, 172
Reinhardt, C., 70, 83
Reynolds, J.D., 179, 201
Ribaric, R.F., 131, 137, 158, 175
Ross, N.V., 180, 200
Rowell, J.C., 180, 185, 190, 192, 210
Rupp, P.R., 161, 165, 172
Russell, J.M., 69, 80

S

Saftlas, H.B., 89
Sanders, J.R., 38, 46
Schneier, C.E., 72, 83
Schneller, T., 143, 175
Scott, R.W., 208, 211, 213, 222
Secher, H.P., 20
Secor, M.R., 118, 126, 137
Shire, T.L., 158, 175
Sikula, A.F., 57, 83
Snider, S.W., 116, 137
Spengler, C.D., 67, 81
Steiner, G.A., 26, 27, 31, 46
Stephan, W.G., 74, 81
Stoner, J.A.F., 34, 46, 51, 52, 54
Synnott, W.R., 140, 175

T

Tanner, D., 66, 83
Tanner, L., 66, 83

Theunissen, W., 113, 137
Thomas, K.W., 12, 20
Todor, W.D., 69, 81
Tracey, W., 80
Trentin, H.G., 88, 94, 108

U

U.S. Small Business Administration,
       56, 83, 87, 103, 109, 193, 202
Urwick, L., 7, 18

W

Wadlington, W., 208, 223
Waltz, J.R., 208, 223
Want, J.H., 24, 46
Weber, M., 4, 20
Westlin, B., 103, 108
Wheeler, J.D., 119, 120, 137
Wijeyewardene, G., 19
Wildavsky, A., 88, 109
Worthen, B.R., 38, 46
Wright, B.J., 95, 109

Y

Young, H.C., 90, 109
Yukl, G.A., 3, 4, 6, 14, 20

Z

Zirkel, P., 82

SUBJECT INDEX

A

Abandonment, 210
Accounts payable, 101-102
Actual cause, 211
Adversaries, 37-38
Agreement—trust matrix, 36
AIM (Athletic Injury Management
  Software), 165, 166
Air conditioning, 128-129
ALFIE, 165, 174
Allen and Hanburys, 168
Allies, 36, 37
Alumni organizations, 102, 122. *See
  also* Booster organizations
American Medical Association
  (AMA), 186
American Physical Therapy
  Association (APTA), 187
Application software, 163-168
  Amiga, 174
  Apple, 163, 174
  Atari, 174
  Commodore, 174
  hardware, 160, 161-163, 164, 175
  International Business Machines
    (IBM), 161, 162, 163, 165, 166,
    167, 174
  Macintosh, 161, 162, 163, 165, 166,
    167, 174
  software, 95, 148, 160, 162, 163-
    168, 174, 175
APTA (American Physical Therapy
  Association), 187
Architect, 116, 118, 119, 121, 123
  directory, 117, 136
  relationship to contractor, 124
  selection, 117, 118
Assumption of risk, 212, 213
Athletic Injury Management Software
  (AIM), 165, 166
Athletic Training Services, 61
Authority, 1, 4-6, 14, 17, 49, 52
  honeymoon effect, 5
  legitimacy, 4, 14, 18

B

Bedfellows, 36, 37
Behaviorally anchored rating scales,
  72, 82
Bidding, 96, 97, 122-123, 196
Bidding documents, 123
BITNET, 168
Bloodborne pathogen standard, 157,
  174-175
Booster organizations, 102. *See also*
  Alumni organizations

Bubble diagram, 119, 121
Budget, 85, 87, 88-93, 108, 158, 168
  evaluation, 95, 109
  fixed, 90
  incremental, 88, 93
  line item, 91
  lump sum, 90-91
  performance, 91-92
  planning, 87, 92-93, 109
  PPBES (Planning, programming,
    budgeting, and evaluation
    system), 90, 109
  spending ceiling model, 88, 91, 93
  spending reduction model, 88-89, 91
  variable, 90
  zero-based, 88, 89-90, 93
Bulletin board, 168, 169, 173
Business plan, 121-122
  financial statements, 121
  market analysis, 121

C

CAHEA (Committee on Allied Health
  Education Accreditation), 27
Capital campaign, 122
Capital improvements, 93-94, 97, 100,
  109
  buying, 102-103, 108
  leasing, 102-103, 108
Capitation, 185
Causation, 209, 211-212
Central processing unit (CPU), 161,
  162, 163
Certification, 206-207
CHAMPUS, 185
Change, 7, 11
Charting by exception, 146, 174
Claims processing, 153, 167, 177,
  187, 201
  educational settings, 182, 183, 184,
    187-191
  sports medicine clinics, 185, 186,
    191-193
Clones, 162
Collective bargaining, 61, 65
Commercial loan, 119-122
Commission, 209
Committee on Allied Health Education
  Accreditation (CAHEA), 27
Comparative negligence, 212, 214
Competencies in Athletic Training, 70,
  207, 210, 222
Computer, 100, 130, 139, 140, 158-170
Computerized athletic drug reference,
  168

Computerized inventory. *See*
  Inventory management
Computer program. *See* Applications
  software
Conduct, 208, 209
Confidentiality, 147, 153, 155, 157,
  185-186, 210
Conflict resolution, 1, 11, 20
  accommodation, 12
  avoidance, 13
  collaboration, 13
  competition, 12
  compromise, 13
  cooperation by edict, 11
  flexible reporting relationships, 12
  leadership replacement, 12
  liaison persons, 12
  mediation and arbitration, 12
  negotiations, 11, 13
  organizational structural changes, 12
  personnel rotation, 12
Consortium, 212
Construction, 112, 116
  bid analysis, 123
  contract, 123, 124
  documents, 122, 124
  management, 116, 135
  and minority contractors, 123
  models, 116-117
Contingency theory, 20
Contract
  breach of, 208
  insurance, 180, 184
  service, 95
Cost-benefit analysis, 158
Counterpower, 3
Counter space, 131
CPT (Current Procedural
  Terminology), 186-187, 192
CPU (Central processing unit), 161,
  162, 163
Credentialing, 184, 203, 205-208, 211,
  237
Critical incident reports, 72
Current Procedural Terminology
  (CPT), 186-187, 192

D

Damage, 208, 209, 212
Data base software, 165-167
Data base management system
  (DBMS), 165-167, 174
Data port, 130
dBase III Plus, 166
DBMS (Data base management
  system), 165-167, 174

Decision makers, 114-115
Deductible, 180, 183, 197
Definers, 114, 115
Delegation, 20
Deposition, 214-215
Design/build, 116-117, 137
Dictation, 149
Direct service, 142
Disk drives, 161, 162, 163
Disk operating system (DOS), 163
Documentation, 139, 140, 141-142,
   217
   communication from other
      professionals, 150
   computerized, 146-148
   errors, 143
   special procedures, 144, 149-150
Doors, 125
DOS (disk operating system), 163
Drains, 127
Duty, 209-211, 216, 221

E

E-mail (Electronic mail), 168-170, 173
Emergency information, 150-151
Emotional distress, 212
Endowment, 122, 183
Entrepreneur, 11
Exclusions, 180, 181, 197
Exculpatory clauses, 153, 173
Exemption, 206, 207-208
Experimental treatments, 181, 182,
   201

F

Facility design
   conceptual development, 112
   design process, 113-124
   electrical, 126-127
   elements, 124-133
   lighting, 129
   location, 124-126
   planning committee, 113-115, 123,
      124, 136
   plumbing, 127-128, 131
   specialized function areas, 129-133
   ventilation, 128-129
Fax, 150
Figurehead, 7
Filing, 156, 157-158, 174
First Agency, 189
Floors, 129
   carpet, 131, 132
   reinforcement, 132
   tile, 131, 132
F.O.B. point (Freight-on-board point),
   100
Focus charting, 146, 148, 174
Focus group, 28
Foot pedal activator, 128
Forced choice rating scales, 72
Forecast, 30, 88
Foreseeability of harm, 211-212, 221

Forms
   emergency information, 150-151,
      174
   explanation of benefits form (EOB),
      188-189
   HCFA 1500, 193, 194
   HCFA 1450 (UB-92), 193, 195
   injury evaluation, 144-149, 167
   insurance, 153, 187
   insurance claim registry, 188, 190,
      193
   medical referral, 150, 151
   permission to treat, 151-153
   physical examination, 143-144, 165
   release of medical information, 153,
      154, 185-186
   treatment, 144-149, 166, 167
   UB-92 (HCFA 1450), 193, 195
Freight-on-board point (f.o.b. point),
   100
Funding, 119-122, 123

G

Gannt chart, 33, 34-35
Garza v. Edinburg Consolidated
   Independent School District, 213
General contractor, 116, 123, 124
General treatment area, 131-132
GFI (ground fault interrupter), 126, 137
Gillespie v. Southern Utah State
   College, 211
Good Samaritan, 212, 213-214, 221
Governmental immunity, 212, 213
Graphic rating scales, 72
Ground fault interrupter (gfi), 126, 137

H

Health Care Financing Administration
   (HCFA), 187, 201
Health maintenance organization
   (HMO), 185, 189, 191, 192, 197
Hiring, 57-65, 81
   approval for, 64
   discrimination in, 59-60, 82
HMO (health maintenance
   organization), 185, 189, 191,
   192, 197
Honeymoon effect, 5
Human resources, 47, 80
Hydrotherapy area, 131

I

Idiosyncratic credits, 19
IITS (Integrated Injury Tracking
   System), 165-166, 174
Influence, 9-10, 19
Information control, 20
Information management, 139, 140,
   141, 175
Informed consent, 208, 216
Insurance, 91, 151
   accident, 177, 180, 196, 200
   agent, 193
   catastrophic, 180, 181, 200
   copayments, 197

documentation and, 142
   evaluation, 177, 193
   excess, 183, 197
   fraud, 186
   health, 177, 179, 180, 181, 200
   layered, 196-197
   malpractice, 215, 218
   medical, 177, 178, 180, 181, 182,
      185
   policy, 180, 181, 184
   premium, 180, 182, 183, 184, 197,
      202
   primary, 177, 182, 183, 197
   purchasing, 177, 193-197
   secondary, 177, 182, 183-184, 189,
      197
   self, 177, 182-183
Integrated Injury Tracking System
   (IITS), 165-166, 174
Interface Conflict-Solving Model, 18
INTERNET, 168, 170
Interviewing, 63-64, 81
   on-site, 63, 64, 65
   telephone, 63
Inventory management, 85, 87, 93,
   103-105
   automation of, 104, 108, 167, 168
   storage, 104

J

Job description, 55, 56, 57, 81, 83
Job specification, 55, 56, 83
Joint Commission on Accreditation of
   Healthcare Organizations, 142,
   174
Joint Review Committee for
   Educational Programs in Athletic
   Training, 27, 39, 157

K

Keyboard, 161, 163

L

LAN (local area network), 162, 166,
   168, 172
Laptop computer, 162
Leadership, 1, 6-7, 17, 18, 19, 80
   transactional, 6
   transformational, 7
Legal cause, 211
Legal defenses, 203, 212
Legal liability, 203
   insurance, 200, 218
   strategies for avoidance, 216-218,
      221, 222
Liaison, 8
Licensure, 206
Life insurance, 121
List server, 168, 169
Local area network (LAN), 162, 166,
   168, 172
Lowe v. Texas Tech University, 213
Lump sum bidding, 116

M

Macro, 164
Mainframe, 130, 146, 161-163, 168, 172, 175
Malpractice, 208, 212, 215
Managed care, 189, 191
Management, 7, 13
Management by objectives, 72
Managerial roles, 1, 7-13
   decisional, 7, 11-13
   informational, 7, 8-10
   interpersonal, 7-8
Master outline, 157
Medicaid, 185
Medical records, 125, 129, 140, 143, 173, 174
Medicare, 181, 185, 193
Microcomputer, 146, 161-163, 168, 173
Microsoft Windows, 165, 166
Mission statement, 21, 23-25, 45, 46
Mixing valves, 128
Modem, 161, 162, 163, 168, 193
Monitor, 161, 163
Mouse, 161, 163, 166, 167

N

Narrative charting, 149, 172
NATA (National Athletic Trainers Association), 141, 168, 175, 205, 206, 207
NATABOC (National Athletic Trainers Association Board of Certification), 27
National Athletic Trainers Association (NATA), 141, 168, 175, 205, 206, 207
National Athletic Trainers Association Board of Certification (NATABOC), 27
National Collegiate Athletic Association (NCAA), 27, 168, 180, 182
National Federation of State High School Athletic Associations (NFSHSAA), 28
NCAA (National Collegiate Athletic Association), 27, 168, 180, 182
Needs assessment, 115, 136, 158
Negligence, 153, 203, 208-209, 214, 221
Negotiation, 97, 108
   for price, 98
   for quality, 100
   for shipping, 100
   for supply, 99
   for technical support, 100, 160, 163, 164
Networks, 160, 168, 170, 173
NFSHSAA (National Federation of State High School Athletic Associations), 28
90th percentile fee, 181
Non-medical correspondence, 156
Notebook computer, 162

O

Occupational Safety and Health Administration (OSHA), 141, 157, 174, 175
Office, 129-130
Omission, 209
Operating system, 163
Operational planning, 26, 31, 87
Opponents, 36, 37
Organizational chart, 50, 88
   based on function, 50-51
   based on service, 51-53
   matrix, 53-54, 82
Organizational culture, 49
   collegial, 49, 67
   formalistic, 49-50, 66
   personalistic, 49
Organizational structure, 50
OSHA (Occupational Safety and Health Administration), 141, 157, 174, 175

P

Participation, 20
Participatory management, 49, 68
PC-File, 167
Performance evaluation, 69-76, 80, 81, 83
   methods, 70-73
   records, 156
   standards, 73-76, 82
   status in athletic training, 69-70
   summative, 66
   trait-oriented, 69, 76, 82
Personal computer. *See* Microcomputer
Personnel records, 156
PERT (Program Evaluation and Review Technique), 33, 34, 46
Physical examination, 143-144, 216, 217
Plumbing fixtures, 128
Policy, 31, 49, 59, 105, 205, 217
POMR (problem-oriented medical record), 144-146, 147, 172
Pooled bond issue, 122
Pooled buying consortia, 102
Position description, 55-57, 80, 216
Position vacancy notice, 61
Power, 1, 2-3, 52
   charismatic, 3, 19
   coercive, 3, 18
   expert, 4, 10, 18
   personal, 3-4, 10, 11
   position, 3, 11
   referent, 18
   reward, 18
PPO (preferred provider organization), 185, 189, 191, 192, 197
Practice act, 206, 205
Preferred provider organization (PPO), 185, 189, 191, 192, 197
Primary care provider, 189
Printer, 161, 162, 163

Private examination area, 133
Problem-oriented medical record (POMR), 144-146, 147, 172
Procedural coding, 177, 186-187
Procedures, 33, 49, 59, 75, 105, 182
Processes, 32
Program administration records, 129, 153, 155
Program evaluation, 21, 38-40, 45, 83, 142
   external evaluators, 39
   formative, 39
   reports, 45
   summative, 39
Program Evaluation and Review Technique (PERT), 33, 34, 46
Program statement, 115
Promotion, 57
Proximate cause, 211, 221
Purchase order, 100, 101, 156
Purchasing, 87, 93, 95, 98, 100, 168

R

Random access memory (RAM), 166, 167
Ranking, 72
Receiving, 101
Recruitment, 57, 59
Referral
   form, 150, 151
   process, 125-126
Registration, 206, 207
Rehabilitation area, 132
Relationship chart, 119, 120
Reports to coaches, 155, 164, 165, 166
Request for quotation (RFQ), 96-97, 98, 99, 100
Requests for proposals (RFP), 156
Requisition, 95
Retirement, 59
RFP (requests for proposals), 156
RFQ (Request for quotation), 96-97, 98, 99, 100
Riders, 180, 197
Rules, 19

S

Safety committee, 217
Salary and promotion records, 156
Schematic drawings, 116, 117, 121, 123
   space needs formula, 118, 119, 131
   traffic patterns, 119
Search committee, 62, 64
Self study, 40, 115
Service program, 141-142
Shareware, 163, 167
Shelves, 133
SIMS (Sports Injury Monitoring System), 166
SIRS (Sports Injury Reporting System), 166
Site visit, 117
SOAP note, 146, 147, 174
Social architecture, 49

Sorey v. Kellett, 213
Sovereign immunity, 212, 213
Span of control, 50, 82
Spokesperson, 9-10
Sports Injury Monitoring System
  (SIMS), 166
Sports Injury Reporting System
  (SIRS), 166
SportsWare Injury Tracking System,
  167
Spreadsheet program, 167-168
Staff selection, 54-65, 81, 83
Standard of care, 211, 212, 222
Standards of practice, 141-142, 150,
  157, 175, 211
*Standards of Practice for Athletic
  Training*, 70
Statutes of limitations, 212
Storage area, 132-133
Strategic planning, 21, 57, 87, 225
  inside interests, 29
  outside interests, 26
Subcontractor, 116, 124
Subpoena, 215

Supervision 50, 83, 210
  clinical model, 67-68, 80
  developmental model, 68
  inspection-production model, 66-67
  physician, 205

T
Tables
  taping, 130, 131, 135
  treatment, 131, 132, 137
Taping area, 119, 129, 130-131
Task oriented performance evaluation
  system (TOPES), 72, 81
Tax exempt bonds, 122
Terminals, 162, 168
Termination, 59
Testimony, 203, 214-215
Thermostat, 128
Third-party, 184, 185
Third-party reimbursement, 177, 179,
  184, 201
TOPES (Task oriented performance
  evaluation system), 72, 81
Tort, 208, 213
Transfer, 57

U
UCR fee (usual, customary, and
  reasonable fee), 181-182
Uniform guidelines on employee
  selection procedures, 81
United States Olympic Committee
  (USOC), 168
Usual, customary, and reasonable fee
  (UCR), 181-182

V
Vision statement, 21, 22-23

W
Walls, 129, 132
Warranty, 100
  express, 100
  implied, 100
Word processing, 163, 164, 167
Work sampling, 67, 72, 81
WOTS UP analysis, 31, 225-235
Written essays, 72

Z
Zone of indifference, 4, 17

ABOUT THE AUTHOR

Richard Ray is the head athletic trainer and an associate professor of physical education at Hope College in Holland, Michigan. He has directed the school's sports medicine program since 1982 and is a recognized leader in the field of athletic training administration. Having worked closely with both students and practitioners in a variety of settings, including four NCAA Division III championship events and the JABBA-KIRIN World Basketball Tournament in Japan, Ray knows the many administrative problems confronting today's athletic trainers.

Ray received an MA in physical education from Western Michigan University in 1980 and an EdD in educational leadership from WMU in 1990. He graduated Summa Cum Laude in both graduate programs and was honored as a Graduate Research and Creative Scholar by the school in 1990.

In addition to being a member of the National Athletic Trainers Association (NATA), Dr. Ray is a member and past president of both the Great Lakes Athletic Trainers Association and the Michigan Athletic Trainers Society. He is also a member of the NATA Board of Certification Task Force on Examination Qualifications. In 1993 Ray was named to the Educational Advisory Board of the Gatorade Sport Science Institute. His favorite leisure activities include camping, reading, playing golf, and coaching summer youth sports.